THE BAD CHILD

A Cultural Critique Book

Cesare Casarino, Frieda Ekotto, Maggie Hennefeld, John Mowitt, and Simona Sawhney, editors

The Bad Child

A MARIA JANION READER

Maria Janion

EDITED AND TRANSLATED BY MARTA FIGLEROWICZ

A Cultural Critique Book

University of Minnesota Press
Minneapolis
London

This book was published with the assistance of the Frederick W. Hilles Publication Fund of Yale University.

Portions of the Introduction were previously published in a different form as "Poland's Other Pope: Re-Appreciating Maria Janion," *Critical Quarterly* 65, no. 4 (December 2023): 12–23. Chapter 1 was previously published as "Uncanny Slavdom," *PMLA* 138, no. 1 (January 2023): 110–26.

Maria Janion's writings are translated and published by permission of her literary executor, Kazimiera Szczuka. Publication information is on page 257.

Published by the University of Minnesota Press
111 Third Avenue South, Suite 290
Minneapolis, MN 55401-2520
http://www.upress.umn.edu

ISBN 978-1-5179-1967-2 (hc)
ISBN 978-1-5179-1968-9 (pb)

A Cataloging-in-Publication record for this book is available from the Library of Congress.

Printed in the United States of America on acid-free paper

UMP BmB 2025

Contents

Introduction vii
MARTA FIGLEROWICZ

Translator's Note xxiii
MARTA FIGLEROWICZ

A MARIA JANION READER

PART I. A Theory of Eastern Europe

1. Uncanny Slavdom 5

2. Poland's Location in Europe 29

3. Between Death and Laughter: The Art of Jacek Malczewski 63

PART II. Socialism, Patriotism, Nationhood

4. The Patriot-as-Madman 85

5. Socialism as a Prometheism 107

PART III. Aesthetics, History, and Critical Method

6. The Project of Phantasmatic Critique 119

7. The History of Literature and the History of Ideas 139

8. Notes on Horror and Melodrama 153

PART IV. The Authority of the Other

9. Adam Mickiewicz's Jewish Legion 179

10. Fragments from a Lover's Discourse 205

11. The Bad Child: Interviews 219

Translator's Acknowledgments 255
Publication History 257
Index 259

Introduction

MARTA FIGLEROWICZ

How does national pride shade into fascism? Is patriotism a form of insanity? Can we shed the illusions that our cultures cause us to develop about ourselves?

Maria Janion spent her life examining such questions while watching the communities around her wrestle with them. Born in 1926, shortly after Poland's regaining of independence in 1918, Janion lived through her country's turn to authoritarian nationalism in the 1930s; its German occupation between 1939 and 1945; its inclusion in the Soviet Bloc after 1945; and then—after 1989—its fraught attempts to integrate itself into Western Europe. Shortly before her death in 2020, this last transition's abruptness had once again bred a nationalist backlash.

As recently as 2010, the confusions and whiplashes of these political turns seemed like a particularly Eastern European problem. Today, they loom as exemplars of a much broader geopolitical shift toward the right, a reawakening of nationalist discourses that Western countries—at least—had hoped to have relegated to the nineteenth and early twentieth centuries. At a time when Anglophone thinkers yearn for tools that might help them move through this historical condition, Janion's writing offers a lifeline to readers far beyond her native region.

I first read Janion during the pandemic. I came to her looking for alternatives to that particularly Western, liberal association of critical thought with abstraction, irony, and detachment. As a queer adult immigrant to the United States, I was watching its political tides turn with growing fear. I had migrated westward to escape nationalism, authoritarianism, and protofascism, whose shadows loomed over Poland in the late 1990s. When MAGA supporters stormed the Capitol on January 6, 2021, I realized that the democracy I now lived in was no less fragile than the one I had left. Once again, I found myself facing the situation that had felt insurmountable twenty years earlier, in the face of which I had fled abroad. This time, there was nowhere to escape.

Searching for answers, I dipped into one of Janion's books, then another, with increasing urgency. A profoundly original theorist of nationalism, fascism, and collective fantasizing, she writes from a perspective that is equally skeptical toward Western discourses of globality and Soviet models of internationalism. Her writing highlights the dangers of denying or mocking the creature comforts human beings find in the experience of cultural and social belonging. Only by acknowledging and exploring these affective needs, she shows, can we curb their potential for exclusionary violence.

Janion's life story is built from layers of exceptionality and marginalization. She was one of very few queer Polish intellectuals of her generation; a female scholar who fought her way through an academic environment entrenched in misogyny; a devoted leftist who chose to stay in Poland, and to remain a Marxist, amid her growing, fearlessly voiced distaste for Soviet rule. Throughout her life, she spoke up against authoritarian governance as well as her compatriots' anti-Semitism, homophobia, racism, and xenophobia. As she defended the excluded and often found herself on her communities' margins, she did not lose hope in the possibility of intersectional coalition-building around shared—if complicated and conflictual—histories and heritages.

With the West's self-assurance crumbling in the face of rising illiberal forces both within and beyond it, readers might finally be ready to learn from a Polish thinker who is not a liberal émigré. For most of the twentieth century, Polish culture was known abroad through its dissidents. Liberal-leaning escapees from beyond the Iron Curtain such as Leszek Kołakowski and Czesław Miłosz were celebrated in the West for both their genuine talents and the ways their diagnoses of the country they fled dovetailed with Western European condemnation of the USSR and its satellite states. After the fall of the Berlin Wall, as Poland moved away from communism, it remained common to equate innovative twentieth-century Polish thought with liberalism. It seemed that the best thinking Kołakowski's and Miłosz's generation had done had happened in solidarity with the capitalist West. Janion's legacy sharply contradicts such assumptions. Throughout her long career, she urged her fellow Eastern Europeans to embrace their non-

Westernness and resist the ideals of individualism and ironic detachment. Her work speaks presciently, and directly, not just to Eastern Europeans, but also—now more than ever—to Westerners trying to understand the increasingly polarized societies they live in and to acknowledge liberalism's role in their polarization.

Eastern Europe's turbulent history made it something of a laboratory for different shades and theories of collective cohesion. Throughout the nineteenth century, the Polish nation—like the Czech nation, the Serbian nation, and most other Slavic nations west of Russia—were merely imagined communities. This was true not only in Benedict Anderson's sense of the term, but also in a more literal one: as Eastern Europe's ethnic groups strove to define themselves, they also struggled for political autonomy from their more powerful neighbors.

The sense of cultural belonging Eastern Europeans developed amid these upheavals forms a confusing hybrid of self-assertion and self-abnegation, an identification with Western Europe but also a vehement pull against it. Following their dramatic shifts in sovereignty, allegiance, and identification, Eastern European communities have remained plagued by a sense of inferiority to the West. Especially in the last decades, this sense of inferiority has fomented pervasive right-wing sentiments throughout the region.

Janion takes Eastern Europe as a cipher for much larger cultural impasses and conflicts. The region offers a liminal case study for the ways non-Westerners' sense of themselves is warped by the West's political and economic dominance. Eastern Europe's unique combination of cultural hybridity and archival lacunae also provides fertile ground for examining nationalism and fascism as forms of pseudo-historical fantasizing. A thinker who engaged extensively with Western as well as Soviet Marxism, Janion is well aware of the generalizability of her insights and effortlessly links them to these broader intellectual networks.

Poland's Other Pope

Though few Western readers have heard of Janion, she has long been a towering intellectual figure in Eastern Europe. To give a sense of her sway over her fellow Polish leftists' critical and creative imaginations, one might begin with the short lyrical play that the celebrated poet Miron Białoszewski presented to her in 1978 as a Christmas present.

The play begins with humanity leaving Earth because of an unnamed cataclysm. Having found a habitable planet, the survivors take stock of whom and what they have brought along in their hurried departure. "The pyramids" have fortunately been stowed in the hold of a spaceship, but the survivors had "forgotten" to stow away the pope. "Not to worry," a character identified as Janion says. "We can elect a pope from among us." "That's a good form of governance," pipes in another voice. A conclave is called, and Janion is unanimously elected. Renaming herself "Adam Juliusz Zygmunt Maria Maryna Małgorzata Janiocentina the First," she blesses those gathered around her "in the name of the father and the son—and of the mother and the daughter."[1]

Janion was fifty-two when Białoszewski presented her with this gift. Just a few months earlier, John Paul II had been elected as the new Catholic pope, the first Pole ever to assume this position. Białoszewski's poem echoes the Polish public's fervent enthusiasm at his election and redirects it. The poet depicts Janion as a woman who carries both male and female names, an unbeliever who can serve as humanity's chief priestess. By this point in the 1970s, Janion had gathered around her a large following of intellectuals and students. Troubled by their culture's legacy of Romantic self-aggrandizement, she and her fellow travelers sought to harness their compatriots' religiously tainted nationalistic fantasies and fervor to a more empathic understanding of the people Polish culture marginalized. In her guise as Poland's other pope, Janion speaks for these multitudes and contains them.

Powerful though it became, Janion's voice barely escaped archival silence. She grew up in poverty in a village outside Vilnius, the daughter of a working-class mother who had left an abusive husband and was raising her two children alone. In the deeply stratified interwar Polish society of her early teenage years, her class background tracked her into blue-collar professions. A path toward a university education only opened once Poland became one of Soviet Russia's satellite states and these prewar class hierarchies were upended. Throughout her life, Janion never forgot this early lesson. She also never forgot her experience of World War II, where she witnessed Nazi persecutions and the mass genocide of the region's Jewish population.

Transplanted to Łódź, a city in central Poland, after the war, Janion attended lectures on Polish literature alongside former partisans and war veterans from throughout the country. With the young people she met there, especially the women, she formed a close-knit scholarly community that was as fiercely committed to leftist ideals as it was to the spirit of debate. In interviews she gave late in life, Janion describes the shock some of her older colleagues felt at her group's intellectual ferocity and independence. Her mother, she recalls, once recounted to her with amusement the gossip that had spread after Janion and a close friend of hers, Maria Żmigrodzka, presented papers at an annual conference of Polish literature teachers. Janion's offense, in her mother's retelling, amounted to "not much—basically nothing. 'They just stood there and talked' is what my mother's friend related to her. The witness from whom she'd heard about it had been appalled to see young women behave that way. To get into polemics with everyone around you, that's just not proper female behavior. The story emphasized gender norms and rules of propriety, and how we'd contravened against them."[2] These generational clashes created tensions between Janion and her advisors both in Łódź, where she got her master's degree, and at the Institute of Literary Studies in Warsaw, where she held her first academic position. The advisors, most of them orthodox Marxist critics, wanted Janion and their other advisees to produce synthetic, programmatic works of materialist literary critique. Grand syntheses, as Janion retroactively describes them, "helped one understand how popular literary venues can be used to educate the general population. And they had a well-articulated, consistent cultural and scholarly politics."[3] But—and this troubled her—they were not finely attuned to the nuances of different subject positions within socialist or nonsocialist societies. They did not account for how embodied sensory and affective experience contributed to one's understanding of a social system, its history, and possible alternatives to it.

Prometheism and Phantasmatic Critique

Janion looked to Romanticism to understand better the subjective dimensions of historical experience and appreciate the role of human creativity within history. Choosing to specialize in Romantic poetry, particularly its so-called minor, regional strands, Janion discovered in this poetry a complicated story of how conservative and progressive, egalitarian and elitist, public and intimate fantasies interpenetrate and transform each other in social milieus. She became a staunch critic of the ways in which Romantic fantasies of subjective or national uniqueness contribute to Polish culture's political blind spots, including its xenophobia and homophobia. But she also sought to recuperate what the Romantics could be at their best. With them, Janion embraced a belief that affective attachments to local cultural histories and geographies could be reconciled with a commitment to inclusivity and the equitable sharing of communal resources. It had to be possible to be a culturally rooted socialist without thereby becoming a *national* socialist on the fascist model. However, only a more speculative and optimistic version of Marxism, different from Stalinism, could offer such utopian possibilities. To imagine something more than a critique of capitalism—or an attempt to eradicate old bourgeois culture—Marxists needed to think more boldly and speculatively.

In one early essay that articulates this position, Janion seeks to recover what she calls a "Promethean" version of Marxism committed to—and optimistic about—socialism as a way of remaking social reality. Calling out the Christian undertones of her more pessimistic Marxist contemporaries, Janion insists:

> It all comes down to how we understand human nature. Did we commit original sin? Are we always at war with one another? Either of these original conditions would compel us to curb our aspirations to self-making, self-saving, and self-liberation as harmful forms of willfulness. Still, in practice, neither of these concepts of humanity accords sufficient weight to the condition of the oppressed, the suffering, the humiliated, and the persecuted (however much John Paul II might be trying to change this). Empathic attention to the marginalized has always been the domain of Promethean socialism, since it assumes that humans are not intrinsically evil.[4]

To stand with the marginalized requires critique, but also faith that society is not yet irrecoverably broken and that its members might be able to embrace change. In the Eastern Europe of her time, this seemed like boundless optimism, which Janion recognized. However, she insisted that without such a radical premise, no positive social change could ever occur.

Janion refined her political vision through an engagement with Western Marxism, which she began to read voraciously in the 1960s. Around this time, she became famous for spearheading a series of seminars and a book series, both called Transgresje (Transgressions), through which Polish students were able, for the first time, to read translations of the works of writers such as Georges Bataille, Jean Genet, Gilles Deleuze, and Michel Foucault.[5] Janion undertook this project, as she retroactively describes it, because "we wanted humanists to think with social categories such as gender and class, with an emphasis on the former. To that end, we discussed forms of exclusion and otherness, of marginality to normative social structures and conventions."[6] As Janion read Western Marxists within an Eastern European context, she frequently reinterpreted them in striking ways. Her readings were informed not only by a spirit of critique, but also by an imperative to enter the experiences and beliefs of marginalized others. "Becoming a madman and becoming a proletarian" seemed to her to be two strikingly similar processes; cultural and socioeconomic exclusion mirroring and revealing each other.[7]

Janion called the mode of thinking she developed in this space between speculation and analysis "phantasmatic critique."[8] This approach seeks to recover, and give clearer form to, suppressed collective histories and desires. In the following description of Witold Gombrowicz's attitude toward daydreaming, taken from her "Notes on Horror and Melodrama" (chapter 8), Janion implicitly voices her own perspective:

> In a wonderful article published in 1936, Witold Gombrowicz calls attention to the great "power of secret fantasies." Setting official and popular culture in sharp contrast with each other, Gombrowicz names secret dreams and fantasies as the domain of the latter. He also describes the kinds of people who indulge in them, who tend to be young: "Their taste for illusion is typical for young people. The cinema, the potboiler romance, the street ad, an illustration in a newspaper: all this arouses them. With nobody to stop them, they forge private daydreams and keep them secret from others. [. . .] The poet and the literary writer who dream lucidly, within boring official frameworks, cannot imagine what lurks inside the heads of these secretive, conspiratorial dreamers." Gombrowicz describes perspicaciously the urban background where these furtive fantasies take shape. He feels tempted to take on the role of "these secret fantasies' leader."

Drawing on Freud's theory of daydreams, Janion describes popular culture as a space where individuals' private fantasies can be shared with others. It gives its audiences relief by showing that what they might have assumed to be their unique, perverse longings are quite commonplace. The job of the popular artist—which, for Janion as for Gombrowicz, includes those working in new media such as cinema—is not to disenchant, but to give form to collective fantasies and enchantments so that they can be processed interpersonally as a collective therapy of sorts. In a way that is not far from how Lauren Berlant, some decades later, would describe the benefits and temptations of melodrama, Janion praises popular culture for not letting collective fantasies fester in the unconscious, and instead releasing some of their energies and acknowledging them.

Janion is quick to note that Gombrowicz's embrace of these "secret fantasies" was not untinged with irony: "Gombrowicz is ultimately too ironic, too drawn to the gesture of unmasking, to take on such a task disingenuously." Hers is a more hopeful, syncretic position, to the point that some of her detractors accused her of New Age–style optimism.[9] Something of an affect theorist *avant la lettre,* she embraced popular culture and its phantasms as means by which a society can better know itself and process its collective anxieties and traumas. Critical of extreme nationalism, Janion sought to articulate a kind of attachment to one's culture and community that was *creative* rather than reactionary because it stemmed from a secure and capacious affection for what is one's own.

Summoning Ghosts

When Janion began writing about phantasms, Poland was still part of the so-called Second World; shortly after she turned sixty, worker strikes were beginning successfully to undermine this Soviet influence. By that point, Janion had long become disenchanted with the Polish communist party, which had expelled her from its ranks in the 1970s. All the same, she witnessed the fall of the Berlin Wall with an enthusiasm tempered by considerable caution. In the European Union, she saw an opportunity for Eastern Europe's growth but also cultural self-abnegation and forgetfulness. In the fervor of post–Cold War transformations, it was tempting for her contemporaries to valorize Polish culture and history only to the extent that it tended toward or imitated the European West. "We are headed back into Europe, but we must bring our dead along with us," Janion quipped in the early 2000s, commenting on these dynamics.[10] How, she wondered, can Polish society accept Western influence without implicitly accepting a position of inferiority to it? And how can it be prevented from displacing some of these feelings of inferiority onto Slavic nations farther east, increasing the nationalist frictions among them?

Janion addresses both these questions in *Niesamowita słowiańszczyzna* (Uncanny Slavdom, 2006), one of her last and most famous works (sections of which are reproduced in chapters 1 and 2). The book lays bare the complicated networks of fantasies and projections that Polish nationalists have long held about the West on the one hand, and Ukraine and Belarus on the other. As Janion describes it, Poles' relationship to Ukraine and Belarus as their country's Eastern "borderlands" is deeply ambivalent. Her compatriots idealize them as spaces where Slavs are more truly themselves because their culture is unadulterated by German or Austrian influences. Conversely, they also see these regions as backward and "barbaric," always in need of civilizing. Janion shows how entrenched such stereotypes are in her contemporaries' mindsets. "For centuries," she writes, citing the scholar Andrzej Żbikowski,

> "the phrase 'borderland people' has been enmeshed with a perception of Polish colonization as a civilizing, culturally creative force, of Polish identity as a stronghold against a sea of barbarism."[11] These views have had lasting consequences: the history of the Galicia region of the Eastern Borderlands has rightly been described as one "of traumas and irreversible ruptures."[12] They also had a long afterlife: after the Cold War, an intoxication with the lost Polish Borderlands resurged in Polish literature and nonfiction. Though post-1989 Poland acknowledged the independence of Ukraine, "paradoxically, acknowledging the sovereign national borders of its eastern neighbors does not yet go hand in hand with ceasing to treat them as peripheries of the Polish state."[13]

Today, as the war in Ukraine continues, Janion's analyses have become even more pertinent as diagnoses of the projections layered onto Ukraine from East and West alike. She does not hesitate to describe the historical relationship between the Polish state and its Eastern neighbors as colonial. She also argues that, as Poles enter the European Union, they carry with them the unacknowledged burden of seeing themselves as needing, or deserving, to be colonized themselves.

Why are Eastern Europeans trapped in these schemata of projected or assumed cultural inferiority? Janion's answer to this question forms the core of *Niesamowita słowiańszczyzna* and constitutes its most provocative claim. A more conventional argument would find the roots of these stereotypes in the nineteenth century, a period during which Poland had lost its independence and Polish-speaking people were frequently compelled to attend German- or Russian-language schools, fighting to preserve their national identity amid forceful acculturation by overpowering political forces. Janion does not deny the importance of this collective experience, but to find the origins of the cultural dynamic she diagnoses, she looks much further back, toward the Middle Ages. Poland was officially recognized as a duchy, then a kingdom, by its Western neighbors in the late tenth century CE. To achieve this recognition, it had to undergo a hasty process of Christianization. Citing historians who study this period, Janion emphasizes that conversion occurred under duress and amid fear of violence. Polish subjects were summarily baptized in mass ceremonies. Meanwhile, any and all signs of their previous beliefs and customs were destroyed: Idols were burned, traditional rituals were abolished, and pagan priests were banished from the region.[14] As a result of the rapidity and brutality of this forced conversion, very few traces of Poland's lost pagan culture persist in the historical archive. Historians have even speculated, improbably enough, that unlike any other cultural community known to anthropology, Eastern Europeans had no Indigenous beliefs and mythologies at all.

In the aftermath of this traumatically suppressed event, Poles cling forcibly to Catholicism as their supposed heritage and birthright. Meanwhile, as Janion demonstrates through masterful readings of Polish literature from the Romantic era into the present, Poland's pagan past is never completely lost from sight: Writers continue to speculate about it and call it back into being. To overcome its sense of inferiority to the West, Polish society needs to work through this huge cultural loss and through the sense of self-doubt and self-alienation it generated. In art and popular culture, Janion sees a potential for expressing collective fantasies and imagining their fulfillment, which she believes could serve as a means to heal these wounds. She wants to draw Poles away from violent self-assertion and toward the proper mourning of a past, and a cultural sense of self, they have irretrievably lost.

As many thinkers wonder about the origins of the recent global turn toward the right, and seek to reverse it, Janion's affectively attuned, speculative Marxism strikes one as surprisingly *realist* in its aspirations. Her work shows that communities will continue to cling to narratives of their exceptionality and purity unless they find a different way to work through the affective needs these narratives satisfy. Additionally, it's essential that both critics and laypeople acknowledge that these needs cannot be simply repressed. The answer to nationalism is not detachment, but a renewed, intellectual as well as affective commitment to the cultural heritages that nationalist ideology hijacks and oversimplifies. Janion shows the importance of this work and gives her readers tools for undertaking it.

Janion authored hundreds of essays and dozens of books in her lifetime. Culling some representative selections from her prodigious output was no small task. No less challenging was the process of deciding which of her essays most easily speak to an Anglophone readership unfamiliar with Eastern European cultural references. To help my reader orient themselves within Janion's copious body of work, I have arranged my selections from it thematically rather than chronologically. Divided into four sections, the *Reader* opens with Janion's analyses of the cultural histories and counterhistories of Eastern Europe from the Middle Ages into the present. The second section focuses on Janion's interventions into Marxist thought and political theories of nationhood. Part III collects Janion's major contributions to aesthetic theory and her manifesto on "phantasmatic critique." The last section gathers some of Janion's theorizations of otherness within an Eastern and Central European context, and ends with an extended excerpt from Janion's own account of her life's intellectual arc.

Part I, "A Theory of Eastern Europe," gathers three essays that illustrate the range and depth of Janion's engagements with Eastern European cultural dynamics. Together, these essays coalesce into an account of Eastern European history as paradoxically marked by both an excess of cultural influences and crucial absences within its cultural archives. "Uncanny Slavdom," the opening chapter of *Niesamowita słowiańszczyzna,* synthesizes much of Janion's prior writing on how Eastern European national identities were crafted and altered. It polemically applies her knowledge of Polish literature and culture, from the medieval period to the present, to contemporary discussions about race, postcoloniality, Orientalism, and collective cultural consciousness in Eastern Europe and beyond. It also relates these historical insights to more recent cultural and literary phenomena, ranging from contemporary Polish right-wing politics to the novels of the Jewish American writer Isaac Bashevis Singer.

"Poland's Location in Europe," taken from the middle section of *Niesamowita słowiańszczyzna,* is of particular interest as a proleptic analysis of the current political crisis in Ukraine. A case study for the book's central thesis, it examines the affects, legends, and histories that reinforce Eastern European nations' liminality as territories that are "east of the West and west of the East." Particularly striking and pertinent to present-day debates is Janion's discussion of Ukraine as a territory that Polish as well as Russian culture tend to portray, at once, as a borderland and as the original wellspring of Slavdom. Janion traces the genealogy of these projections back to Eastern Europe's turbulent conversion to Christianity. She shows why the long shadow of these histories has impeded Poland's and Russia's capacity to recognize Ukraine as culturally and politically separate from themselves.

These two opening essays discuss the vestiges of Eastern European folk culture in broad strokes. "Between Death and Laughter: The Art of Jacek Malczewski" (2001) zeroes in on a singular example. Through the prism of the paintings of Jacek Malczewski, it pursues a critical feminist genealogy of the *rusałka,* a demonic water spirit from Eastern European folklore. Western readers might know this water spirit from Antonin Dvořák's eponymous opera. In Eastern Europe, legends about it constitute one of the most lasting traces of the region's pagan past. Janion's genealogy of the *rusałka* powerfully instantiates her broader account of Eastern Europe's religiously syncretic, internally conflicted collective symbolisms. In addition to offering a case study in the persistence and transformations of folklore in Polish nation-building, Janion's essay provides an accessible introduction to the work of Malczewski, one of Poland's great modernist painters, who remains relatively unknown in the West.

The second section of this reader, "Socialism, Patriotism, Nationhood," reveals Janion's acumen as a political theorist concerned with Eastern Europe's nationalist tendencies and the imperfections of Soviet-style socialism. In "The Patriot-as-Madman" (1989), an essay from a collection of writings on the problem of evil, Janion confronts the dark side of Polish patriotism. In the nineteenth century, Polish writers depicted patriotic attachment to the nation as a form of madness that was both metaphorical and *literal.* After Poland's threefold partition and loss of independence to its neighbors, one had to be insane to still hope for its return to sovereignty. Yet, a good patriot also *ought* to fall into this madness, even if it caused him to lose his senses in all other respects as well. As she tracks the self-destructive patriot-madman in nineteenth-century Polish literature and culture, Janion finds in this trope a deeply self-hating, but also intriguingly anti-Darwinian, non-fascistic form of nationalism.

The second essay in this section, "Socialism as a Prometheism" (1989), seeks to renew Marxist theory by recovering Karl Marx's original view of human nature. Janion gradually became disillusioned with Soviet Marxism, but Western, existentialist-inflected Marxism did not satisfy her, either. Calling for a return to an abandoned form of leftism, Janion emphasizes ideas that had been espoused by Marx himself. She argues that leftists need to move away from both Soviet dogmas and an existentialist, Sisyphean notion of social progress as painful and interminable. Her preferred kind of socialism is neither Stalinist nor Sisyphean, but Promethean. This Promethean socialism goes back to Marx's love of this Greek myth, which he absorbed through Johann Wolfgang von Goethe's poems. Janion urges her readers to reappreciate this Promethean metaphor because it disconnects human labor and creativity from the specter of original sin while drawing attention to socialism's duty to support the weak and marginalized. This essay provides a striking example of Janion's role as a mediating figure between Western European, Eastern European, and Soviet Marxisms.

Part III, "Aesthetics, History, and Critical Method," spotlights Janion's theory of personal, literary, and cinematic fantasies and phantasms. Readers might recognize in this section some surprising, productively estranging parallels to affect theory. "The Project of Phantasmatic Critique" (1991) presents a manifesto for Janion's approach to fantasizing. *Phantasm*, a key term in her theory of literature and cultural politics, connotes an act of imagination that hovers on the brink between daydreaming and unconscious dreamwork, between collective stereotypes and individual creativity. To Janion, phantasmatic figures such as vampires or *rusałki* (the plural form of *rusałka*) offer crucial models for the shared social realities cultures create. To perform what she calls "phantasmatic critique," one must not seek to disenchant the phantasm, but learn to think with and through it. Only by coming to appreciate phantasms' ineluctable place in her own and other people's thinking, and by learning to speak through them, can a thinker understand and communicate with her community. This exposition of Janion's literary–critical method articulates how her readers might apply phantasmatic critique to Eastern European imaginaries, as well as how they might carry it elsewhere.

The second essay in this section, "The History of Literature and the History of Ideas" (1980), offers one of Janion's clearest and most forceful statements about aesthetics as a scholarly and creative framework. Janion self-identified as a historian of both literature and ideas. In this essay, she lays out these two pursuits' synergies, as well as the tensions between them. For ideas to travel and develop, they must be portable and repeatable; but to command aesthetic attention, literature must militate against its ideological portability. Whereas ideas are intended to exist and evolve in linear time, pieces of writing are literary to the extent that they are written against time, for a putative eternal present. Even when historians of literature and ideas look at the same primary sources, they do not see the same objects; their spatiotemporal premises and points of reference are radically different. Janion locates human experience at the intersection between literary works and ideas. She senses intellectual danger where human achievement is too closely associated with only one of them.

"Notes on Horror and Melodrama" (1980) applies Janion's phantasmatic critique to these two literary and cinematic genres. A lifelong lover of cinema, Janion offers a speculative theory of its cultural genealogies in Europe. Friedrich Kittler connects cinema to the unconscious; Janion argues that it has stronger ties to conscious phantasms such as daydreams. She combines this insight with a generic one: For her, the cinematic sensibility has its roots in Romantic reckonings with tragedy. Romantic writers fractured tragedy into melodrama and gothic horror. Cinema retreads and transforms this distinction, deepening nineteenth-century accounts of how daydreaming shapes our sense of ourselves.

Part IV of the reader, "The Authority of the Other," circles back to Janion's commitment to the perspectives of those whom her surrounding communities stigmatize or exclude. These essays highlight minorities whom Eastern Europeans need to acknowledge and embrace as part of their collective "we." The first essay in this section, "Adam Mickiewicz's Jewish Legion" (2009), presents a lesser-known chapter of cross-fertilization between Polish Romanticism and an emergent Zionism. Adam Mickiewicz, seen by many as Poland's greatest

Romantic poet (or greatest poet *tout court*), articulated his idea of Polish nationhood under the influence of Jewish mysticism. Toward the end of his life, he worked with early Zionists to create a Jewish military legion that was to fight for Poland's independence alongside Polish Christians, with a view to creating a shared Polish–Jewish "chosen nation." After Mickiewicz's untimely death, this utopian vision was never realized. Janion insists that Polish anti-Semitism remains virulent, in great part, because of Polish culture's deeply repressed identification with its Jewish influences.

The next essay, "Fragments from a Lover's Discourse" (1996), explores how normative conservative society marginalizes its sexual minorities. Janion generally kept silent about her private life—she only publicly came out at the age of eighty-six—but long before then, her love for women was an open secret, and veiled engagements with homosexuality appear in many of her published writings. In this playful essay, Janion imitates the form of Roland Barthes's *A Lover's Discourse* in an extended review of then-recent fiction by female-identified German writers. The review rapidly turns into a broader reflection on intimacy, homosexuality, and the different conventions of representing love between men and love between women. Throughout, it pursues a coyly self-reflexive Barthesian meditation on homosexuality and closetedness as writerly subject positions.

In the final essay in this section and volume, Janion discusses her writing while looking back on the long arc of her life. "The Bad Child: Interviews" (2012) collates excerpts from an extended, two-volume interview that Kazimiera Szczuka conducted with Janion eight years before her death. These conversations bring out Janion's personal voice and highlight her incisiveness and intellectual generosity as a teacher, editor, activist, and institutional leader. The fragments I have selected touch on Janion's adolescence in war torn Vilnius; her recognition of her queerness; her early postwar years as an enthusiastic young Marxist and feminist; her decision to remain in Poland despite a growing frustration with the Polish communist party; and her work as a groundbreaking disseminator of Western critical theory throughout Eastern Europe. A self-described archival hoarder and compulsive reader, a "polygamist" and "monogamist" in different senses of these terms, Janion looks back on her life with irony and warmth. She highlights how intimately even her abstract political concerns are informed by a closely examined, boldly singular personal life.

Notes

1. Maria Janion and Kazimiera Szczuka, *Transe, traumy, transgresje* (Warsaw: Wydawnictwo Krytyki Politycznej, 2012), 2:5–6.
2. Janion and Szczuka, *Transe, traumy, transgresje,* 1:61.
3. Janion and Szczuka, *Transe, traumy, transgresje,* 1:105.
4. Maria Janion, *Wobec zła* (Warsaw: Verba, 1989), 156.
5. For an extended account of the resonances of these translations, see Michał Paweł Markowski, "Projekt Janion," *Tygodnik Powszechny,* nos. 51–52 (2016): https://www.tygodnikpowszechny.pl/projekt-janion-146050.
6. Janion and Szczuka, *Transe, traumy, transgresje,* 1:151.
7. Janion and Szczuka, *Transe, traumy, transgresje,* 1:151.
8. Maria Janion, *Projekt krytyki fantazmatycznej* (Warsaw: PEN, 1991), 30–59.
9. Brigitta Helbig-Mischewski, "Guru przełomu tysiąclecia," *Teksty Drugie,* nos. 1–2 (1997): 165–92.
10. Maria Janion, *Niesamowita słowiańszczyzna* (Kraków: Wydawnictwo Literackie, 2006), 32.
11. Andrzej Żbikowski, *U genezy Jedwabnego: Żydzi na Kresach Północno-Wschodnich II Rzeczypospolitej. Wrzesień 1939–lipiec 1941* (Warsaw: Żydowski Instytut Historyczny, 2006), 235.
12. Delphine Bechtel, "'Galizien, Galicja, Galitsye, Halatchyna': Mit Galicji od zaniku do wskrzeszenia," *Borussia* 31 (2003): 85.
13. Daniel Beauvois, *Trójkąt ukraiński: Szlachta, carat i lud na Wołyniu, Podolu i Kijowszczyźnie, 1793–1914* (Lublin: Wydawnictwo Uniwersytetu im. Marii Curie-Skłodowskiej, 2005), 16–17.
14. Not all of Janion's readers agreed with this interpretation of the gaps in Poland's medieval archives. For polemics against *Niesamowita słowiańszczyzna,* see Julia Tazbir, "Cienie zapomnianych przodków," *Tygodnik Powszechny,* no. 3 (2007): https://www.tygodnikpowszechny.pl/cienie-zapomnianych-przodkow-137939; Marek Piechota, "Bolesna utrata własnej mitologii: Jeszcze o *Niesamowitej słowiańszczyźnie* profesor Marii Janion," *Śląskie Studia Polonistyczne,* nos. 1–2 (2012): 283–90; Jan Jakóbczyk, "Niesamowita/samowita Maria Janion," *Nowa Polszczyzna* 4 (2007): 59–60; and Dariusz Skórczewski, "Trudności z tożsamością: Na marginesie *Niesamowitej słowiańszczyzny,*" *Porównania* 5 (2008): 127–42.

Translator's Note

MARTA FIGLEROWICZ

Maria Janion knew Russian, French, English, and German and read widely across European, Soviet, and American philosophy, critical theory, historiography, and literature. She saw herself as not only a scholar but also a mediator of the international cultural traditions into which she tapped, within which she wanted her students to situate themselves. Her writings provided Polish readers with their first introduction to figures such as Edward Said, Michel Foucault, and Julia Kristeva, among many others. Janion herself obtained many of these sources with difficulty, at times illegally, as friends smuggled them back to her from across the Iron Curtain. As a result, Janion's essays usually serve a double pedagogical purpose: Alongside her original arguments, she devotes considerable space to summarizing sources that she assumes her readers could not access otherwise. Janion's early writing often gives very limited bibliographical information about the works she cites, possibly because they would not have been available in Polish libraries. Her later essays compensate for this tendency by featuring increasingly long, discursive notes that include extensive bibliographic references.

I follow Janion's bibliographic method in each essay translated here: Where she provides notes and references, I do so as well. To help the twenty-first-century Anglophone reader grasp the originality and force of Janion's writing, I have reduced the expository apparatus in her later essays and also occasionally elided passages where Janion engages in local scholarly debates. My reductions of her notes are unmarked, and my elisions in the body of the text are marked by ellipses in square brackets. Ellipses *without* square brackets are Janion's own. In square brackets, I also occasionally offer translations of the names of untranslated Polish sources and other editorial clarifications. When

Janion quotes from texts originally published in English or with an established English translation, I refer to these original or standard sources and cite only their English titles. When Janion quotes from works untranslated into English, I provide my own translations in square brackets.

A MARIA JANION READER

PART I

A Theory of Eastern Europe

CHAPTER 1

Uncanny Slavdom

What Story Should the Humanities Tell Poland?

Polish intellectuals began to debate the universal and local value of our national culture in the eighteenth century. These debates briefly intensified in the wake of the Cold War; today, they are at an impasse. This standstill stems from our general public's inability to read and interpret Poland's cultural past. The Polish public reaches back into its heritage, if at all, as a trove of propagandistically useful quotations. But even that does not happen very often. In the aptly named "Szachownica bez szachów" [Chessboard without pieces], Stanisław Lem stated quite accurately, if with great bitterness, that our contemporary culture has become "maddeningly flattened." Present-day Poland displays "complete amnesia" about its history; it has also pushed literature to the margins. In the past, when aspiring writers visited Lem, he would counsel them to flee toward business school or computer science. "Today," he confesses, "I would no longer be so radical." No one is there to take up the "heaviest of topics," as he calls them.[1] It's as if all of Poland's forty million citizens have become spellbound by fear and listlessness.

The humanities are frequently the object and addressee of grievances such as Lem's. We would, therefore, do well to reflect on our discipline's current condition. *Transformation, modernization:* these words have dominated Poles' vocabularies in the past fifteen years. They describe our economy, of course, but our culture as well. As postcommunist countries such as Poland shifted toward democracy and capitalism, the working class, as well as other social classes, lost considerable economic and symbolic capital. At the same time, another facet of our modernization—the so-called media revolution—has transformed Polish politics into mass politics. Pop culture has come to dominate the public sphere. High culture has fallen into crisis; in the eyes of many, culture *as such* has done so as well. Older ideals of community, many of which were grounded in an unspoken but widely shared popular commitment to independence and freedom, have not survived Poland's transition out of communism. Amid the rise of globalization, Poland's technocratic elites have lost interest in national culture, and traditional notions of identity have come to feel obsolescent.

Contemporary Polish prose bears witness to these processes through what our writers say as well as through what they do not. "The intelligentsia has fallen silent," writes Barbara Skarga. She makes this diagnosis while refusing to name any still-existing bastions of critical high culture, "lest she should thus expose them to attacks, or inspire someone to destroy them."[2] [. . .] Indeed, the Polish intelligentsia has fallen into silence and its influence has diminished. The quality of readership has eroded as well. Janusz Sławiński describes its erosion in grim terms: "The reader who demands something of literature, or hopes for, or expects something from it—that reader no longer exists. What does reach audiences seems uniformly uninteresting to them."[3] [. . .]

Finally, let me name the third and most important consequence of Poland's modernization: Mass communication has become its main medium and point of reference. Przemysław Czapliński writes passionately about this shift as a return to standardization and banal, ready-made formulas. Being unrevelatory has become our cultural norm and desideratum. Whatever social consensus we might form in such a public sphere is necessarily superficial; indeed, it might be merely the appearance of a consensus. Without deeper humanistic knowledge of and exchange about our communities' diversity, Polish democracy lacks a foundation. Czapliński describes the effects of these new conditions on contemporary Polish literature as the "passivity effect": "An ideological aversion to further change has stilled social communication."[4] We drown in the idiom of mass media, to which writers have forfeited "the field on which battles are fought for social attention, by means of newly discovered mimetic forms."[5] Literature ought to forge new ways of speaking. Instead, it has apprenticed itself to journalistic realism and seeks to imitate the language of the news.

How can literature and the humanities renew themselves? I believe that humanistic knowledge is at its most meaningful in the act of *recounting*. It does not suffice to observe human experience, live through it, or even comprehend it. One must also know how to tell stories about it. Whether aesthetic or not in intent, these stories inevitably tend toward some formal structure. Without a form, they would become incomprehensible. A humanistic narrative can follow one of a few basic genres. Hayden White lists them as romance, comedy, tragedy, and satire, adding that these four genres frequently mix and combine into subgenres.[6] [. . .] By telling them, we orient ourselves within the world. The humanities are supposed to do some of this work for us. Storytelling draws its power from a sensitivity to the other, the one to whom our story is told and to whom we must afterward listen, in a circle of empathy and compassion that constitutes a special mode of understanding. Whenever we tell a story, we enter a compact within which narratives can be exchanged both ways.

So, what new forms or genres should our stories take? Perhaps those of postcolonial critique, for which I look to Edward W. Said. In *Orientalism,* Said analyzes the half-mythical "Orient" conjured up by Westerners as they tried to subjugate the non-Western nonhistory of the East to their own genres and schemata. Norman Davis rightly notes that Western studies of Eastern Europe often replicate similar Orientalist prejudices and distortions. Does that mean we should use the terms of postcolonial critique in the narratives we recount about Slavdom and Poland? I want to consider this question here.

Said described the two principles of his groundbreaking work as humanism and "humanistic critique." Humanism is a mode of understanding grounded in rationality as well as in history. It sustains and is sustained by a sense of community with other commentators, societies, and periods. Following Giambattista Vico, Said argues against cultural and biological essentialisms. As he puts it, "The secular world is the world of history as created by human beings" and "human beings must create their own history." The critical method Said embraces, as following these principles, is comparative literature as practiced by Goethe, Humboldt, Dilthey, Nietzsche, Gadamer, Auerbach, Spitzer, and Curtius. Said describes these comparatists' shared method, philology, as "the most basic and creative of the interpretative arts." Through philological practice, comparative literature interprets its sources concretely, but also sensitively and intuitively; it delves deep into their contexts at the time of their composition and in their subsequent reception. Said invokes Dilthey's term *Einfühlen* to describe this attitude. Thus understood, a humanistic education is not "a sentimental piety enjoining us to return to traditional values or the classics but . . . the active practice of worldly secular rational discourse." Contemporary technologies might be diminishing this humanistic education's effects. "Instead of reading in the real sense of the word, our students today are often distracted by the fragmented knowledge available on the internet and in the mass media."[7] We must, therefore, revisit the tradition of philology and turn our attention back toward cultural texts of a more old-fashioned sort.

A thousand years ago, a religious and cultural boundary began to form between the Latinate West and the Greek East, between Rome and Byzantium; this boundary is now often seen as "Europe's most lasting cultural rift."[8] What does this East–West division look like from the vantage point of Poland? We find ourselves, as Sławomir Mrożek ironically put it, east of the West and west of the East. We also often find ourselves—as intellectuals and as members of the public—in the position of trying to tip this balance toward the West, to make ourselves seem more Western than Eastern.

Can the Polish humanities take it upon themselves to *retell these stories*? The task is imperative. The old narratives we need to replace, and which remain in circulation, repeat familiar themes of Poland as a martyred, chosen nation. They continue to resonate with many Poles by force of habit, stereotype, and intellectual inertia. In the nineteenth and twentieth centuries, Poland was partitioned among and effectively colonized by Russia, Germany, and Austria. In response, Poles developed counterfantasies of themselves becoming colonizers of other peoples and lands. The historical reality of being conquered and the dreams of conquest that this reality generated forged a double bind that makes Poland's version of postcolonial consciousness particularly fraught and paradoxical. It expresses itself, on the one hand, in feelings of helplessness and failure. Poland as a country and the stories its people tell seem inadequate and peripheral. On the other hand, in lockstep with these feelings of inferiority, Poles assert a messianic pride in their country's unique suffering and exceptional cultural contributions. They claim themselves to be superior to an "immoral" West; they also see themselves as cultural missionaries to the uncultivated East. This closed circle of perceived inferiority and superiority ultimately results in a sense of powerlessness—and in a constant tug of war between "Europe's false appearances" (which, one fears, might not be completely false or superficial) and "Poland's own truth" (which one strongly suspects of not being absolutely true after all).

What Happened to Slavic Mythology?

An online exchange made a big impression on me recently. It took place in a forum hosted by *Gazeta Wyborcza* titled "Why Don't Our Children Learn about Slavic Mythology?" Readers debated whether a genuinely Slavic mythology or creed had ever existed. Greek, Roman, Scandinavian, or Celtic ones did not invite similar doubts: The forum users saw them as authentic, rich in content, great inspirations of European art. The Slavic mythscape, by contrast, seemed to them like a collage of nineteenth-century pseudoscientific fantasies and well-intentioned speculations. To cite one of the online comments, "There is so little we can say about Slavic mythology that it's just not worth talking about."[9]

[. . .] This online discussion laid bare a major cultural trauma. Having probably just seen [*The Lord of the Rings*,] a wildly successful film adaptation of Celtic mythology as retold by Tolkien, the writers of these comments must have asked themselves the inevitable, painful question: Do they have an equivalent one of their own? . . . And then, they rapidly suppressed this question by vehemently affirming that Mediterranean culture is superior to all others.

Such traumatic reactions should bring to mind the way Poland adopted Christianity and the attitudes the Roman Catholic missionaries bore toward the paganism of the Slavs. These missionaries disdained Slavic myths and beliefs and systematically worked to eradicate them. Their success in doing so is marked by the absence from the historical record of any written sources mentioning pre-Christian Slavic religious practices. This absence is so complete that, for a time, it led scholars to hypothesize that Slavs did not have any Indigenous religion at all. "Christian missionaries to the region and their medieval chroniclers lacked any deeper interest in, sensitivity to, or curiosity about the spiritual lives of the peoples they had been sent to convert."[10] The region's past was erased, leaving a gap in the archive that produced an only-recently overturned conviction that the Slavs did not believe in any gods and did not tell any stories about these gods' lives, deeds, or familial relations. If this were indeed the case, it would make Slavs what one major religious historian of the region has called "a deeply bizarre and singular exception to global patterns of human culture." That such a "bizarre" hypothesis persisted for so long says much about the unwarranted but real national and international conviction about the Slavs' overwhelming "primitiveness."[11]

Consider, by way of counterexample, the cultural condition of early medieval Ireland. Converted to Christianity in the fifth century but never incorporated into the Roman Empire, Ireland adopted Latin while managing to maintain much of its own cultural distinctiveness. As Thomas Cahill puts it, "The survival of an Irish psychological identity is one of the marvels of the Irish story."[12] The Irish did not work very hard to eradicate pagan customs; Halloween, for one, remains with us to this day. When their monks mastered Greek and Latin, they used it to preserve Greco-Roman and Judeo-Christian works that, at the time, were actively endangered elsewhere; they also used these same skills to set down in writing the products of Celtic culture. "It is thanks to [the Irish] scribes," Cahill points out, "that we now have the rich trove of early Irish literature, the earliest vernacular literature of Europe to survive."[13] Pre-Christian, Slavic Poland was not nearly so privileged.

Pagan Polish culture was less fortunate than that of the Celts during the Middle Ages, but also thereafter; efforts at its belated reconstruction have been plagued by ill luck. In 1818, Zorian Dołęga Chodakowski dreamed of composing "a major treatise on Slavic mythology that would enhance our poetry and give it an unusual, singular quality."[14] This treatise, which Chodakowski hoped would inspire Polish poets and redirect them from classical myths, never took shape. Between 1847 and 1848, Bronisław Trentowski worked on a copious manuscript titled *Wiara słowiańska lub etyka piastująca wszechświat* [Slavic beliefs: An ethic of universal care]. It remained unpublished until 1998, when it came out in a highly abridged version. Trentowski's work was indebted to the outline of Slavic mythology that Adam Naruszewicz laid out in the still-available second volume of his *Historia narodu polskiego* [History of the Polish nation, 1776–79]; but many of his other sources, including oral ones, have now been lost. Trentowski's present-day editor, Tadeusz Linkner, claims that some of his research did trickle out into the nineteenth-century public when parts of his manuscript, as well as sections of his *Dictionary of the Polish Language,* were plagiarized by Joachim A. Szyc in *Słowiańscy bogowie* [Slavic gods, 1865]. Nevertheless, Linkner sees the greatly delayed publication of Trentowski's study as a huge missed cultural opportunity: "Had Trentowski managed to publish *Slavic Beliefs* in his time, it would have been the first such compendium of knowledge about pre-Christian religions available to the Polish Romantics. It bears comparison only to *Die Wissenschaft des slawischen Mythus* [The study of Slavic myth, 1842], by Trentowski's contemporary Ignaz Johann Hanusch; and even as the two scholars' aims and perspectives were similar, the former's work promised to be much richer and more resonant in its attentiveness to gaps in the historical archive."[15]

Around the recent premiere of Marek Koterski's *Wszyscy jesteśmy Chrystusami* [We are all Christs], the star of this film, Marek Kondrat, gave several important interviews. In all of them, he reflected on the following question: How did Poles acquire their particular cultural "genetic code," predicated on a strong sense of superiority ("We're obsessed with ourselves!") as well as on a painful sense of inferiority toward "the West of which we dream"? Kondrat responds as follows: "I am persuaded by the following hypothesis, though I will state it with some apprehension: Poland remains a relatively new part of the Old World. The tenth century is a late starting point for a European nation, especially since we bear no relation to what came before then."[16]

But perhaps Poles *do* bear some relation to a cultural past prior to the tenth century, even if we do not realize it. Many signs point in that direction. A certain strand of Polish Romanticism speculates whether Slavs' conversion to Christianity was a "bad" one, marked by cultural and physical violence, by means of which Slavs were forcefully torn away from their old beliefs. Such a violent cultural transformation would have sparked in Slavs a sense of fragmentation and inferiority, a feeling of diminishment that might have persisted over centuries.

Consider the dramatic events surrounding the conversion of the Slavs of the Polabi region [in present-day Czechia]. Bruno of Kwerfurt, who led the Christianizing mission to the Polabi Slavs, described the twofold principle of his task as *compelle intrare*: he was to *compel* the Polabi peoples *willingly* to accept their new faith. As Henryk Łowmiański clarifies, the term *compelle intrare* refers to a legal act, a public declaration that the collectives into which the Slavs organized themselves had to make for Bruno's task to be complete. German scholarship on this subject emphasizes the voluntary aspect of this declaration. Łowmiański pushes back: "We can only speculate about the feelings with which tenth- and eleventh-century Polabi Slavs took on their new faith; but what we do know for sure are facts, and in this case, these are the facts of military conquest."[17] We also know that missionaries from the West insisted on the superiority of Christianity and the contemptible nature of paganism. Hasty and superficial in their conversion efforts, they were more interested in eradicating pagan rites and destroying pagan temples and idols than in teaching their converts about the Christian faith.[18]

The fall of Cape Arkona, known as the "Troy of the North," closed the final chapter of the Polabi Slavs' independence from their Saxon and Danish invaders. Much has been written about the new, Christian order the latter created. But one should also "see the conversion of Eastern Europe's barbarian peoples as a destructive act." As Karol Modzelewski writes, "The missionaries insisted that sacred pagan idols and places of worship had to be demolished before collective baptisms could take place; these acts of destruction took place in public, before the eyes of the believers, in purposefully shocking fashion."[19] In *Barbarzyńska Europa* [Barbarian Europe], Modzelewski quotes medieval Christian chroniclers who describe the fear and dread with which the pagans witnessed the ruin and defilement of their ancient cults. "After Arkona was conquered by the Danes, crowds of pagan believers watched their armed conquerors violate successive circles of local religious taboos. They saw the Danes take down the fences built around their temples and rip the veils covering their sacred sculptures; they saw the Danes order henchmen to cut off a holy idol's legs, put a noose around its neck, and drag it to the victors' encampment, where kitchen help cut it up for firewood." The chroniclers add that the pagans assembled to witness these spectacles of desecration often cried in despair at the hurt done to their idols by the horses that dragged them and the soldiers who struck them.[20] This despair would have resonated across the centuries; a powerful historical trauma, it must have left some traces in the cultures of the Slavic peoples.

Historians further remind us that, had pagan Poles refused to adopt this new Christian, European, monarchical social system, we would have been reduced to a small, deeply peripheral ethnic minority within Western European states—not unlike the Luzitsi tribes [Łużyczanie] crushed by and absorbed into Germany, whom historians now see as the "last living witnesses" of Polabi Slavdom.[21] In a chapter titled "How We Might Not Have Existed," Zdzisław Skok dramatically asserts that "the emergence of the Polish state was by no means an inevitable consequence of its surrounding historical processes."[22] When Mieszko I [the founder of Poland's first royal dynasty] created a Polish state and worked to incorporate it into Europe, this transformation "came at the cost of immense bloodshed, and of violence done to pagan tribal leaders, gods, and priests; pursuing this violent politics against its own people was the only means by which Poland could assert itself as independent."[23] By contrast, Poland's Polabi neighbors perished because of their fierce loyalty to both their pagan deities and their principles of cooperative, group-based decision-making.

In the course of their defeat and brutal conversion to Christianity and Latinate culture, Slavs, especially Western Slavs like the Polabi, lost their cultural memory and the communal imaginaries their Indigenous mythologies subtended. [. . .] Modzelewski stresses that the converted Slavs "did not fear baptism itself. What they did fear was the radical, demonstrative destruction of the old cults that grounded the world in which they lived. [. . .] Their traditional cultures did not make distinctions between the sacred and the profane that might have allowed their members to redescribe themselves in secular terms. With the death of their gods, their whole cosmos perished as well."[24] The world as they knew it had been defiled and overturned, even as they were never quite integrated into the world of their conquerors.

A sense of contempt toward the supposed inferiority and ignorance of Slavic pagans established itself firmly and persistently in non-Slavic Central Europe. "In 1108, the archbishop of Aldegoza in the Magdeburg province wrote a letter that called on his community to invade the lands of the pagan Slavs; he described them as inhabited by 'the worst kinds of peoples' and their conquest as bearing a double advantage: 'Saxons, Franks, Lothringians, Flandrians—all you glorious victors—this task will bring you eternal salvation, and, if you like, it will also yield excellent lands for you to settle in.'"[25] Christianization went hand in hand with colonization, as it did in the Teutonic Knights' "civilizing" mission "to the East." The process of subjugating Slavs through and within European culture continued for centuries. Granted, during this time, Poland enjoyed some periods of political and socioeconomic success. But for the most part, Europeans saw Slavdom as "a reservoir of slave labor to be exploited";[26] they described Slavs as slavish, passive, and submissive in character, and as therefore deserving conquest and enslavement.

Nineteenth-century German nationalism was nourished by such stereotypes and gave them even more aggressive, expansionist meanings and aims. [. . .] Twentieth-century German propaganda whose aim was to increase German Lebensraum in the East made use of the preexisting image of the Slav as innately a slave. In the middle of

December 1941, Hitler justified the invasion of Eastern Europe as follows: "Slavs are a mass of slaves by birth; they invariably follow their master and ask themselves only who this master is. . . . Slavic nations were not meant to lead an independent life of their own. They know as much, and we should not try to convince them otherwise."[27] These oppositions of masters and slaves, racial superiority and inferiority, had murderous consequences.

In a book called *L'ingratitude,* in reference to the ingratitude of Western Europe toward Eastern Europe, Alain Finkielkraut writes that the agreement Western European nations signed with Hitler in Munich in 1938 [which allowed Germany to invade Czechia] was rendered possible not only by the West's cowardice but also by the contempt all the countries involved shared toward Eastern Europe's "unimportant nations."[28] In Germans, it was motivated by racial aggression; other Westerners looked down on Eastern Europeans because, unlike themselves, they did not belong to the "civilized part of humanity."[29] One hears echoes of this contempt, Finkielkraut remarks, in a recent French intellectual's insulting response to the reintegration of Eastern European countries into cooperative Western institutions [such as NATO] from which they had been separated since 1945. The intellectual in question described it as the continent's "balkanization."[30]

Balkanization: What a terrible word, with its undertones of chaos, fragmentation, and war! So much lies hidden beneath it. Georges Corm describes the Balkans and the Near East as victims of the same historical transformation that gave rise to Western Europe as we now know it. The dissolution of the multiethnic Ottoman, Austro-Hungarian, and Russian empires of which the Balkans and the Near East were major constituents coincided with the strengthening of Western Europe's power-hungry nation-states. The former regions' "balkanization" and "becoming-Lebanon," as Corm also calls it, were processes to which these latter states' predominance and mutual rivalries strongly contributed. However, the "culturally narcissistic" West insists on its natural and not just historically contingent superiority to these other civilizations from whose political decline it benefited. This narcissism led Western nation-states to express contempt toward the so-called East and see themselves as its educators. It also simplified Western views of political conflicts into "a Manichean system: with rationalism and democracy on one side, irrationalism, fanaticism, archaism, ethnocentrism, and tribalism on the other."[31] Such simplifications persist even today.

Let us return to the question of Slavic mythology. Western Europe's cultural disdain for "all these small Eastern nations" makes us furious, bitter, and sad.[32] I would not advocate that we overcome these feelings by teaching schoolchildren about Slavic belief systems, praising our ancestors' pagan deities, or glorifying neopagan nationalists such as Jan Stachniuk. However, to improve our mental balance, we do need to become better aware of the long history from which both our helpless sense of marginality and our fantasies of being a special, chosen nation stem. If we take some historical distance from ourselves, we will appreciate more fully the harmfulness of our habitual oppositions between "better" and "worse" cultures. From this transhistorical standpoint, the humanities can properly commence retelling our cultural narrative to ourselves.

What Do We Fear about Slavdom?

Such a retelling could indeed begin with the concept of Slavdom, even while adorning this concept with many dramatic question marks. I know that many of us would rather not discuss our imagined notions of Slavdom and focus instead on a revised notion of Central Europe. In one such evasion, Angelus, the literary award cosponsored by the city of Wrocław and the national daily newspaper *Rzeczpospolita*, introduces

> a new understanding of Central Europe. For us, this term does not, as would be more traditional, designate the territories of the former Hapsburg Empire. Nor does it follow a range of other definitions developed in the numerous literary and political debates that have surrounded this subject since the 1980s. Instead, for the purposes of this award, the term encompasses the following twenty countries: Austria, Belarus, Bosnia and Herzegovina, Bulgaria, Czechia, Estonia, Lithuania, Latvia, Macedonia, Moldova, Germany, Poland, Russia (as far as the Ural Mountains), Romania, Serbia, Slovakia, Slovenia, Ukraine, and Hungary. Including all the countries of the former Soviet Bloc as well as their neighbors, this designation reminds us of the shared, profound imprint that the two totalitarian regimes of the twentieth century have had on all of them.[33]

Such contemporary reconstructions of Central Europe refer back to, and then step away from, a political and cultural myth that was first established and debated twenty years earlier. Formulated by Milan Kundera in a 1984 essay, it sparked much discussion before becoming a means of regional self-definition. For Kundera and his followers, to speak of *Central Europe* was to protest the despotism of Russia and the USSR's totalitarian domination over the Second World. It suggested that Soviet Russia tore away from Western Europe countries that culturally belonged to the West, to which they had made unique contributions through their literature, architecture, and music. Kazimierz Brakoniecki has subjected this myth of Central Europe to devastating critique. He describes Kundera's Central Europe as a "hybrid entity impossible to locate in time and space," which was moreover rendered anachronistic in 1989 by the fall of communism and the contradictory national interests postcommunism awakened amid the USSR's former vassals. "The history and heritage of countries such as Poland, Czechia, Slovakia, Germany, Hungary, Romania, Bulgaria, Serbia, Slovenia, Austria, et cetera," writes Brakoniecki, "have no shared origins that the term *Central Europe* could designate."[34]

The notion of Central Europe put forth by Angelus is capacious by comparison. Indeed, it is perhaps *too* capacious since the constellation of states it creates is so diverse as to seem arbitrary. Spanning "the countries of the former Soviet Bloc as well as their neighbors"—Austria and Germany, that is—it forges their connective tissue out of a shared totalitarian [i.e., Nazi as well as Soviet] past. I am not interested in evaluating the aptness of this connection. I think, however, that the notion of Slavdom ought to be available to us as an alternative tool of thinking. Moreover, it should be possible to use this term in a nonessentialist way.

Brakoniecki sees Slavdom as a mythologized idea of "our East." It fascinates but also frightens him as "a myth that threatens our collective moral and social health even more than the corpse of the Weimar Triangle."[35] I understand his reservations, which stem from a particularly Polish fear: that embracing Slavdom might make one a "slavophile" or a "pan-Slav." Both labels—as well as calls for "Slavic unity" and "Slavic brotherhood"—are well-worn masks donned by Russian imperialism. As soon as one mentions them, the history of Polish–Russian relations rears its ugly head. But here, I will try to sidestep its specter: I want to approach the issue of Slavdom less spasmodically than usual, and with less concern for boundary demarcations.

To speak of Slavdom also brings up a second fear: Like any myth of ethnic or tribal belonging, it can easily fuel nationalist and even fascist ideation. [. . .] Today's nationalist radicals are drawn to the ideas of prewar theorist Jan Stachniuk, for whom Slavic nationhood evolved from and should revert to *zadruga,* the putative social unit of Eastern Europe's ancient tribal communities. Stachniuk wanted the Polish nation to self-liberate by rejecting Catholicism as "a faith imposed on Poles from the outside, by a foreign agent," and reembracing paganism. This fantasy of a neopagan national collectivity that might recover its ancient Slavic roots bred further backward-looking utopias. Stachniuk was "haunted by the need to reconstruct Poles' self-understanding around their culture's as yet poorly understood and underdescribed, original proto-Slavic paradigms."[36] Today, Stachniuk's racist and nationalist inheritors tell us that "on one level, we embrace national socialism; on another level, we embrace Slavdom. We want to fuse them into one powerful social movement"; and that "faced with the multiracial decadence of the West, only a united Slavia can fulfill the hopes of the white race; a Westerner who does not support the Slavs betrays the white race and himself."[37] To hitch their movement to imperial Russia's Eurasianism is the Polish neofascists' ultimate goal.

"I have taken myth away from the fascists," Thomas Mann once proudly announced. Perhaps that is the challenge we should undertake: When necessary, can we—and *how* can we—take Slavdom away from the fascists? Slavoj Žižek sees this as an impossible task: For him, national and ethnic identity are inseparable from fundamentalism. To be sustained, these identities require an Other who can be loathed, accused, and persecuted for appropriating, poisoning, and depleting some most precious, if inarticulable, "spirit of the nation." Such fundamentalism feeds on violence and hatred. Žižek argues that one cannot meaningfully distinguish between a "'healthy' national identity" or a "'healthy' nationalism" built around a circumscribed national self-awareness, and an "'excessive' nationalism" that becomes "xenophobic" and "aggressive."[38] Still, such a distinction is precisely what I will try to establish and reflect on here. I want to assume that it is possible, in principle, to speak of and maintain a national identity that is neither aggressive nor xenophobic. Wolfgang Sofsky observes that "the dream of the absolute gives rise to absolute violence."[39] When a nation is conceived of as an absolute value, it gives rise to violence as well. But can that process of absolutization be avoided?

"We Slavs Love an Idyll"

Over two hundred years ago, Europe's elites found out that Slavs were destined to lead their continent on a mission of cultural and social renewal. The man who delivered this news was one of the Enlightenment's great thinkers, Johann Gottfried Herder. The ancient Slavs Herder imagined "manufactured salt, fabricated linen, brewed mead, planted fruit trees, and led, after their fashion, a gay, musical life." These cheerful lovers of rural freedom were hospitable to the point of extravagance. They enjoyed farming, hated wars, and wanted to spend their lives by the family hearth. Our supposed progenitors came close to epitomizing Herder's notion of a pure human society. But they carried one crucial flaw: Their gentleness made them easy targets of conquest and enslavement. "Many nations, chiefly of German origin, injuriously oppressed them. . . . In whole provinces the Slavians were extirpated, or made bondsmen, and their lands divided among bishops and nobles." Herder compared this process to colonization; he underlined that the fate of Slavs within Europe invites analogies to the conquest of South America: "Their remains in Germany were reduced to that state, to which the Peruvians were subjected by the Spaniards." In both cases, Christianity served as a pretext for European invasion. Herder believed that this forced conversion temporarily transformed the character of the Slavic people: The softness with which they initially responded to their Christian masters and raiders turned into "the artful, cruel indolence of a slave." In assessments such as these, Herder did not mince words about the condition of his Slavic contemporaries; still, he did not see their condition as irreparable. After all, as he believed, "the wheel of changing time . . . revolves without ceasing." With its future revolutions, Slavs would go back to peaceful, exemplary practices of farming and trade within what Herder saw as the "finest lands of Europe."[40] His ideas about this innate, rediscoverable superiority of the Slavs gave fodder for several incarnations of Slavic nationalisms and myths of ethnic chosenness.

As a utopian thinker, Herder did not care about the actual political and religious differences that divided his contemporaneous Slavs.

Instead, he saw Slavdom as a homogenous territory within which his vision of an ideal society could realize itself. Slavs' perceived "non-historic" quality, as Hegel later termed it, made them a prime canvas for utopian thinking. The "Slavian chapter" of Herder's *Philosophy of the History of Man* thus crucially contributed to spreading idyllic visions of the Slavs both within their own territories and beyond them. Even Adam Mickiewicz, Poland's greatest Romantic poet, would thus say, though not without irony, that "we Slavs love an idyll" *[Sławianie, my lubimy sielanki]*.[41]

The Spellings of Slavery

Should the word *Slavs* be spelled *Słowianie* or *Sławianie*? Mickiewicz's choice of the latter, in the passage I just quoted, contributes to a broader Romantic debate about this old tribal name. *Sławianie* could derive from *sława,* glory; as the eighteenth-century Archbishop Jan Paweł Woronicz put it, it makes Slavs "sons of glory." *Słowianie,* on the other hand, recalls *słowo,* the word, thus perhaps also the "one who is called the Word."[42] Mickiewicz made the latter point in a series of lectures he delivered in Paris: "*Słowianie* means people of the word, the Word of God"; *słowo* "invokes piety and creative power."[43] Meanwhile, behind these glorious etymologies lurked a third one: *der Slawe–der Sklave* [both from the medieval Latin *sclavus*]. The Slav is the subject, the captive, the slave. Slavic territories were objects of conquest as well as sources of human bodies for the slave trade. Enslaved Slavs were often bought by Scandinavian merchants, who saw them as "a product to be traded on the markets of the Islamic world, where it carried much value."[44]

Herder writes that "the figure made by the Slavian nations in history is far from proportionate to [i.e., much smaller than] the extent of country they occupied."[45] Why would that be? Fifty years after Herder, Mickiewicz set out to solve this riddle in front of audiences assembled for his lectures at the Collège de France. He put forth two definitions of history: "that which is built and written" and "that which accretes to the Spirit." By the first definition, the spoils of history belong to the West; but by the second, he argued, they belong to the Slavs. It is the latter's destiny to fulfill and make manifest the spirit of history. In geographic terms, Slavdom "occupies a vast global territory."[46] The vastness of this space does not find adequate reflection in Western-style historical achievements. But the submissiveness that has prevented Slavs from exercising more historical agency is God-given. It is a sign not of their weakness, but of their anticipated future fate. From birth, they intuit and await a divine calling. For Mickiewicz, his people's seemingly passive attitude of hopeful waiting marks a defining feature of their implicit philosophy of history. He transforms Herder's utopian Slavic idylls into a full-blown messianic vision of Slavs as the world's spiritual saviors (though, as Mickiewicz also hastens to add to the assembled Parisians, the Slavs cannot accomplish this mission without help from France).

Utopias, legends, mystical visions, myths, ideological and literary phantasms: those are the warp on which our modern images of Slavdom were woven. As the Romantics wove these images, they did so in open conflict with Western prejudices about the "organic inadequacy of nonwestern peoples,"[47] forging for themselves a new myth of origin. They did so by revendicating the hidden, the forgotten, the repressed, the marginal, the superstitious, the strange, and the unhinged. The cultural forms they thereby sought to ennoble formed their period's unofficial counterculture. From an initial focus on local folklore, their reparative work went on to embrace all that was pagan, anti-Latinate, Slavic, and Northern. These Romantic efforts met with considerable resistance from proponents of classical Greco-Roman culture, some of whom also saw themselves as members of Polish Romanticism's subbranches. These other Romantics insistently identified their culture with the cultures of the Mediterranean; by going back to the Renaissance, they wanted to restore cultural harmony between Poland and the Greco-Roman South and Southwest.

Against these counterarguments, the main branch of Polish Romanticism refused to hope for cultural harmony and reconciliation. They rejected all things Latinate because they were convinced that their surrounding folk culture had preserved an older, pagan network of pre-Christian beliefs and customs from which they could draw their inspiration instead. These writers insisted that their local folk sources were not merely different from Greco-Roman ones, but intellectually and aesthetically on par with them. They believed that, as Gieysztor wrote two centuries later, "even today, Slavic folklore preserves a core pre-Christian view of the world and of the sacred."[48]

The Polish Romantics had thus intuited a possibility that would come to preoccupy twentieth-century microhistorians such as Norbert

Schindler and Carlo Ginzburg: "Popular culture [is] a social formation distinct from élite culture that possesses a practice of autonomous symbolic actions of its own."[49] "The ecclesiastical and theological influence on popular life, which is largely conceived of as a totality," is easily overestimated by historians.[50] By contrast, members of Poland's Romantic movement saw folk culture and official church culture as dramatically opposed to each other, at times even as each other's antinomies. In *The Cheese and the Worms*—a fascinating work—Ginzburg describes the "savage" religiosity of the common people, an orally transmitted "peasant religion." Ginzburg's protagonist, a "simple" miller named Menocchio, developed out of these traditions his own philosophical view about the nature of the cosmos. His pronouncements seemed so dangerous that the Catholic Inquisition investigated them and sentenced Menocchio to death. By studying the transcripts of this trial, which include the accused's own statements, Ginzburg shed new light on the deep rift between folk beliefs and church orthodoxy.[51] But the Romantics had already known a lot about it.

As Polish Romantics explored their cultural past through its folkloric traces, they recognized how mysterious and laden with secrets it was. Monika Rudaś-Grodzka writes that "from our contemporary point of view, we recognize these Romantic figures as discovering a previously undiagnosed collective cultural amnesia. They diagnosed this amnesia, because of which Poles have no past in which to recognize themselves, as one of our constitutive identity markers."[52] Romantic and post-Romantic writers continued to revisit and deepen this sense of painful oblivion and misrecognition. They also drew attention to the many symptoms of our cultural trauma, which manifests itself in feelings of identification with the weak and the oppressed; with the enslaved and the humiliated; with the dispossessed and the unfairly forgotten; with those who were cast aside or crushed in the gears of so-called historical progress.

Within their murky cultural past, the Romantics sensed the vestigial presence of some huge communal catastrophe. The aftershocks of this event reached them in billows of explosive, frenetic imageries of destruction and dread. The uncanny Slavdom they discovered was properly *unheimlich:* at once strange and familiar, marked by a sense of rupture, pregnant with a repressed non-Latin, maternal, autochthonous unconscious. At times, it would manifest itself in a secret rite of speaking with the dead that the common folk hid from their lords and their priests (and which Mickiewicz represents in *Dziady* [Forefathers' eve, 1832]). At other times, it would resurge as a semi-utopian vision of the past as both idyllic and intensely violent, inspired by both Herder's view of Slavdom and Nikolai Karamzin's *History of Russia* (1816) in which "the ruler's charisma stems from his cruelty," as in Juliusz Słowacki's *Król-Duch* [The spirit-king, 1847].[53] It sometimes inspired the Romantics to write quasi-historical tales of how Christianity and feudalism were forcefully imposed on a previously free Slavic people (such as Ryszard Wincenty Berwiński's *Bogunka na Gople* [Bogunka on the Lake Gopło, 1840]). At other times, Romantic writers gestured toward this Slavic uncanny through narratives that were at once very local and intensely foreign—as does the young Zygmunt Krasiński in his tale of a vampiric, Transylvanian-esque Slavic princess who lives under the village of Opinogóra. In his many novels, especially *Masław* (1877), Józef Kraszewski depicts it through vague images of unspecified defeats, destructions, and ruins. Well into the modernist period, Stanisław Wyspiański resurrects these visions of Slavdom as equal parts homely and demonic in a series of stage plays.

Józef Kraszewski and Isaac Bashevis Singer

Józef Kraszewski's *Stara Baśń* [An ancient tale, 1876] best exemplifies all these tendencies. Amid its idyllic, fairy-tale ancient Slavic landscape, this novel contains many scenes of concentrated violence. Kraszewski releases this violence into his represented world, as if to acknowledge the catastrophic cultural rift that is to come after the period whose realities he imagines. But he ultimately smooths out these turbulences by means of rather simplistic ideological schemata taken from the Roman Catholic playbook. Rudaś-Grodzka argues that Kraszewski cannot conceive of actually going back to Poland's pre-Christian Slavic roots or constructing a present-day identity around them; the tale he spins, he insists, is only a tale. Indeed, in his eyes, only with Christianity does the *real* story of Slavdom begin. Poles need it to enlighten their world and set their society on the right path. As Rudaś-Grodzka puts it, "Kraszewski repeats the old narrative that the conversion of Poland marked a necessary step in its refinement as a nation. This is the official narrative handed down by Polish history's political and military victors."[54]

Against this backdrop, consider Isaac Bashevis Singer's *King of the*

Fields (1988), which creatively rewrites Kraszewski's novel. This work, the last one Singer published before his death, imagines a mythical Polish prehistory in which agrarian communities—the tribes of the fields—alternately fight and cooperate with the Lesniks, hunter-gatherer tribes of the surrounding forests. Singer finds inspiration in old Jewish legends, according to which

> Jews used to live in Polish territories even before their conversion to Christianity. One such legend embroiders on a very well-known Polish folk tale about an evil pre-Christian ninth- or eighth-century prince named Popiel. [In the latter, better-known legend, Popiel and his Germanic wife are eaten alive by rats and mice as divine punishment for their cruelty and are immediately succeeded by Piast the Wheelwright, the legendary founder of the first Polish royal dynasty.] The Jewish legend on which Singer draws adds one more prince between Popiel and Piast. It imagines, as Popiel's immediate successor, a Jewish man named Abraham who eventually, peacefully, hands Poland over to Piast.[55]

In the spirit of this legend, Singer's fictional panorama of prehistoric Poland includes Ben Dosa, a Jewish cobbler who writes down the Polish language in Hebrew letters and preaches to the pagan Poles about the monotheistic God. But a blond, Christian stranger, Bishop Mieczyslaw, arrives on the scene. "He was tall, young, erect; he had a blond beard, a long cloak, a feathered hat, and spurs on his boots. He rode a white horse on a saddle trimmed with dangling tassels. His face was thin and pale, his eyes were blue." Mieczyslaw denounces Ben Dosa as a descendant of the One God's killers. The Jewish cobbler, whom the pagan community had embraced, is forced to flee the "land called Poland." A new royal conqueror named Yodla arrives on the scene: "On a white horse with an ornamented saddle, rode a man with a long mustache and a hat from which a feather dangled. His coat was richly embroidered with red and white threads. There were spurs on his boots." His feathered cap and fancy heel spurs presage the fashions of the Christian oligarchs and nobles of early modern Poland. King Yodla speaks of the need to "become one large nation, to speak one language, to live in one land."[56] In the course of the tale, a fabricated conflict separates Judaism and Christianity, even though they share the same point of origin; this conflict is then entangled with Poland's embrace of Christendom. This is how Singer portrays the emergence of Polish anti-Semitism and its inextricability from the history and identity of the Polish nation.

Herder's Hour?

In an instance of great historical irony, Hans-Georg Gadamer claimed in the 1980s that Herder's philosophy of history would soon need to be revisited and reappreciated. "Herder's hour," as he called it, did come, but in horrific guise. As Joanna Rapacka powerfully argues in her study of the cultural and historical context of the war in the former Yugoslavia, Herder's idea of history came back to life in the Balkan conflict. In the process, utopian hopes that Slavdom might be the source of Europe's political deliverance were cruelly dashed. The holiness of nations and their divine right to sustain their being by fomenting war, contempt, and hatred were also definitively called into question.[57] The "patriarchal–heroic Romanticism" of Slavic identity formation had revealed its nationalistic visage. In her celebrated book of essays *The Culture of Lies,* Croatian-born writer Dubravka Ugrešić takes inspiration from Paweł Pawlikowski's *Serbian Epics* (1992) to paint a vicious portrait of the Serbian leader Radovan Karadžić, "the psychiatrist, a doctor of science, a poet and a murderer." Grotesque, but also dangerous, this "king of the gusle-playing bards" and his murderous supporters coalesce into a "brotherhood of emphatic rhythms." As the ring they form around the besieged Sarajevo tightens, their attacks themselves become circle dances; they are confident that "the hypnotic 'gusle' will be there to sing of Serbian heroism and heroes for the 'n'th time on the smoking ruins." Criminals become national heroes to the beat of the ancient musical–mythical genre of the "Serbian epic," a genre that the Slavic Romantics also loved. Ugrešić writes how Karadžić's bardic "gusle storytelling" is reinforced by "gusle journalism," which "sings of contemporary events, summoning the memory of glorious forebears, with whom the new men stand in an unbroken necrophiliac connection."[58] In his reading of Emir Kusturica's *Underground* (1995), Žižek similarly highlights this heady, intoxicating soundtrack of the Serbian genocides. The film, he argues, "unknowingly provides the libidinal economy of the Serbian ethnic slaughter in Bosnia: the pseudo-Bataillean trance of excessive expenditure, the continuous mad rhythm of drinking-eating-singing-fornicating." Karadžić's being a poet is, for Žižek, anything but accidental: "Ethnic cleansing in Bosnia was the continuation of a (kind of) *poetry* with the admixture of other means."[59] The war in Yugoslavia thus definitively discredited prior attempts at a racial idealization of the Slavs.

A Bond We Cannot Sever

We are headed back into Europe, but we must bring our dead along with us. The pre-Christian Slavic ritual of *dziady* insists on the connectedness between the living and the dead. Mickiewicz saw this belief as our culture's most foundational, and most invigorating, principle. The chain of being *dziady* imagines transcends national, ethnic, and religious boundaries. Death does not sever the bonds that tie our lives together, nor can history sever them, though the process of history-making often requires one to forget more than one ends up remembering. Repeating the rites of *dziady* places one in a life-giving state of mourning. Here in Poland, these rituals might make us think mostly of those who died while fighting for our country's independence or were persecuted by its foreign occupants and conquerors.

But we have much more to mourn for. Speaking at the Collège de France in 1844, Mickiewicz described the destinies of Poland and Israel as mystically intertwined. "Our land has come to also belong to that oldest and most mysterious of nations: the Jewish nation." On Polish soil, "destiny entangled with each other these two peoples who would seem so mutually alien."[60] Mickiewicz was convinced that, through their mystical union, the Poles and the Jews were bound toward a joint, messianic fate, and that Poland served as a replacement for the lost territory of the promised land.

In 1957, Maria Czapska returns to this theme of Jewish–Polish entanglement in very different circumstances that Mickiewicz could not have anticipated: the aftermath of the Holocaust. She writes, "The globally unprecedented genocide of several million Jewish people took place in Poland, whose territory Hitler chose for the site of their execution. Their blood and ashes have become absorbed into our soil. It is not in our power to sever the bond this creates between Poland and the Jewish people. We may not be directly responsible for these crimes; but we share responsibility for offering reparations for the damage they caused."[61]

How are we to understand this statement? What reparations can a culture defined by *dziady* offer? . . . We must live in an excess of pain, an awareness of irretrievable damage. At stake is not a one- or two-year mourning period, but an unending one. The ethical awareness it builds, and the statement it makes, should be shared by all of Europe. Poland in particular must not try to avoid this mourning process. In *The Jewish War*, Henryk Grynberg powerfully conveys what it means to live on land marked by the reality as well as the specters of genocide. The protagonist of the novel, a young boy, comes to Warsaw while the Holocaust is under way. The sheer number of people he sees there shocks him. "I hadn't thought there were so many people left alive in the world. How was I to suspect it? After my town had disappeared, I had assumed that all other towns and cities had also been destroyed, and that the fields and forests where we hid were all that was left."[62] The Slavic rites of *dziady* commune with these lost lives as well.

Notes

1. Stanisław Lem, "Szachownica bez szachów," *Tygodnik Powszechny*, December 18, 2005, https://www.tygodnikpowszechny.pl/szachownica-bez-szachow-127242.
2. Barbara Skarga, "Inteligencja zamilkła," *Gazeta Wyborcza*, December 13, 2006, https://classic.wyborcza.pl/archiwumGW/4557258/Inteligencja-zamilkla.
3. Janusz Sławiński, "Potrzebujemy nowej zasadniczości," *Europa*, November 2, 2005.
4. Przemysław Czapliński, *Efekt bierności: Literatura w czasie normalnym* (Kraków: Wydawnictwo Literackie, 2004), 130.
5. Przemysław Czapliński, "Powrót centrali?," *Kresy* 1, no. 2 (2005): 31.
6. See Hayden White, *Metahistory* (Baltimore: Johns Hopkins University Press, 1975).
7. Edward Said, *Orientalism* (1979; repr., New York: Vintage Books, 2002), xxiv, xiv, xxix, xxvi.
8. Jerzy Kłoczkowski, *Młodsza Europa: Europa Środkowo-Wschodnia w kręgu cywilizacji chrześcijańskiej średniowiecza* (Warsaw: PIW, 2003), 12.
9. "Dlaczego w szkole nie uczą mitologii słowian?," *Gazeta Wyborcza*, December 12, 2005, https://forum.gazeta.pl/forum/w,29,33004288,33004288,Dlaczego_w_szkole_nie_ucza_mitologii_slowianskiej_.html.
10. Andrzej Szyjewski, *Religia Słowian* (Kraków: WAM, 2003), 9.
11. Szyjewski, *Religia Słowian*, 11.
12. Thomas Cahill, *How the Irish Saved Civilization* (London: Anchor, 1996), 148.
13. Cahill, *How the Irish Saved Civilization*, 160.
14. Zorian Dołęga Chodakowski, *O Słowiańszczyźnie przed chrześcijaństwem*

oraz inne pisma i listy, ed. Julian Maślanka (Warsaw: Biblioteka Tradycji Słowiańskiej, 1967), 41.

15. Tadeusz Linkner, *Słowiańskie bogi i demony: Z rękopisu Bronisława Trentowskiego* (Gdańsk: Wydawnictwo Marpress, 1998), 9.
16. Marek Kondrat, "Czasy się zmieniają, ale aktorzy zastygli w romantycznej pozie," *Dziennik*, April 20, 2006.
17. Henryk Łowmiański, *Religia Słowian i jej upadek* (Warsaw: PIW, 1979), 260.
18. Łowmiański, *Religia Słowian i jej upadek*, 260–63, 273–81.
19. Karol Modzelewski, *Barbarzyńska Europa* (Warsaw: Iskry, 2004): 455.
20. Modzelewski, *Barbarzyńska Europa*, 458.
21. Jerzy Strzelczyk, *Słowianie połabscy* (Poznań: Wydawnictwo poznańskie, 2002), 80.
22. Zdzisław Skok, *Słowiańska moc, czyli o niezwykłym wkroczeniu naszych przodków na europejską arenę* (Warsaw: Iskry, 2006).
23. Skok, *Słowiańska moc*, 109.
24. Modzelewski, *Barbarzyńska Europa*, 458, 460.
25. Henryk Samsonowicz, *Miejsce Polski w Europie* (Warsaw: Bellona, 1995), 44.
26. Monika Rudaś-Grodzka, "Słowiańszczyzna zniewolona," in *Romantik und Geschichte: Polnisches Paradigma, europäischer Kontext, deutsch-polnische Perspektive*, ed. Alfred Gall et al. (Wiesbaden: Harrassowitz, 2007), 222.
27. Jerzy Borejsza, *Antyslawizm Adolfa Hitlera* (Warsaw: Czytelnik, 1988), 32.
28. Alain Finkielkraut, *L'ingratitude: Conversation sur notre temps* (Paris: Gallimard, 1999), 25.
29. Finkielkraut, *L'ingratitude*, 25.
30. Finkielkraut, *L'ingratitude*, 15.
31. Georges Corm, *L'Europe et l'Orient: De la balkanisation à la libanisation* (Paris: Editions Bouchène, 1990), xviii.
32. István Bibó, *Misère des petits états d'Europe de l'Est* (Paris: Albin Michel, 1986).
33. "Wydarzenia roku 2006," *Rzeczpospolita*, April 7, 2006, https://ksiazki.wp.pl/wydarzenia-roku-2006-6145578251823233g/12.
34. Kazimierz Brakoniecki, "Widmo Europy Środkowej," *Borussia* 31 (2003): 24–25.
35. Brakoniecki, "Widmo Europy Środkowej," 25.
36. Jan Stachniuk, *Neognoza polska* (Kraków: Wydawnictwo Uniwersytetu Jagiellońskiego, 2004), 17.
37. Rafał Pankowski, "Poseł ze swastyką w podpisie," *Gazeta Wyborcza*, January 22, 2006, https://forum.gazeta.pl/forum/w,12217,35484917,35484917,Posel_ze_swastyka_w_podpisie.html.
38. Slavoj Žižek, *The Plague of Fantasies* (New York: Verso Books, 1997), 62.
39. Wolfgang Sofsky, *Traktat über die Gewalt* (Frankfurt am Main: Fischer, 1996), 226.
40. Johann Gottfried Herder, *Outlines of a Philosophy of the History of Man*, trans. T. O. Churchill (New York: Bergman Publishers, 1966), 483.
41. Adam Mickiewicz, *Dzieła* (Warsaw: Czytelnik, 1998).

42. John 1:1 (CEV).
43. Mickiewicz, *Dzieła*, XI.76.
44. Henryk Samsonowicz, *Miejsce Polski w Europie* (Warsaw: Bellona, 1995), 17.
45. Herder, *Outlines of a Philosophy of the History of Man*, 482.
46. Mickiewicz, *Dzieła*, X.176.
47. Ewa Thompson, *Imperial Knowledge: Russian Literature and Colonialism* (Westport, Conn.: Greenwood Press, 2000), 5.
48. Aleksander Gieysztor, *Mitologia Słowian* (1982; repr., Warsaw: Wydawnictwo Uniwersytetu Warszawskiego, 2006), 259.
49. Norbert Schindler, *Rebellion, Community, and Custom in Early Modern Germany*, trans. Pamela E. Selwyn (Cambridge, U.K.: Cambridge University Press, 1992), 94.
50. Schindler, *Rebellion*, 95.
51. Carlo Ginsburg, *The Cheese and the Worms* (New York: Routledge, 1980).
52. Monika Rudaś-Grodzka, "Słowiańszczyzna: Pamięć i zapomnienie w wykładach Adama Mickiewicza i powieściach Józefa Ignacego Kraszewskiego," *Konteksty* 1, no. 2 (2003): 217.
53. Boris Andriejewicz Uspienski and Wiktor M. Żywow, *Car i bóg: Semiotyczne aspekty sakralizacji monarchii w Rosji*, trans. Henryk Paprocki (Warsaw: PIW, 1992), 22.
54. Rudaś-Grodzka, "Słowiańszczyzna," 222.
55. Monika Adamczyk-Garbowska, *Polska Isaaca Bashevisa Singera: Rozstanie i powrót* (Lublin: Wydawnictwo Uniwersytetu im. Marii Curie-Skłodowskiej, 1994), 57–58.
56. Isaac Bashevis Singer, *King of the Fields* (New York: Farrar, Straus and Giroux, 1988), 170, 1, 211, 213.
57. Joanna Rapacka, *Godzina Herdera: O Serbach, Chorwatach i idei jugosłowiańskiej* (Warsaw: Energeia, 1995), 32–33.
58. Dubravka Ugrešić, *The Culture of Lies: Antipolitical Essays*, trans. Celia Hawkesworth (Philadelphia: University of Pennsylvania Press, 1998), 137–39.
59. Žižek, *Plague of Fantasies*, 64.
60. Mickiewicz, *Dzieła*, XI.138.
61. Maria Czapska, "W odpowiedzi redaktorowi Turowiczowi," *Kultura* 6 (1957): 53.
62. Henryk Grynberg, *Żydowska wojna i zwycięstwo* (Warsaw: Czytelnik, 1965), 46.

CHAPTER 2

Poland's Location in Europe

Ukraine and the Border

Antiquity knew a distinction between "civilization" and "barbarism." Its present-day equivalent is the distinction between the "West" and the "East." Edward Said shows how profoundly the Western understanding of this binary shaped nations' self-assessments far beyond the West. His *Orientalism* concerns itself "with Western conceptions and treatments of the Other but also with the singularly important role played by Western culture in what Giambattista Vico called the world of nations."[1] Europe's national mythologies typically equate the East with barbarism and, thus, inferiority. The eminent nineteenth-century historian Leopold von Ranke saw European history as a tumultuous, stirring struggle between Roman and Germanic nations. The "peripheral" nations of Eastern Europe were, on his account, merely onlookers or extras to this central drama, from which their national boundaries excluded them.

Throughout its history, Poland's intermediate placement between the East and the West frequently put it in a difficult position. Poland aspired to, but could not consistently maintain, the appearance of Westernness; meanwhile, it could not quite own up to being Eastern. To reconstruct its double, Eastern–Western national consciousness, we must look to literary, philosophical, as well as sociological and historical sources.

Pierre Chaunu observes that the lines between Eastern and Western Europe, like those between Northern and Southern Europe, have not historically been clear: "It is difficult to name Eastern Europe's exact dimensions." This boundary remained blurry, partly because of the uneven distribution of Europe's population and the resultant inconsistency of its communication networks. The farther east one traveled, the thinner the continent's population and its infrastructures became. Soon, the Europe of paved roads came to an end; instead, the traveler faced endless expanses of swamp and mud. One could cite many travel accounts of voyages to Eastern Europe that express astonishment at the amount of water that pools in Polish fields in springtime and terror at the severity of Polish winters. Today, we have drained most of our swamps, but our communication networks remain comparatively thin and inadequate. Chaunu also draws attention to a significant cultural shift that decisively separated Slavic Eastern Europe from the West over the course of the seventeenth century: The attempts of Latinate Slavs [i.e., those from Poland and Czechia] to self-Westernize and to sever ties with their eastern neighbors contributed to isolating these eastern neighbors from the rest of Europe.[2]

I cannot fully agree with Chaunu, especially when I consider the history of Poland's southeastern border. Let us reflect on the territories around this border, which the Polish "mythical–symbolic complex" designates as *Kresy* [the Borderlands].[3] At first, the term referred to military outposts scattered throughout Poland's southeastern territories, protecting them from Cossack and Tatar raids. Eventually, Kresy came to designate all the southeastern territories of Poland as demarcated by its 1772 borders—and that is the broader meaning the term has retained. Piotr Grabowski, the sixteenth-century writer born in southeastern Poland, to whom we owe the first efflorescence of the mythologies that surround it, vehemently defended its reputation. He described it as a broad, vaguely delineated band of transitional landscapes "whose boundaries were fuzzy and based on common usage." Grabowski waxes poetic about these landscapes and their military significance. "Our might comes from our arms, chests, and throats—and from our mountains, rivers, castles, walls, and embankments," he writes in 1595. Melchior Wańkowicz cites this phrase in the chapter of his memoirs devoted to his childhood, titled "Granica niepojęta jak śmierć" [A border as incomprehensible as death].[4] For him, too, the borderlands carry a mystical, mysterious aura, not unlike the Tatar steppe of Dino Buzzati's 1940 novel.

Kresy, the Eastern Borderlands between present-day Poland and Ukraine, attracted migrants from all sides. Religions (especially Catholicism and Russian Orthodoxy) mingled and clashed there, as did cultures: Ukrainian, Polish, Jewish, Russian. Zenon Fisz, the nineteenth-century author of travel sketches from the region, emphasizes that mid-eighteenth-century Ukraine "was populated by migrants from all corners of Poland, many of whom had no family trees and no last names."[5] Mysterious people moved there, and no one asked where they came from. These nameless migrants blended with waves of other newcomers, many of whom were fleeing war or serfdom. Henry Tyrell claims that the Cossacks, the dominant cultural community of the region, were mostly deserters from Europe's various armies. Ukraine gradually filled with refugees from societies' margins. "They opened their arms to recruits from every nation and were joined by the outcasts whose crimes compelled them to abandon civilized society. In this manner, they ceased to be fugitives and became a people." However, "as may be supposed, their habits revealed the taint that sullied their origins."[6] Polish representations of Cossacks drew attention to their apparent rootlessness and its stamp on Cossack culture. But Cossack life also seemed ineluctably "picturesque." As Andrew Wilson describes it, "The Cossacks were (from the Turkish *qazaq*) 'free men,' who took advantage of the 'wild field' *(dike pole)*, the no-man's-land in the open steppe, to establish autonomous farming and raiding communities beyond the reach of the formal authority of the main regional powers—the Polish Commonwealth, Muscovy, and the Crimean Tatars and Ottoman Turks. Most early Cossacks were originally fleeing serfdom or religious persecution, but eventually the free-booting lifestyle became an attraction in itself."[7] "Cossack freedom," an unstable social structure that often shaded into anarchy, held value for Polish as well as Ukrainian writers. It evoked great, open spaces and the spirit of adventure.

The Ukrainian steppe loomed large in the cultural imaginary as the most picturesque of landscapes to live in or to write about. The Romantics elevated and foregrounded its appeal, turning it into a metaphor for infinity. They frequently compared the steppe to a sea or an ocean. Maria Zadencka rightly points out that the maritime mythology with which these comparisons associated the steppe could be deeply ambivalent: "Ukrainian steppes offer a space of freedom as well as anxiety. Nothing is stable there, and anything can happen: unexpected twists of fate as well as sudden catastrophes and storms." The steppe brings up other connotations as well. Some writers portray Ukraine as a sea to foreground not its "exterritoriality," but the opposite: "the destruction of maritime freedoms."[8] The latter happens as the steppes succumb to colonial interests, the machinations of surrounding states, or the workings of large merchant companies.

A similar ambivalence marks cultural depictions of the Cossacks.

On the one hand, Polish Romantics saw them as the quintessential free people: bold, combative, poetic, famed for their songs, the apex of folk artistry. Let me offer just one example, among hundreds, of how this attraction to Cossack aesthetics manifested among the Polish upper classes: King John III Sobieski, otherwise fond of French chamber music, also took great pleasure in listening to Cossack *dumy* (singular *duma*). He had these long epic poems sung to him by a Cossack *kobzar* in his employ.[9] On the other hand, Polish nobles also perceived Cossacks as guileful rebels who slaughtered large numbers of Polish gentry. Seweryn Goszczyński's Romantic poem *Zamek kaniowski* [The castle of Kaniów, 1828] features a vengeful Cossack leader named Nebab who calls for revenge on Ukraine's Polish masters for all the crimes and suffering they have inflicted on his people.

Between these extremes, Polish literature construed Cossacks as beautiful savages—as epitomized by Henryk Sienkiewicz in *With Fire and Sword* (1884). One corrective to these construals did appear half a century before Sienkiewicz's novel: Nikolai Gogol's *Taras Bulba* (1835) depicts Cossacks, above all, as Orthodox Christian defenders of the unity of Russia locked in a struggle against their Polish masters. Across both sides of this political and aesthetic barricade, amid torrents of blood, betrayal, and depravity, there crystalizes the trope of a Cossack who is passionately, madly in love with a beautiful *Laszka* [i.e., Polish woman]. This tragic passion often serves as a metaphor for Poland's complicated political and ethnic relationship to Ukraine.

The Romantic aura in which Polish culture wraps the Eastern Borderlands most directly resembles the American mythology of the Wild West. In his study of the American Renaissance, Vernon Luis Parrington underlines how many of this new country's settlers were castaways, bandits, and social pariahs. The American West, with its immense forests and steppes inhabited by Indigenous tribes, was unscrupulously exploited by incoming settler writers "as frankly as their fellow adventurers were exploiting the material resources."[10] From the 1830s to the present, the best-known voice of this literary tendency has been James Fenimore Cooper, with his portrayals of Native Americans as noble savages and his admiration for man in the state of nature. Zenon Fisz, whom I mention above, remarks on the great similarities between the backwaters of the Taśmina River (a tributary of the Dniester) and the landscapes described by Cooper. "Before first visiting the Taśmina region, I happened upon one of Cooper's novels. The novel made me fall in love with the mysterious forests of America; I dreamed of them and longed for them. The *Leatherstocking Tales* loomed vividly in my mind's eye. After having read Cooper, how could I not be drawn to the landscapes around Taśmina, with all the enthusiasm of my youth, when they so clearly resembled the uninhabited regions of Delaware?"[11]

These aesthetic raptures over the Borderland and its people spread from the Polish Romantics onto Sienkiewicz and, from there, onto Polish literature as such. Sienkiewicz praises Wincenty Pol's Romantic poem *Mohort* (1855), which portrays a pious knight of the Eastern Borderlands who guards the Polish border with his life, as "a monument to all that was good about the Polish tradition; a monument so grand that it is hard to turn one's eyes away from it."[12] Such effusive praise, from Sienkiewicz and others, came in reaction to the younger, positivist generation's critiques of the Romantics' idealized notion of history. Wincenty Pol saw the Eastern Borderlands as the stronghold of the Polish gentry's true virtues: as the place where chivalric ideals still retained their normative power. He claimed that "the borderland steppes of Ukraine gave rise to a different kind of personality."[13] They fostered a love of simple soldierly life, a severe, intractable sense of duty, and a commitment to serving the Republic of Poland unto death.

One must remember, of course, that these borderland personalities developed under what were essentially colonial circumstances. In 1936, Bogumił Jasinowski [. . .] published a memorable article in the Polish literary magazine *Pamiętnik Literacki* under the striking title "The Foundational Significance of the Southeastern Borderlands in the Formation of the Collective Polish National Consciousness." Jasinowski's piece lauded both the centuries-long eastward expansion of Poland and the Polish people's will to dominate that it revealed. He saw this historical process as the source of Poles' national pride and as the reason why this pride remained unshattered even after Poland's own conquest by its neighbors in the nineteenth century. We may have been colonized throughout the nineteenth century, he argues, but we survived because of our pride in having once been colonizers ourselves. These depictions of Poland as a historical colonizer of the East persisted throughout the interwar period, motivating Poles to regain their former dominance in Ukraine and once again to subdue its people.

One must be careful in assessing how Polish–Ukrainian relations developed throughout this long history. Jan Kieniewicz describes Poland's cultural influences in the Ukrainian Borderlands as "the means by which the region became Europeanized. Polish influence impeded local, Ukrainian nation-building. At the same time, it mediated new cultural values, ideas, models, and challenges that enabled Ukrainians to conceive of national consciousness as their goal."[14] Kieniewicz summarily depicts Polish influences as European ones; this is especially true, he argues, in the seventeenth century, when Polish literature and learning—themselves shaped by Western European influences—were often imitated in the European East. The Ukrainian historian Ihor Ševčenko underlines "Poland's success in transplanting Western culture onto Ukrainian soil."[15] The frequent dangers posed to Polish settlers in Ukraine by both Russia as well as the slow self-emancipation of Ukrainian peasants solidified these settlers' self-image as particularly "tough" in character. That is how people in mainland Poland perceived them as well.

Thus, the Borderlands continued to accrue ever more fantastical mythological significance. Daniel Beauvois observes that studying Polish national myths about the Borderlands reveals a persistent chasm between collective imagination and historical reality. The country's "historical frustrations breed a certain schizophrenia that we should recognize as a constant of Polish cultural–historical imaginaries."[16] Polish settler landowners defined themselves as "generous patrons" while exploiting the populations they governed. Fighters for Poland's national independence failed to recognize, let alone support, parallel national strivings in Ukraine and Belarus. The Polish gentry of the Borderlands were hardly ascetic knights and soldiers. We should more appropriately describe them as an assemblage of marginalized individuals, frequently tyrannical and cruel in character, who took possession of huge latifundia and lorded over them with no one to restrain their follies.

Beauvois's publications set him apart as one of the foremost critics of the Polish myth of the Borderlands. A central part of our collective consciousness, this myth asserts Poland's superiority to the East and highlights the nation's mission to civilize and convert neighboring regions. During the nineteenth and twentieth centuries, this narrative assumed an outsized cultural presence, becoming a nostalgic symbol of lost greatness nourished by "pious beliefs about the supposed communion between Poles and Ukrainians."[17] In the nineteenth century, "the Polish gentry's understanding of their presence in Ukraine shifted: they no longer perceived themselves as the bulwark of Christianity but, more so, as economic outposts that preserved these lands' connection to Poland." Beauvois cites turn-of-the-century Polish novelist Zofia Kossak-Szczucka, whose writings "spread anti-Ukrainian Polish racism." Kossak-Szczucka felt convinced that "the Polish people were the true masters and lords of Ukraine as defined by tradition, common knowledge, and historical fact."[18]

Trójkąt ukraiński [The Ukrainian triangle], as Beauvois describes it, becomes Poland's equivalent of the Bermuda triangle, full of dangerous riddles, illusions, and misperceptions. Beauvois grounds his argument in rigorous archival research. A Frenchman unburdened by Polish national self-centeredness who—like many of his compatriots—experienced a problematic nostalgia after France's loss of Algeria, he seeks to write "history from a human rights perspective," without which "Eastern and Western Europe will not be able to coexist with each other." An exacting historian, he reorients his readers from a sentimental to a factually grounded perspective, leaving behind "the beautiful, fantastical myth" that Polish lovers of the Borderlands have spun out since Sienkiewicz and well into our present moment. Beauvois does not mince his words: "The relations between the Polish gentry and their Ukrainian serfs most closely resembled the relationship between slave owners and enslaved populations." He cites as evidence the testimony of the Polish Romantic Józef Ignacy Kraszewski, "one of the few if not the only Pole of his generation who was prepared to condemn his compatriots' treatment of their serfs."[19] In *Wspomnienia Wołynia, Polesia i Litwy* [Recollections from Wołyń, Polesie, and Lithuania, 1840], Kraszewski bemoans the hatred and violence that pervade this region. "The Polish masters oppressed the local people terribly. This oppression caused, or at least catalyzed, the great, bloody rebellion led by Chmielnicki [in 1648]. The constantly increasing number of taxes, tithes, and various other payments placed a nearly unbearable burden on those whom the Polish masters subjugated."[20]

The beauty of the mansions Polish nobles built in Ukraine, the culture that these mansions' inhabitants forged, the modernization of farming and industrialization of manufacture that Polish settlers spearheaded in the late nineteenth and early twentieth centuries cannot outweigh the toll their presence took on an oppressed, exploited Ukrainian peasant population and the local tenant gentry whom

Polish settlers betrayed and forced out of their homes (and whose fates Beauvois is the first ever historian to narrate).

Consider the now-symbolic episode in which Polish nobles handed out to Ukrainian peasants copies of Złota Hramota [The golden book], a decree that emancipated them and gave them the right to land ownership. They issued this decree during the 1863 insurrection against Russia; promising freedom to Ukrainian peasants, it portrayed Poles as their true allies and friends. Ukrainian peasants responded to this offering with aggression and hatred: they massacred or handed over to the tzar's police the Polish nobles and social idealists who had come to deliver it. Jarosław Iwaszkiewicz beautifully depicts these national and class-based Polish–Ukrainian tensions in a short story titled "Zarudzie," in which a group of innocent and well-meaning "Polish youths" try to make peace with the Ukrainian people by walking among them, unarmed. Their vulnerability meets a horrific, bloody end. The Cossack–peasant uprising led by Chmielnicki in the seventeenth century, the eighteenth-century massacre of Uman in which Cossack and peasant rebels murdered defenseless Polish and Jewish civilians, and many other events of this sort cast a long shadow on the region's nineteenth and twentieth centuries.

To return to the Borderland Polish settlers' collective "personality," nineteenth- and twentieth-century Polish literature persistently idealizes them, especially in memoirs. Beauvois documents these idealizations in the chapter of *Trójkąt ukraiński* titled "Ziemiański prestiż i życie publiczne" [The landowners' prestige in public life]. "In the face of immense political pressures and religious persecution from Russians, and of the latter's attempts to assimilate them culturally, Polish landowners in Ukraine had only one reliable means of asserting their public significance: increasing their already considerable economic dominance in the region." Polish landowners' economic advantages over local populations made them feel like the rulers of the region. Zofia Kossak-Szczucka depicts this dynamic in *Pożoga* [The raging fire], her autobiographical novel from 1922 that recounts the massacres of Polish nobles that took place in Wołyń immediately after the October Revolution. "Because of how long they had occupied Ukraine," Beauvois writes, "the Poles did not perceive themselves as colonizers, merely as its more fortunate inhabitants." And so, "the Polish gentry's consciences felt clear, serene, and angelic."[21]

During the interwar period, the newly independent Poland did not extend as far eastward as it had in the eighteenth century; all the same, the myth of the Polish settler persisted. Andrzej Żbikowski describes these self-identified, supposedly active and courageous "Borderland people" as, "for the most part, supporters of Polish nationalist groups: the National Democrats and the right wing of Piłsudski's Sanacja [Sanation] movement. Their ideology hinged on a xenophobic understanding of Polish national identity. For centuries, the phrase 'borderland people' has been enmeshed with a perception of Polish colonization as a civilizing, culturally creative force, of Polish identity as a stronghold against a sea of barbarism."[22] These views have had lasting consequences: the history of the Galicia region of the Eastern Borderlands has rightly been described as one "of traumas and irreversible ruptures."[23] They also had a long afterlife: after the Cold War, an intoxication with the lost Polish Borderlands resurged in Polish literature and nonfiction. Though post-1989 Poland acknowledged the independence of Ukraine, "paradoxically, acknowledging the sovereign national borders of its eastern neighbors does not yet go hand in hand with ceasing to treat them as peripheries of the Polish state."[24]

Toward the end of the interwar period, the great Polish artist and writer Stanisław Ignacy Witkiewicz (usually referred to as Witkacy) dismissed these national borderland mythologies as pernicious and worthless. In a slim book titled *Niemyte dusze* [Unwashed souls], he deploys psychoanalysis to "wash" the stained souls of the Polish people. Witkacy writes that the Eastern Borderlands remain "an open wound upon the body of the Polish state." He sees their occupation by Polish nobles as "a not-particularly-moral enterprise that created an oppressive power differential between the landowners and the peasantry, one that exceeded the equivalent gap between masters and serfs in mainland Poland. Within this framework, Ukrainian peasants were stereotyped as *barely tamed colonial savages.*"[25]

Power differentials between the social classes of the Borderlands seemed greater to Witkacy because of the additional ethnic, linguistic, and religious divides between them. Throughout the region, Catholicism and Eastern Orthodoxy maintained a tense coexistence. Especially following the Union of Brest (1595–96) [in which the Ruthenian Orthodox Church of the Polish–Lithuanian Commonwealth broke with the Eastern Orthodox Church and entered into communion with Roman Catholicism], Poles came to be seen as active persecutors of the Orthodoxy.

The myth of Poland as the outer bulwark of European Christianity, which emerged in this context, has proven surprisingly persistent. Janusz Tazbir shows that Poles saw their presence in the Borderlands as a rampart against not just Islam but also the Orthodox Church, which they did not perceive as Christian. "To concede that members of the Eastern Orthodox Church followed the same religion as the Catholics would have undermined the idea of Poland as a rampart between Christians and non-Christians." Poles boasted that their country marked the outer edge of the Christian world, "beyond which God has no more worshippers."[26] Poland defends Europe against the onslaught of barbarian, pagan nations—while gradually introducing the "true faith" to them. Even today, these stereotypes live on in the commonly expressed opinion that Poland ought to civilize Russia and convert it to our true religion.

Sarmatians at the Border

Let us now consider the Borderlands from a different angle. This shift of perspective requires us to embrace contemporary historians' reevaluation of the term *barbarian*. It is already a key term for Herodotus, the fulcrum of what François Hartog describes as his "discourse of alterity."[27] When Athenians fought against the Persians, they had to ask themselves what differentiates them from their enemies, "us" from "them." They found this crucial difference in their settled lifestyle, which made them "superior" to their nomadic, "barbarian" enemies. But then these Eastern "barbarians" turned out to have some estimable skills and qualities of mind that contributed to the development of Western civilization. Polish nobles identified with Herodotus's "barbarians." They claimed as their true ancestors an ancient tribe of Iranian nomads known as the Sarmatians, who used to live along the banks of the Danube. This belief gave rise to another ethnic myth about Poland, its status as the "Sarmatia of Europe." Maciej of Miechów, a sixteenth-century chronicler, voices a version of this myth when he describes the Polish Jagiellonian monarchy and Moscow as "European Sarmatia" and Tatar-occupied territories as "Asian Sarmatia."[28]

In the first half of the twentieth century, Tadeusz Sulimirski launched a convincing polemic against the common belief that the Polish nobility's "Sarmatian" roots were a historical fiction. Perhaps, he argues, this association is more than a myth forged by fifteenth- and sixteenth-century Polish chroniclers, and real Sarmatians lie at the root of the Polish preoccupation with them. Sulimirski believes that this ethnic group played a considerable, if underrecognized, role in the history of our part of the European continent, especially toward the end of antiquity and the beginning of the Middle Ages. Their cultural imprint on Eastern European nations remains legible, he believes, even if members of these nations have frequently forgotten or tend to deny it.[29] Sarmatian influences on Polish traditional culture supposedly originate from the great migrations of the fifth-century CE. Sulimirski claims that the religious, ritual, and ethical dimensions of proto-Slavic culture were influenced by people who came from present-day Iran. Because proto-Slavs shared a common language, these influences spread quickly across large territories. Sulimirski argues that Iranian culture left its marks on Slavs sometime between the second and sixth century CE. During this period, Sarmatian settlers were slowly integrated and assimilated into the local population, even while introducing into this new environment some important features of their culture of origin.

The concept of a border*land* undoes the fixity and absoluteness of a *border*. It implies transcultural contact, interpenetration, and cross contamination, as well as the hybridization and ethnic indeterminacy of social formations that emerge within it. In this regard, a sense of being the "eastern part of the West" or the "western part of the East" pervades not only Poland's Eastern Borderlands, but all of Poland. Many examples could be adduced to make this point: Here, I will focus on the links between Sarmatism and Orientalism. In his research on borderlands and spheres of cultural transfer, Tadeusz Chrzanowski discerns in medieval and early modern Polish Orientalism "an ease of assimilation and syncretism" characteristic of Sarmatian culture. The latter's early influence "explains Polish culture's capacity to assimilate aspects of Mediterranean as well as Eastern cultures into itself."[30] The supposed similarity between Poles and Sarmatians hinges on their shared willingness to hybridize Eastern and Western influences. Marina Ciccarini reframes this observation in the context of European attitudes toward otherness. Throughout the seventeenth century, the Near East may have been Poland's towering religious and political Other. But early modern Polish people also felt the pull of that region's culture, especially its more lavish and more visual elements. *Indeed, Poles may have adopted Near Eastern aesthetics in their* *homes and their clothing to highlight their own otherness from Western Europe.*[31]

Scholars have often emphasized that the Polish, putatively Sarmatian, nobleman wore long, flowing Eastern robes. He fought with a Turkish saber. ("Unlike the European sword, the saber develops among the nomadic peoples of the Eurasian steppe.")[32] He filled his manor with luxurious Persian carpets and tapestries, as well as many other products of Eastern artisanship. His predilection for Eastern weaponry was often explained as due to Poland's constant military conflicts with Tatars, to whose fighting style the Polish nobility needed to adjust their own. But the real reasons for such borrowings ran deeper, stemming from a sense of affinity with Eastern culture. When Polish nobles donned their Sarmatian garb, they did not see themselves as wearing a costume. Przemysław Mrozowski underlines that, toward the end of the sixteenth century, "Oriental garments become not only commonplace but customary throughout Poland. This is no longer a passing fashion . . . the *żupan* and the *delia* come to be seen as the Polish people's own, national clothes. The ideal Polish man could not do without them: this outfit testified not only to a person's good taste, but also to his noble roots and to his pride in the fatherland. The tendency continued well into the eighteenth century."[33] Paradoxically, the Polish Sarmatian self-Orientalized so freely because he felt confident in his (hybrid, Western–Eastern) national and ethnic identity.

In 1683, during the Siege of Vienna in which the Polish King John III Sobieski dealt a decisive blow to the invading Ottoman Empire, "the Polish troops looked so much like the enemy that they were obliged to wear a straw cockade, in case their Habsburg allies mistook them for Turks." Bringing up this spectacular example of cultural interpenetration, Neal Ascherson notes that "Poland still today insists on its 'European,' Western allegiance, now based not only on the Catholic faith but on diligently Western institutions and tastes. And yet in subtle ways Poland is a much more oriental culture than Russia." Ascherson's statement may seem shocking; it stems from his conviction that, while Muscovites hid from the Mongols in their kingdom's northern forests, Poles were open to cultural influences from the steppes around the Black Sea. The Polish nobility's Oriental lifestyle testified to this openness. Ascherson goes so far as to suggest that the Polish nobility's ideas of democracy were inspired not by the Roman Republic, but by the *quriltai*, "the assembly of Mongol–Tatar nobles and clan chiefs who gathered to elect a new khan"—a political formation that the Poles adopted from Crimean Tatars.[34]

I do not mean to endorse the full breadth of these speculations. But I mention them here to highlight the possibility of an alternative way of thinking about our place within Europe. We need not define ourselves by drawing uncrossable boundary lines between the East and the West. We also ought to reject the suggestion that, as incompletely Western, we are an immature nation, a "worse" and an "inferior" one. Such a shift of perspective releases us from the constant pressure to imitate and measure ourselves up to the European West.

Bogurodzica

Pre-Christian Poland or Christian Poland of the Slavic rite? The year 966 marks Poland's adoption of Catholicism. But starting around 870, there may have already existed within its territories an earlier form of Christianity.

The possibility that Poland might have converted to Christianity before 966, in the spirit of Cyril and Methodius's Greek Orthodox mission, has fascinated many scholars. Michał Miniat, the author of a sizeable popular treatment of Cyril and Methodius's mission to the Slavic East, describes this possibility as "well-known, still unresolved, and, in many ways, controversial." In Polish historiography, it remains a touchy subject. Miniat sees Polish historians' lack of objectivity in this regard as an expression of Roman Catholic fears of Reformation-era aspirations toward a national Christian Church . . . or as an attempt to defend Polish Christianity from tsarist pan-Slavism and to prevent Russia from using Methodius's mission as an excuse to pull Slavic Catholics toward Russian Orthodoxy. "Several generations of Polish historians grew up amid these fears."[35]

Adolf Stender-Petersen did not, and he sees the matter quite differently. He believes that, between the ninth and the eleventh centuries, a cultural community may have existed in the territories spanning Czechia/Moravia and Poland that shared the language, rites, and terminology of Old Church Slavonic. Even up to the early twelfth century, the tradition of Cyril and Methodius may have flourished in Poland. A road not taken. Used throughout Eastern Europe, Old Church Slavonic was directly understandable to everyone and successfully competed with Latin.[36] Roman Jakobson adduces many pieces of evidence that its cultural influence penetrated Poland from Czechia. For instance, he highlights the famous fragment from the medieval Polish chronicler Gallus Anonimus that describes all of Poland mourning the passing of Bolesław I the Brave, "Latinorum et Slavorum, quotque estis incolae": "For anyone with a passing knowledge of early medieval Czech-Latin sources and of their language, it is self-evident" that the words *Latinorum* and *Slavorum* refer, respectively, to Christians of the Latin and the Slavic rite.[37]

This is a sensitive but crucial question. Many experts have drawn attention to the historical conflict between early medieval Europe's Germanic and Slavic peoples; Slavs resisted conversion to the Latin Christian rite because of its perceived association with Germany. Christianity in Poland may have initially followed two parallel tracks, and Latin universalism only eventually suppressed what its ministers described as the "misguided Slavic rite." Conversations about this suppression often return to arguments about how the shared use of Latin tied together medieval European cultures; by acceding to it, Slavs were able to join the united European cultural sphere. But Stender-Petersen argues that, at its core, the Latinization of Slavdom did not have such benign motivations. The newly established, well-organized Holy Roman Empire, which spearheaded this effort, was driven by a desire to subordinate Christian Slavic peoples to German–Roman spirituality and its rising imperial ambitions.[38] In an excellent essay published in 1905, Karol Potkański describes how German clergy "leaned on the most powerful institution in existence," the Roman Catholic Church, which was "the inheritor of the old organization of the world-dominant Roman Empire," to put pressure on Slavs to convert to Catholicism, triggering a conflict between the Slavic peoples and the papacy.[39] From Stender-Petersen's mid-twentieth-century perspective, Old Church Slavonic, as Slavdom's lingua franca, could have served as a unifying force for the region and thereby posed a threat to the German Empire. Through the Holy Roman Empire's efforts, that did not come to pass.[40]

The unhealed wound of Slavdom's division into two churches—those of the East and the West—recently manifested right before us. In 1985, John Paul II, the "Slavic pope," published an encyclical titled *Slavorum Apostoli* devoted to the holy apostles Cyril and Methodius's mission to Slavdom. Prominently on display in this encyclical is a policy that the Catholic Church developed after the Second Vatican

Council. Following the council's conclusions, the encyclical advocates that the church catechize and educate those around it, sharing its eternal truths, but also recommends that it adapt its message to local cultural contexts. This injunction toward "inculturation"—the incorporation of the Gospels into native cultures in a way that acknowledges their separateness and reckons with the mentalities of the newly converted and their local conditions—charges the Catholic Church with considerable internal change; it also makes the mission of Cyril and Methodius seem radically progressive by comparison. In the encyclical, the pope reminds his faithful that Cyril and Methodius did not impose Greek, their native language, on the people they encountered; instead, they created "rich, refined texts" in the Slavic tongue. They treated Old Church Slavonic as equal in stature to Latin. John Paul II also underlines that pagan and Greek Orthodox medieval Slavs "were defending their own identity against the military and cultural pressure of the new Romano-Germanic Empire, and . . . attempting to resist forms of life which they felt to be foreign."[41] Within this context, the early medieval state of Great Moravia, where Eastern and Western influences crossed freely, could have played a powerful role in converting communities to Christianity while preserving their native tongues.

The encyclical states that it remains historically unproven whether a Christian church in the Slavic rite was ever established within the territory of present-day Poland. However, John Paul II concedes that "the fact remains that the beginnings of Christianity in Poland are in a way linked with the work of the Brothers who set out from distant Salonika."[42] The pope's acknowledgment of Poland as a point of contact between Catholicism and Greek Orthodoxy marks a significant triumph for those who see early Polish Christianity as essentially dual. John Paul II underlines that both traditions—the Eastern and the Western one—come from the womb of one Christian Church; he longs for these two sister churches to reunify.

Quoting the Russian poet Vyacheslav Ivanov, John Paul II describes the Eastern and Western churches as the "two lungs" of the Christian Church and the "two lungs of Europe." Ten years later, in 1995, he penned a pastoral epistle titled *Orientale lumen* in which "John Paul II's Slavic theology of ecumenism" comes fully into its own, giving rise to "a beautiful description of Orthodox Christianity." But as Andrzej Walicki puts it, "The last few years have unfortunately seen a regression in the dialogue between Catholic and Orthodox Christianity."[43]

In 2000, with the knowledge and consent of John Paul II, Cardinal Joseph Ratzinger published a document *(Dominus Iesus)* that stated that "the Church of Christ, despite the divisions which exist among Christians, continues to exist fully only in the Catholic Church" and that the "one true religion continues to exist in the Catholic and Apostolic Church."[44] Meanwhile, the Bishops' Council in Moscow recently described Catholics as members of a schism with whom one should not enter into compromises.

The wound created by this enmity continues to fester. Within this context, one would do well to return to Bogurodzica [Mother of God], the medieval Polish *carmen patrium* that bears unforgettable witness to the combined Easternness and Westernness of Polish culture.

The astonishing two first stanzas of Bogurodzica have been the object of an ongoing theological and philological debate that spans more than a century, and which has yielded copious publications. It concerns the relationship the hymn establishes between Christ, the Virgin Mary, and John the Baptist. Józef Birkenmajer, an important voice in these conversations, unearthed Bogurodzica's Greek–Byzantine roots by noting that this triad invokes what Eastern Christianity knows as *deesis:* the Greek iconographic triangulation of the Mother of God, John the Baptist, and Christ Pantocrator. He also highlights the hymn's close relation to Greek Christian hymnography. "One will search in vain within this hymn for signs of the West's unified Roman liturgy, as established by Gregory VII's reforms at the end of the eleventh century. But Bogurodzica does bear obvious marks of a *liturgical compromise between the East and the West,* of the kind that was in evidence in many Slavic countries between the tenth century and the second half of the eleventh century."[45] Stender-Petersen also draws attention to the association between Mary and John the Baptist prevalent in the Czech variant of the tradition of Cyril and Methodius. He sees the presence of *deesis* in Bogurodzica as evidence for the Byzantine–Slavic provenance of the hymn. Toward the end of his essay, he mocks attempts to treat the archaisms of the first part of Bogurodzica as borrowings from Russian. He also hypothesizes that, prior to the Battle of Grunwald [which took place in 1410, in a memorable turning point in the Polish–Lithuanian War against the Teutonic Knights], the Bogurodzica had not been the anthem of the Catholic Polish army, but of its Lithuanian–Russian supporting regiments. According to Stender-Petersen, critics who argue otherwise simply cannot acknowledge the Byzantine–

Orthodox roots of this hymn.[46] Stanisław Urbańczyk leans on a large body of prior research to stress Bogurodzica's ties to Czech language and literary culture [. . .]. Urbańczyk shows that a rich literary culture developed throughout Moravia and Czechia among continued users of Old Church Slavonic and preserved many traces of the old Slavic Christian liturgy. We must not overlook the influence that this corpus of Old Church Slavonic literature had on Western Slavs.[47] [. . .] Roman Mazurkiewicz, who as of now has had the last interesting word on this subject, sees Bogurodzica as testimony to our hybrid Byzantine–Slavic and Western–Latin heritage. He concludes that the hymn, Poland's first national anthem, was "the deepest 'breath' that our Christianity ever took, with both the Western and the Eastern lung of our thousand-year-old tradition."[48]

Whence come all the misunderstandings that surround this hymn? How can the great late nineteenth-century scholar of early Polish culture Aleksander Brückner no longer have known where the hymn's invocation of John the Baptist came from? Mazurkiewicz, an expert on the figure of *deesis,* shows that "the form of religiosity and spirituality developed in Polish Catholicism after the Council of Trent (1545–63) focused on Jesus and the Virgin Mary." This shift of focus marginalized the more ancient cult of John the Baptist as Christ's closest predecessor and mediator. "The Gothic period definitively 'occidentalized' our religiosity," to the point where *deesis* lost its "legibility" within it.[49] One might add that, in the aftermath of the Council of Trent, Polish religious practice became increasingly hostile toward perceived schisms and heresies, bearing particular animosity toward Russian Orthodoxy. This attitude became a defining feature of Polish nobility, and eventually also of Polish culture as such—which came to understand itself as intrinsically Catholic. That is why it requires some intellectual and emotional effort properly to read Bogurodzica—to see and hear, in our mind's eyes and ears, the "two lungs" of early Polish culture.

Germans and Russians

Poland disappeared from the map of Europe toward the end of the eighteenth century through the combined efforts of three states: Russia, Prussia, and Austria. The partition of Poland among them had decisive consequences for our national consciousness. It also inspired an ongoing search for our proper place in Europe, as a nation without a state. In the course of the nineteenth century, Poles' relationship to Europe became hypersensitive to the point of neurosis. It fell to the Romantics constantly to remind Europeans about Poland: to highlight Europe's debts to it, look for foreign allies in the cause of Polish independence, and develop philosophies of history in which Europe could not attain political equilibrium without an independent Polish state.

Upon this soil grew many varieties of Polish messianism, among them Adam Mickiewicz's Napoleonic notion of Slavs and the French as Europe's twin messiahs.[50] Another major Polish Romantic, Zygmunt Krasiński, wrote letters to Europe's spiritual and political giants (Pius IX on the one hand, Napoleon III on the other), imploring them to support the cause of Poland's oppressed nationhood. Krasiński saw the true "people's church" as forged from nations rather than from individuals; each nation formed an independent spiritual whole, suffused with the Holy Spirit. "This is why," he argued, "the integrity of nations is sacred and untouchable." Poland's occupants, particularly Russia, had violated these sacred principles. But in its oppression, Poland becomes "a planetary archetype of the immortality of nations." The spirit of this great nation will recognize (and others will be forced to acknowledge) that "despite its faults and sins, Poland remains the purest European nation, the one least guilty of historical crimes and misdeeds, the one closest to Christ: More selfless than other nations, it continually brought succor and salvation to others and sacrificed itself in the process."[51] It is no wonder that for Krasiński, the Polish national spirit is the greatest among all Slavs'; it embodies no less than Christ himself. In their tenor, Krasiński's megalomaniac pronouncements were not far from statements issued by other Polish messianic writers; like these others, Krasiński made a very feeble impression on his politically powerful European addressees. Especially after several European nations joined forces to defeat Napoleon with pivotal help from Russia, the Holy Alliance tightened the bonds among the extant European nations; they did not need an independent Poland added to the mix.

During the Romantic period and in its immediate aftermath, Poles allegorically depicted their nation as Polonia: a proud, unhappy, persecuted woman held in chains, thrown into a grave, nevertheless maintaining her composure and shaking her manacled arms. This feminized image of Poland matches quite precisely Simone de Beauvoir's assessment of the roles typically accorded to women in history. Women, as Beauvoir describes it, are never depicted as world-historical actors. "Martyrdom remains allowed for the oppressed; during Christian persecutions and in the aftermath of social or national defeats, women played this role of witness; but a martyr has never changed the face of the world."[52] Such was also the case with Poland-as-Polonia.

Throughout the nineteenth century, Poles fought to regain independence by means of plots, insurrections, and diplomatic intrigues. This effort crucially defined their relationship to their occupants, Germany and Russia, in a way that carried forward into the twentieth century. As late as the 1990s, Poland remained dominated by a Romantic cultural paradigm; if anything, the Cold War had breathed new life into it. This paradigm shaped all aspects of Polish life, giving rise to what I call our "religious patriotism." The Romantics' patriotic messianism bore the intensity of religious heresy. Many, including Czesław Miłosz, have since condemned it for mistaking the fatherland for the Absolute itself. In his interpretation of the third part of Adam Mickiewicz's *Dziady* (1832), Miłosz comments on the double identity of the Polish messiah as both the one meant to resurrect a nation and that same nation crucified: "No, no. . . . Whoever deals in the religion of God who became a Man, the religion of Incarnation, in order to redefine the Messiah as a national collective, has lost his bearings and his sense of proportion."[53]

Few Romantics escaped the fog of these messianic illusions; most, like Krasiński, merely modified and universalized them. Two brief quotations will suffice to highlight the peculiarity of this national "religion." At the end of the Great Improvisation, Konrad's famous monologue in part III of *Dziady,* the speaker threatens God, as the Devil tempts him to do: "*Konrad:* I will declare that you are not the world's father, but . . . *The Devil:* its tsar!" In Juliusz Słowacki's *Kordian* (1834), the titular hero visits the Vatican, only to hear the pope say, "I will be the first to curse the defeated Poles." (The latter alludes to Pope George XVI's condemnation of the Polish insurrection of 1830 in his 1832 encyclical *Cum primum,* which calls on Poles to obey their "magnanimous emperor," Tsar Nicolas I.) Between the pope and the tsar, there was no room left for Poland. So, the Romantics sought refuge by turning patriotism itself into an absolute. The church frequently condemned them for preferring their earthly homeland to the heavenly one.

Let us consider how Poland's relationships to Germany and Russia figured in its national consciousness. In general, Polish culture represents knowledge and morality as intrinsically related to each other. To thirst for knowledge in a way that exceeds all bounds, especially the bounds of divine law, easily comes to seem immoral and depraving. It is interesting to consider the Polish reception of Goethe's *Faust* from that perspective. For example, in an 1897 essay about the "idea of Poland," Stanisław Szczepanowski underlines the fundamental differences between Polish and German national philosophical and literary styles through a comparison of the second part of *Faust* and the third part of *Dziady,* both of which were published in 1832. The Polish writer's fundamental drive is toward justice; the German's, toward *Erkenntnis,* knowledge of all things.[54] At stake here is not merely a superficial, knee-jerk Polish antipathy toward German aphorizing. The point goes far deeper—and Mickiewicz's *Dziady* helps one understand it.

The two works, *Faust* and *Dziady,* depict two fundamentally different worlds. In *Dziady,* "insatiable lust for knowledge and for pleasure, which *Faust* foregrounds, are explicitly condemned. And that which is missing from *Faust*—faith and conscience—appear front and center." Szczepanowski believes that Goethe wrote *Faust* while thinking about the Book of Job, that staggering tale of a man who asks questions about God, evil, and justice. But then Goethe purposefully moves away from his inspiration. "What had been a question of the heart and of justice in Job becomes, in *Faust,* a question of reason, imagination, and knowledge." Goethe enacts a striking conceptual substitution: The problems of knowledge and the intellect replace Job's moral problem of justice. Meanwhile, morality and justice remain at the center of part III of *Dziady.* For Szczepanowski, the Polish mind cannot accept the Faustian values of knowledge and self-knowledge because they lack a moral sense. Faust must give way to the moral hero depicted by Mickiewicz.[55]

By the 1840s, Mickiewicz argued explicitly that a powerful man need not be irreligious, and that great power need not bind one to Satan. In his arguments against the supposed diabolical origins of political force and authority, Mickiewicz formulated a moral framework in which love compels human beings equally, and concurrently, toward faith and action. Humans' capacity to act cannot be intrinsically impure or contaminating, fundamentally opposed to our transcendent aims. This is because human nature can only reveal itself in action and activity, working toward the ideals it sets for itself. Mickiewicz, like other Romantics, and like the many later figures who drew inspiration from them—including General Józef Piłsudski, the de facto leader of the Second Polish Republic between 1918 and 1935—refused to treat politics as something dirty and shameful that a true and transcendent life ought to marginalize. Politics and the spirit had everything to do with each other—and as a result, politics was inextricable from the pursuit of a moral life.

The present-day Catholic thinker Karol Ludwik Koniński describes the Romantics' state of mind exceptionally well in his aphorisms. "*Polish religion:* One grounded in a fundamentally modern idea of conscience and the religious beliefs of the old pagan philosophers. The religion of Krasiński and Słowacki, Mickiewicz, Orzeszkowa, and Prus, is heretical. But perhaps their heresy is the same as the heresy of the Gospels? . . . At the end of the day, the best kind of religion is the one that releases its believers to do the greatest amount of noble, creative, unrestrained work."[56]

The Polish Romantics' understanding of action does not succumb to the "German sin" of disconnecting the Spirit and politics from each other. In his 1945 lecture on *Germany and the Germans* as well as in his novel *Doctor Faustus* (1947), Thomas Mann describes the "German problem" in those terms. He treats German music and German attitudes toward music as a source of national greatness, but also as a threat to it. German music radically, definitively separates spirit from life itself. For Mann, Martin Luther already fell prone to this error when he made distinctions between the "liberty of the Christian" and the "liberty of the citizen." Setting human beings' speculative energies apart from the sociopolitical realm, such distinctions accord an absolute supremacy to the former. Mann believes that the Germans' false understanding of liberty ultimately gave rise to fascism. Attuned to spirituality alone, the German philosopher and politician alike treat politics as inherently evil. "He regards politics as nothing but falsehood, murder, deceit, and violence, as something completely and one-sidedly filthy. . . . Since he thinks it is unalloyed evil, he believes he has to be a devil to pursue it."[57]

Szczepanowski criticizes Schiller's division between reality and the ideal. He believes that such a division feeds into "that typically German notion that a worthy individual could happen to serve a bad cause. Schiller grants each such individual forgiveness by fiat: After all, since ideals can never be completely fulfilled, can one say that these worthy individuals had betrayed them?"[58] Against this background, Szczepanowski describes Polish people as struggling to reconcile ideals and reality with each other: to fuse spirit and life, morality and politics. Politics should be moral: That is the call of Polish independence movements. Granted, it often tempted Poles to twist their moral codes to fit their politics, rather than the other way around.

This struggle to make politics more moral was aimed at Poland's nineteenth-century occupants, especially Russia. The Romantics pitted Poland against Russia as Slavdom's two mutually hostile powers bound to fundamentally antagonistic codes: liberty and despotism. Russia was figured as the "East" and Orientalized according to Western European stereotypes: as inert, immobile, belated, backward, irrational, and tyrannical. Since the Romantic period and into the present, Poles have assumed the right to be Russia's harshest critics, with expertise on the inequities of tsarist as well as Soviet Russia. They continue to underline that Russia is not, and cannot be, part of Europe.

Zygmunt Krasiński hated Russia passionately, as the embodiment of Asian barbarism and Mongol cruelty. He reiterated an idea that would later be taken up, within the fields of history and the history of philosophy, by Jan Kucharzewski's *Od białego caratu do czerwonego* (From the White tsardom to the Red one, 1923–35). Krasiński and Kucharzewski both insist on parallels between tsardom and the revolution as powerful political systems that use the same principles of violence. This view of Russia as an evil force threatening Europe from the East persisted throughout the nineteenth century and gained force during the Polish–Soviet War of 1919–21. Poles see themselves as superior to Muscovites because, unlike the latter, they are part of Western civilization and the Roman Catholic Christian community. The copious anti-Bolshevik poems written around this time repeat this antinomy between "Europe" and "Asia," the "West" and the "East."[59]

But the shoe is also on the other foot: Other Eastern European nations often describe Poland as the Judas of the Slavs, and Russia as its betrayed sister. Such metaphors highlight these other nations' sense that their shared cultural heritage binds Slavs together in emotionally deep ways. Roman Catholicism, with the figure of the "Catholic Pole" at its center, plays a crucial role both in internal and in external polarizations of Poland against Russia. The idea of Polish people as intrinsically Catholic was first articulated in the seventeenth century, amid major regional conflicts over borderland territories and following the Catholic Church's fracturing by the Reformation. It gained increased importance in the nineteenth century after Poland had lost its independence as a state. During the interwar period, Catholicism and nationalism became further entwined; under the People's Republic of Poland, their association accrued an additional anticommunist edge.

An essay coauthored by Mirosław Marody and Sławomir Mandes sheds new light on this subject. The authors show that during the Cold War, churches were the only institutions where the persistent Romantic–ethnic idea of the Polish nation could be ritually maintained. John Paul II, who named the Polish nation as "the basic, autonomous form of Polish identity," brought back into his sermons "the old topoi of nineteenth-century Romantic nationalism" and messianism. Polish people felt that their nation deserved to be elevated above others because "they had maintained the Catholic faith in the face of communism." The old idea of the "Catholic Pole" hardened and crystallized.[60]

In the nineteenth and twentieth centuries, when Polish Catholicism was often under threat both as a religious and as an ethnic identity, believers clung to this double self-identification as a solace and refuge. The cult of the Virgin Mary as Our Lady of Consolation spread widely. The ancient Marian hymn known as Sub Tuum Praesidium became one of Poland's most popular prayers. But as it came to be perceived as a source of earthly hope and consolation, Polish religiosity lost touch with its supernatural, transcendent affects and dimensions. When Miłosz edited and translated into Polish the writings of Simone Weil (who believed that "religion as a source of consolation is an obstacle to true faith"), he sought in them a kind of prosthesis for understanding what transcendent faith is like when it is unadulterated by human "interests"—even the loftiest human interests, say, national ones.

Over the centuries, Poles brought a plethora of petitions to God's attention: Their wishes were material and forcefully articulated. One might go so far as to describe the Polish national theodicy as a variant on Leibnitz's theodicy. Poles needed to justify God's presence and choices, given that Poland seemed bad, riddled with oppression and suffering. Messianism offered an explanation: Poland had been singled out for acute oppression by the forces of evil as a sacrificial offering that would redeem the sins of all other nations. Within this context, it makes sense why Romantic culture tended to depict Poland as an angel, setting it apart from other, sinful nations, especially from Russia and Germany.

Believers in Polish messianism sought out signs of God's presence in history, special clues that God may have left for the "long-suffering Polish nation." This form of messianism appealed to Poland's lower classes as well as its elites. It persisted well beyond the nineteenth century and colored Polish people's understanding of major twentieth-century historical events: the Nazi occupation, the Cold War, the martial law of the 1980s. Adoring Poland as an innocent victim also necessitated treating its persecutors as embodiments of the Devil. In the nineteenth century, Russia took on that role: As Mickiewicz liked to put it, in political terms Russia *was* Satan. Bolshevik Russia fell under similar suspicion; our projections here found easy affinity with Ronald Reagan's naming the USSR the "evil empire."

These long-standing views have still not lost their power. Alongside judicious, competent voices such as Andrzej Walicki's and Andrzej de Lazari's, one frequently encounters obviously post-Romantic journalistic takedowns and unmaskings of Russia's evils. In an article from 1995 devoted to the eastern borders of Europe, Alain Besançon thus follows the Polish Romantics and their epigones in accusing Russia of trying to blur the otherwise "clear" border between Europe and Asia. Russia does so, he claims, "through the mouths of its rulers—Peter, Catherine, or Alexander." These rulers' express wish to become European was never authentic and never decisively Westernized Russian social structures. Russian rulers only claimed to desire Westernization, Besançon argues, in order to further Russia's westward imperial expansion. Martin Malia persuasively shows that arguments like Besançon's do not acknowledge how similar these Russian colonial policies are to those of the French, Dutch, Belgian, or Portuguese empires. "Though these similarities are—or ought to be—beyond serious empirical dispute, we have also seen that Western Europeans as often as not failed to see Russia in such 'rational' fashion—because of the persisting belief . . . that Russian despotism (despite some 'enlightened' interludes) was an intrinsically alien, threatening civilization."[61] In another familiar gesture, Besançon brings up the supposed continuities between the Russia of the tsars and that of the commissars: In both cases, Russia's state power construes itself as "an occupying army in a conquered nation." Europe, he claims, must remain on guard against Russia and its unceasing imperial fantasies. We protect the boundary between "us" and "them," lest our sense of identity cease to feel clear and absolute. "Were Europe to count Russia as part of itself, the boundaries of our world would become definitively blurred. We would, moreover, entangle ourselves in Russia's intractable territorial problems. Having come into being as an empire and been one for most of its historical existence, Russia does not recognize the borders between its various ethnic groups."[62] Clearly, matters are very serious.

I do not agree with Besançon. In Western Europe as well as in Poland, we would do well to revise views like his. The Russians themselves can help us toward this end. Mikhail Rikhlin shows that the idea of an "Eternal Russia," set in opposition to an "Eternal Europe," comes from a book titled *Russia in 1839,* published in 1843 by a Frenchman, the Marquis de Custine. Besançon admires this nineteenth-century treatise. Most of our topoi and stereotypes of what Russia looks like under foreign eyes do in fact originate in Custine's volume. However, the boundaries Custine draws between "Eternal Russia" and "Eternal Europe" are arbitrary and inconsistent; as Rikhlin puts it, "However absolute these differences may have seemed to Custine, [from our perspective] they seem temporary and superficial." Custine's distinctions between Russia and Europe, Rikhlin argues, cannot reasonably ground an absolute understanding of the two regions. Strikingly, when Custine tries to name the "essence" of Russia, he can only do so through binary contrasts against Europe. What is "good" about Europe becomes "bad" about Russia—and vice versa. "No Russian 'shibboleth' exists on one side or the other; the predictable differences Custine lists stem from mutual projections."[63]

The "Orientalizing" of Russia by Europe generally hinges on such strong binary contrasts. They have been deconstructed by many scholars, however little their deconstruction has penetrated Polish consciousness. Most recently, Viktor Erofeyev persuasively dismantled the notion of the "Russian soul," which enjoys such popularity in the West. Erofeyev demystifies this concept in a series of short vignettes whose fragmentary nature in itself undermines the logic of Russia as Europe's "mirror image." One of these fragments, "The Russian European," makes his point with wonderful, nondialectical irony:

> Inside myself, I have created a French Russia and a Russian Paris. I carry them within me, even though they don't really exist: I have

> invented, crossbred them. I am most likely a Russian European—that is, neither one nor the other.
>
> I have achieved a rare outcome. Shall I be counted among successful hybrids? No norms seem absolute to me anymore. Because my two worlds don't overlap, my morality feels unstable.
>
> I accept [my European] others as my people and deal well with them; but I also accept Russians as my people, and I can deal with them, too (somewhat less well). At the crossroads of Montparnasse and Raspail, I am my own person, but I don't know who else would recognize my existence. If I went back to living in only one world, I would feel constrained. I need to be in one world after the other—or better still, in both worlds at the same time, coextensively.[64]

Exactly: no absolute criteria distinguish Europe from Russia. Acknowledging that they are coextensive with each other would dispel their illusory binary differences. But the reception Erofeev's book has enjoyed in Poland does not indicate that such a revisionist process is taking place. Its reviewers continue to revert to binary oppositions; they cannot think more flexibly about this calcified, "eternal" line between Russia and Europe.

"Here in Our Auschwitz"

Poland's best narratives about the Nazi concentration camps and the Soviet gulags—the short stories of Tadeusz Borowski and Gustaw Herling-Grudziński's *A World Apart* (1951)—are renowned works of world literature. Borowski and Herling-Grudziński do not endorse a belief in Poland's supposedly unadulterated intrinsic moral superiority or in the equally intrinsic, complete immorality of Poland's Russian and German persecutors.

Herling-Grudziński, a former prisoner of the gulag, rejects the common Polish memoir convention of demonizing his communist oppressor. He fought hard, and successfully, to cleanse his style of the ethnic stereotypes of Polish national martyrology. Indeed, he accused Joseph Conrad of showing anti-Russian bias in *Under Western Eyes* (1911), thus failing to espouse the art of distance: an art that any Pole writing about Russian topics needs to perfect.

Herling-Grudziński absorbed this crucial lesson from Daniel Defoe's *A Journal of the Plague Year* (1772). He summarizes the insight as follows: "Certain chapters of the 'dark' history of humanity—cataclysms, plagues, exterminations, barbarian conquests, genocides—can only be reconstituted from the perspective of an anonymous . . . absolutely impersonal . . . chronicler. This chronicler must be scrupulous to the point of pedantry, so measured as to seem not like a human being, but like a hand moved by a faceless crowd, the needle in a seismograph."[65] Herling-Grudziński draws attention to the anonymity of mass killings, whose descriptions can end up inciting only indifference. Defoe's narrative method "remains unsurpassable to this day when it comes to eliciting dramatic tension from the anonymous deaths of masses of people, whose numbers threaten to blur the sum of human individuals into mere digits."[66]

This is, more or less, how Herling-Grudziński wrote *A World Apart*—though sometimes, especially in his biographies of Russian prisoners, he allowed himself some aesthetic flourish. He examines these prisoners with the detachment of a Stendhal; as Miłosz puts it, he balances the beautiful and the horrific against each other. Even in the most extreme situations, when his characters touch bottom "without religious consolation," Herling-Grudziński finds "a modicum of humanity." His understanding of the human condition as fundamentally tragic resembles the views of Camus and the heroic existentialist stance. But those parallels do not take away from his originality, or from his writing's uniqueness on a national and a European scale. In the gulag, he paid a high price for this distinctness.

Personal experience also informs Borowski's short stories about survival in a German concentration camp. One of these, titled "Here in Our Auschwitz," takes the form of a letter. The original title of the story, "U nas, w Auschwitzu," is not just thematically but grammatically unsettling. Though it uses the German name of the Polish city of Oświęcim, it modifies the word *Auschwitz* following the rules of Polish declension—making Auschwitz seem German, but partly Polish as well. The story names experiences that no one before Borowski, or after him, had ever written about in quite that way. His narrator's relationship to the reader is perverse: whereas the latter lives within a horizon circumscribed by moral values, the former does not. This difference gives rise to a disturbing, tragic irony.

Describing how tens of thousands of people are routinely killed in the concentration camp, Borowski makes the procedure seem infinitely trivial:

> But look here: first of all, one country barn painted white and—they're suffocating people in it. Then four larger buildings—it's nothing to suffocate twenty thousand people. Without magic, without poisons, without hypnosis. A couple of people directing traffic to prevent a jam, and the people flow like water from a pipe when the faucet is turned on. This goes on amid the anemic trees of a smoke-covered woods. Ordinary trucks deliver the people, drive back as if on a conveyor belt, return with another delivery. Without magic, without poisons, without hypnosis.[67]

Borowski's style—which is itself "without magic, without poisons, without hypnosis"—ingeniously reflects a reality that has become godless but also demonless: a reality in which Jews are brought into the gas chambers of Brzezinka–Birkenau on an assembly line, ferried into the camp by the truckload—unless, before they reach the camp, they are murdered in a stable or a nearby forest. What does it mean to represent mass killings in this fashion? Some saw this style as a sign of Borowski's loss of empathy, his insensitivity to suffering. He has even been called a nihilist. I read these stories very differently.

Wolfgang Sofsky underlines that "the perpetrator [of violence] feels euphoria, waxing enthusiastic over what he is doing. Every new idea, every further victim killed heightens his elation. Yet he is not 'beside himself' but expanding from within, extending himself, gaining the terrain of absolute liberty." What is "absolute liberty"? Above all, it is freedom from dying. "This dance of violence gives its perpetrator a strange feeling of inner unity. . . . The old ego is extinguished, the need for individuation and the fear of death are suddenly cast off. Transformation has reached its ultimate point. The festival of violence is a leap into a utopian state which fulfills an ancient yearning: the dream of absolute power, of absolute freedom and wholeness, of the return to paradise."[68] When Borowski's narrator later enjoins his reader to "behold the wondrous possession of one man by another," that is exactly what he has in mind: The SS establishes and reinforces its members' absolute freedom from dying.[69]

Borowski's stories also describe a different practice of absolute freedom. His narrator experiences this freedom at the expense of the prisoner whose body and spirit have been destroyed, one who is ready to go into the crematorium and whom other prisoners therefore isolate and hold in contempt—but who remains abjectly alive. In concentration camps, these people were called *Muselmänner* (Muslims). Despite or indeed precisely because of their abjection, these figures form the concentration camp's emotional and philosophical center. Sofsky argues that "the *Muselmann* embodies the anthropological meaning of absolute power in an especially radical form. Power abrogates itself in the act of killing. The death of the other puts an end to the social relationship. But by starving the other, it gains time. It erects a third realm, a limbo between life and death. Like the pile of corpses, the *Muselmänner* document the total triumph of power over the human being. Although still nominally alive, they are nameless hulks."[70] Bruno Bettelheim saw the camps' *Muselmänner* as marking a fluctuating boundary between the human and the inhuman. In his memoir of life in Oświęcim, *Survival in Auschwitz: If This Is a Man* (1947), Primo Levi describes them as the "drowned," "an anonymous mass," the ones who "have no story," the damned of Dante's *Inferno*.[71]

From within this experiment, as Levi calls it, Borowski throws a horrific accusation at European civilization. In the midst of a German concentration camp, he recognizes the course of European history and the prices paid for it. Antiquity was already "a gigantic concentration camp," he argues, one in which some—the majority—were condemned to hard labor and slavery, while others wrote dialogues and tragedies, made history, were transcendentally and aesthetically minded. Beauty, goodness, truth: these concepts all depend on silenced, bloody, cruel suffering inflicted on fellow human beings. Borowski saw ancient Greece and Nazi Germany, which enslaved people like him to "construct the foundations of some kind of new, monstrous civilization," as analogous to each other. Once victorious, the Germans will kill everyone around him. "And no one will know about us. The poets, lawyers, philosophers, priests will drown out our voices. They will create beauty, goodness, and truth. They will create religion."[72]

Borowski accuses Europe as a whole of having birthed the crimes of totalitarianism. He calls Plato a liar and describes "beauty, goodness, and truth" as illusions cast over the reality of the Holocaust. Borowski's cruel assessment of himself and those around him should be a stumbling block in our thinking about Europe and our place within it. Auschwitz is "our home." It is also at home in Europe. Let us place this realization at the core of an empathic, modern-day, tragic viewpoint within which—unlike in ancient tragedy—we cannot hope for catharsis. All that awaits us is an excess of pain and a sense of loss that will remain irretrievable and irreconcilable.

Notes

1. Edward Said, *Orientalism* (1979; repr., New York: Vintage Books, 2002), 24–25.
2. Pierre Chaunu, *La civilisation de l'Europe des Lumières* (Paris: Arthaud, 1971), 62, 65, 54.
3. See Anthony D. Smith, *The Ethnic Origins of Nations* (London: Wiley-Blackwell, 1991). [Janion finds this concept in Ewa M. Thompson, *Imperial Knowledge: Russian Literature and Colonialism* (Westport, Conn.: Greenwood Press, 2000), 7.—Trans.]
4. Melchior Wańkowicz, *Było to dawno*, ed. Tomasz Jodełka-Burzecki (Warsaw: Państwowy Instytut Wydawniczy, 1981), 7–9.
5. Tadeusz Padalica [Zenon Fisz], *Opowiadania i krajobrazy: Szkice z wędrówek po Ukrainie* (Vilnius: Zawadzki, 1856), 2:74.
6. An epigraph from Henry Tyrrell's *History of the Russian Empire* cited from Neal Ascherson's *Black Sea* (New York: Hill and Wang, 1995), 89.
7. Andrew Wilson, *Ukrainians: Unexpected Nation* (2000; repr., New Haven, Conn.: Yale University Press, 2009), 58.
8. Maria Zadencka, "Znaki eksterytorialności: Obrazy Ukrainy w utworach polskich romantyków," in *Romantik und Geschichte: Polnisches Paradigma, europäischer Kontext, deutsch-polnische Perspektive*, ed. Alfred Gall et al. (Wiesbaden: Harrasowitz, 2007).
9. Tadeusz Mańkowski, *Genealogia sarmatyzmu* (Warsaw: Łuk, 1946), 105.
10. Vernon Luis Parrington, *Main Currents in American Thought: Volume 2—The Romantic Revolution in America, 1800–1860* (Norman: University of Oklahoma Press, 1987), 161.
11. Padalica, *Opowiadania i krajobrazy*, 2:47.
12. Henryk Sienkiewicz, *Dzieła* (Warsaw: Państwowy Instytut Wydawniczy, 1950), 2:195.
13. Wincenty Pol, *Wybór poezji*, ed. Maria Janion (Wrocław, Warsaw, Kraków: Zakład Narodowy im. Ossolińskich, 1963), 291.
14. Jan Kieniewicz, "Polska granicą Europy," *Przegląd Powszechny*, nos. 7–8 (1990).
15. Ihor Ševčenko, *Ukraina między Wschodem a Zachodem* (Warsaw: OBTA, 1996), 67.
16. Daniel Beauvois, "Préface," in *Les confins de l'ancienne Pologne*, ed. Beauvois (Lille: Presses Universitaires de Lille, 1988), 8.
17. Daniel Beauvois, *Trójkąt ukraiński: Szlachta, carat i lud na Wołyniu, Podolu i Kijowszczyźnie, 1793–1914* (Lublin: Wydawnictwo Uniwersytetu im. Marii Curie-Skłodowskiej, 2005), 584. [This Polish translation of Beauvois's work combines several of his prior monographs published in French, fused together and partly rewritten by the author. Despite considerable effort, I have not been able to find exact French equivalents of the quota-

tions Janion cites here; therefore, I translate them (in)directly from Polish. —Trans.]

18. Beauvois, *Trójkąt ukraiński,* 737, 260.
19. Beauvois, *Trójkąt ukraiński,* 691–92.
20. Cited in Beauvois, *Trójkąt ukraiński,* 692.
21. Beauvois, *Trójkąt ukraiński,* 698, 319.
22. Andrzej Żbikowski, *U genezy Jedwabnego: Żydzi na Kresach Północno-Wschodnich II Rzeczypospolitej, Wrzesień 1939–lipiec 1941* (Warsaw: Żydowski Instytut Historyczny, 2006), 235.
23. Delphine Bechtel, "'Galizien, Galicja, Galitsye, Halatchyna': Mit Galicji od zaniku do wskrzeszenia," *Borussia* 31 (2003): 85.
24. Beauvois, *Trójkąt ukraiński,* 16–17.
25. Stanisław Ignacy Witkiewicz, *Narkotyki / Niemyte dusze* (Warsaw: Państwowy Instytut Wydawniczy, 1975), 266.
26. Janusz Tazbir, "Przedmurze jako miejsce Polski w Europie," in *Rzeczpospolita i świat: Studia z dziejów kultury XVII wieku* (Wrocław, Warsaw, Kraków, Gdańsk: Zakład Narodowy im. Ossolińskich, 1971), 64–65.
27. See François Hartog, *Le miroir d'Hérodote: Essai sur la représentation de l'autre* (Paris: Folio, 1980).
28. Andrzej Borowski, ed., *Słownik Sarmatyzmu: Idee, pojęcia, symbole* (Kraków: Wydawnictwo Literackie, 2001), 173.
29. Tadeusz Sulimirski, *The Sarmatians* (London: Thames and Hudson, 1970), 166–67, 202–3.
30. Tadeusz Chrzanowski, "Orient i orientalizm w kulturze staropolskiej," in *Orient i orientalizm w sztuce: Materiały Sesji Stowarzyszenia Historyków Sztuki, Kraków, grudzień 1983,* ed. Elżbieta Karwowska (Warsaw: PAN, 1986), 68–69.
31. Marina Ciccarini, "Sarmatyzm i orientalizm w kulturze polskiej XVI wieku," in *Od "Lamentu świętokrzyskiego" do "Adona": Włoskie studia o literaturze staropolskiej,* ed. Giovanna Brogi Bercoff and Teresa Michałowska (Warsaw: Towarzystwo Literackie im. Mickiewicza, 1995), 173. [Janion's emphasis.—Trans.]
32. Borowski, *Słownik sarmatyzmu,* 191.
33. Przemysław Mrozowski, "Orientalizacja stroju szlacheckiego w Polsce na przełomie XVI i XVII wieku," in Karwowska, *Orient i orientalizm,* 258.
34. Ascherson, *Black Sea,* 233, 45.
35. Michał Miniat, Wierność i klątwa: Losy misji Konstantyna i Metodego (Warsaw: Odrodzenie, 1971), 278–79.
36. Adolf Stender-Petersen, "Die cyrillo-methodianische Tradition bei den Polen," in *Cyrillo-Methodiana: Zur Frühgeschichte des Christentums bei den Slaven 863–1963,* ed. M. Hellmann et al. (Cologne and Graz: Böhlau Verlag, 1964), 440–48.
37. Roman Jakobson, "Polska literatura średniowieczna a Czesi," *Kultura* 6 (Paris, 1953): 30.
38. Stender-Petersen, "Die cyrillo-methodianische Tradition bei den Polen," 440–42.

39. Karol Potkański, "Konstantyn i Metodyusz," *Przegląd Powszechny* 6 (1905): 328.
40. Stender-Petersen, "Die cyrillo-methodianische Tradition bei den Polen," 441.
41. Pope John Paul II, *Slavorum Apostoli,* June 2, 1985, https://www.vatican.va/content/john-paul-ii/en/encyclicals/documents/hf_jp-ii_enc_19850602_slavorum-apostoli.html.
42. Pope John Paul II, *Slavorum Apostoli.*
43. Andrzej Walicki, "Wschodnie płuco," *Gazeta Wyborcza,* September 20–21, 2003.
44. Cardinal Joseph Ratzinger, "Declaration *Dominus Iesus* on the Unicity and Salvific Universality of Jesus Christ and the Church," Vatican, August 6, 2000, https://www.vatican.va/roman_curia/congregations/cfaith/documents/rc_con_cfaith_doc_20000806_dominus-iesus_en.html.
45. Józef Birkenmajer, *Bogurodzica dziewica: Analiza tekstu, treści i formy* (L'viv: Filomata, 1937), 109.
46. Stender-Petersen, "Die cyrillo-methodianische Tradition bei den Polen," 469.
47. Stanisław Urbańczyk, "'Bogurodzica': Problemy czasu powstania i tła kulturalnego," *Pamiętnik Literacki* 1 (1978): 38–40.
48. Roman Mazurkiewicz, *Deesis: Idea wstawiennictwa Bogurodzicy i św. Jana Chrzciciela w kulturze średniowiecznej* (Kraków: Universitas, 2002), 298.
49. Mazurkiewicz, *Deesis,* 237–38, 324.
50. See Andrzej Walicki, *Filozofia a mesjanizm: Studia z dziejów filozofii i myśli społeczno-religijnej romantyzmu polskiego* (Warsaw: Państwowy Instytut Wydawniczy, 1970), 280–82.
51. Zygmunt Krasiński, *Pisma filozoficzne i społeczne,* ed. Paweł Hertz (Warsaw: Staszic, 1999), 31, 47, 46.
52. Simone de Beauvoir, *The Second Sex,* trans. Constance Borde and Sheila Malovany-Chevallier (New York: Vintage Books, 2011), 150.
53. Czesław Miłosz, *Szukanie ojczyzny* (Kraków: Znak, 1992), 88.
54. Stanisław Szczepanowski, *Idea polska: Wybór pism,* ed. Stanisław Borzym (Warsaw: Państwowe Wydawnictwo Naukowe, 1987), 325.
55. Szczepanowski, *Idea polska,* 218.
56. Karol Ludwik Koniński, *Ex labyrintho* (Warsaw: Pax, 1962), 122.
57. Thomas Mann, *Germany and the Germans* (Washington, D.C.: Library of Congress, 1945), 8, 13.
58. Szczepanowski, *Idea polska,* 330.
59. See Ewa Pogonowska, *Dzikie biesy: Wizja Rosji sowieckiej w antybolszewickiej poezji polskiej lat 1917–1932* (Lublin: Wydawnictwo Uniwersytetu im. Marii Skłodowskiej Curie, 2002), 93–132.
60. Mirosław Marody and Sławomir Mandes, "Polak katolik: O związkach religijności z tożsamością narodową," *Europa* 24 (June 14, 2006).
61. Martin Malia, *Russia under Western Eyes: From the Bronze Horseman to the Lenin Mausoleum* (Cambridge, Mass.: Belknap Press of Harvard University Press, 1999), 415.
62. Alain Besançon, "Wschodnia granica Europy," *Eurazja* 3, no. 1 (1996): 94.

63. Mikhail Rikhlin, "Rosyjski szibbolet," *Kafka: Kwartalnik środkowoeuropejski* 11 (2003): 60–65.
64. Viktor Erofeyev, *Encyklopedia duszy rosyjskiej: Romans z encyklopedią* (Warsaw: Czytelnik, 2003), 89.
65. Gustaw Herling-Grudziński, *Wyjście z milczenia: Szkice* (Warsaw: Czytelnik, 1998), 324.
66. Herling-Grudziński, *Wyjście z milczenia,* 231.
67. Tadeusz Borowski, "Here in Our Auschwitz," in *"Here in Our Auschwitz" and Other Stories,* trans. Madeline G. Levine (New Haven, Conn.: Yale University Press, 2021), 18.
68. Wolfgang Sofsky, *Violence: Terrorism, Genocide, War* (London: Granta Books, 2003), 30–31.
69. Borowski, "Here in Our Auschwitz," 19.
70. Wolfgang Sofsky, *The Order of Terror: The Concentration Camp,* trans. William Templer (Princeton, N.J.: Princeton University Press, 1993), 199–200.
71. Primo Levi, *Survival in Auschwitz: If This Is a Man,* trans. Stuart Woolf (New York: Simon and Schuster, 1958), 90.
72. Borowski, "Here in Our Auschwitz," 36–37.

CHAPTER 3

Between Death and Laughter

THE ART OF JACEK MALCZEWSKI

The Pond in Wielgie

Teresa Grzybkowska's richly illustrated *Świat obrazów Jacka Malczewskiego* [The world of Jacek Malczewski's paintings] opens with a reproduction of a photograph captioned as follows: "The pond in the village of Wielgie, where Jacek Malczewski lived between 1867 and 1871." Grzybkowska staged the photograph, which she took herself, to invite reflection about its location's charms. She juxtaposes it against a reproduction of one of Malczewski's late works, the 1919 painting titled *Dzieciństwo—Jacek nad stawem w Wielgiem* [Childhood: Jacek by the pond in Wielgie]. This painting, ardently admired by the art critic Kazimierz Wyka (who calls it "one of Malczewski's few complete masterpieces"), places Malczewski's art in a magical sphere that is at once domestic, familial, and aquatic.[1] These three attributes define the genius loci that grounded Malczewski's artistic genius.

Grzybkowska begins her essay with a passage from a letter Jacek wrote to his father in 1876 as a rebellious young man: "I want to paint differently than [my mentor, the historical realist painter Jan] Matejko, or all the world's past masters. I want to paint the living, unadorned world—to represent reality, truth . . . , and my own feelings. I do not want to serve my viewers some predigested slop patronizingly arranged on a platter."[2] His desire for a painterly universe all his own is striking, as is his intuition of the singularity of his vision: a singularity that can withstand "all the world's past masters." *The living has not yet been painted.* The twenty-two-year-old Malczewski takes this as his motto as he aspires to reveal reality, truth, feeling—things that cannot be mediated through preexisting conventions. Many have dreamed such dreams, but Malczewski is among the few who realized these youthful aspirations. He wanted to paint *differently*—and so he did.

Malczewski's correspondence from his early travels abroad conveys a surprising antipathy toward foreign lands. "France and its environs do not interest me. [. . .] I want to breathe our own air and see our own faces." His longing for the homely occasionally found expression in programmatic confessions of faith. Writing to his wife about how little he cared for "this alien world, these well-educated people, this Western civilization," he followed these expressions of repulsion with ones of attachment to things he felt were necessary to his creative practice: "I would prefer to sit by a Polish wheat field, to hide in some forgotten corner and look at the faces of our common people, at our hamlets, swamps, and forests. The nature and the people here leave me indifferent." These self-abnegating patriotic images, which idealize the proverbial wild pear trees growing in the balk, are motivated by a strong formal consciousness. Malczewski searched for "fresh forms"; the ones he found in the West were "worn out and old." Their triteness threatened artistic individuality. As he juxtaposed inspiring familiar landscapes against artistically monotonous foreign ones, he stressed in quite dramatic terms that he would need to wage an inner war against the latter. "I can see that I will come home relaxed, I suppose, but with my head all emptied out or, worse, filled with Western forms that I will need to tear out one after another."[3] This antinomy between "Western forms" and "fresh forms," ones that are fresh because they are homely, traverses Malczewski's work beyond his juvenilia. As an artist, he continually searches for the right modes of representation.

Malczewski understood the art he created as oneiric and phantasmatic. An early painting titled *Sen malarza* [The painter's dream, 1888] depicts an artist musing in a meadow as shadowy specters emerge from his dreamwork.[4] This is an apt metaphor for his creative output as a whole. Jadwiga Puciata-Pawłowska draws attention to the themes that Malczewski's works shares with those of the painter and playwright Stanisław Wyspiański. The latter had once planned to write a play about a painter dying in his studio as various imaginary beings that inspired his art emerge from canvases. Malczewski's *Błędne koło* [Vicious circle, 1895–97] and *Melancholia* [1890–94] directly gave rise to a memorable phrase in Wyspiański's *The Wedding* (1901), which is now often invoked to describe the organizing principle of Malczewski's work: "What music plays in a person's soul, what a person sees in his dreams." Here is how Malczewski himself describes the workings of his imagination in a letter from 1893: "As always, images big and small, bits of light and shade, and various figures, have been moving across my head. Past experiences rise up before me; pictures I had seen come back to me and move out onto canvas or fade underneath others. That's how it is; that's how it will remain all my life."[5] Malczewski's self-description seems accurate: His imagination worked like an alchemical workshop or a film studio converting dreams into paintings and paintings into dreams. The many phantasmatic landscapes and figures that appear in his canvases emerge from this dreamwork, which undergirds the uniqueness of his art.

Rusałki

The first dreamworld Malczewski created according to these principles was that of Slavic female water demons, known in Polish as *rusałki* [sing. *rusałka*]. "Rusałki," writes Grzybkowska, "were the first mythological–legendary creatures to appear on Malczewski's canvas."[6] He depicts them, among others, in *Opętany* [Possessed, 1887] and the four other canvases that form part of the cycle called *Rusałki: Boginka w dziewannach* [Swamp demon amid the mullein, 1888], *On i ona* [He and she, 1887], *Załaskotany* [Tickled to death, 1888], and *Topielec w uściskach dziwożony* [The drowned man embraced by a swamp demon, 1888]. Around 1900, Malczewski also painted "his first and only mermaids" in paintings titled *Wodnik i syrena* [The nix and the mermaid] and *Osobliwy połów* [A strange catch]: They are both worth mentioning in this context as they, too, depict dangerous, aquatic–pastoral fantastical creatures that exist on the boundary between Thanatos and Eros.

Figure 1. *Opętany* [Possessed, 1887]. The first painting in the cycle, it represents a young shepherd falling under the spell of a water demon. The village women look on with concern as he chooses the stranger over them. Image courtesy of the Jagiellonian University Museum in Kraków, Poland.

Figure 2. *Boginka w dziewannach* [Water demon amid the mullein, 1888]. In this painting, the shepherd seduced by the water demon is younger, on the brink of adolescence. Mullein, a medicinal plant, is associated with the Slavic equivalent of the Greek goddess Artemis. Image courtesy of the Jagiellonian University Museum in Kraków, Poland.

Figure 3. *On i Ona* [He and she, 1888]. This is the only painting in the *Rusałki* cycle in which the man and not the demonic woman takes center stage. Catching fish into his hat, he seems to be showing off for her. Image courtesy of the Jagiellonian University Museum in Kraków, Poland.

Scholars have drawn attention to a significant change that occurs in Malczewski's work around this period. Before he paints *Rusałki,* his art focuses on folk themes from a naturalist or ethnographic angle: He depicts evening songs in the village, matchmakers, and so forth. . . . With this new cycle, he steps into the supernatural worlds of folk mythology and fairy tales and begins to draw on them for his main inspiration.

Figure 4. *Załaskotany* [Tickled to death, 1888]. In the last two paintings of the cycle, Malczewski moves from the moment of infatuation to its consequences. Here, the rusałka stands to the side, triumphant, as her demonic sisters examine her kill. Image courtesy of the Jagiellonian University Museum in Kraków, Poland.

Figure 5. *Topielec w uściskach dziwożony* [Drowned man in the embrace of a water demon, 1888]. The fifth painting brings the folk legend to its narrative conclusion: After his death, the drowned man haunts the lake alongside the demonic woman, a warning to others. Image courtesy of the Jagiellonian University Museum in Kraków, Poland.

The rusałka, also called *majka, boginka, bogunka,* or *dziwożona,* features in many Slavic folktales, as do her male equivalents: *utopiec, topich, topczyk, topnik, topielec,* and *topielnica.* Leonard J. Pełka, who specializes in Polish folk demonology, organizes these nature-bound demons that even today haunt popular fantasy into five categories based on the spaces they inhabit: water, the shoreline, swamps, fields, and forests.

Slavic folklore describes all these demons, especially those of the field and the forest, as exceptionally dangerous, especially for men. "Wheat rusałki,"[7] who are young and beautiful, tend to hide in green, rising wheat fields. "When they catch hold of a careless young man who steps into the wheat, they do not release him until they have tickled him to death."[8] So writes the great scholar of Belarussian folklore Michał Federowski. Wheat demons and forest demons embody a free and independent feminine spirit. The former like to laugh; the latter sway in branches, singing and charming humans with their voices. All these magical creatures love to dance and pull unfortunate chosen humans into their revelries. Oskar Kolberg thus "summarized the activities" of a forest rusałka who supposedly lived between Tarnów and Rzeszów: "With her smile, her charms, her sweet singing, she seduces and charms incautious young men; she draws them into the depths of the forest and tickles them until they have laughed so much they can convulse no more."[9] River and lake rusałki like to swim "naked, with their hair down, and to charm and seduce their victims, then tickle them to death or drown them."[10] Those fated to fall prey to rusałki or their brethren cannot escape their fatal allure: "Whoever is destined to fall prey to a *topich* is ineluctably drawn toward water; though fear begins to overwhelm him, though he could still call for help, he stays put. The *topich* pulls him in, and no one can resist the force of his attraction."[11] If a man seduced by a rusałka does not drown or die from laughter amid her tickling, he continues to wander among the living in sadness and melancholy, listening to rusałki's unearthly singing; possessed by longing, he will often end up committing suicide. This seeker of unknown beauties is not unlike the artist himself.

Romanticism built much of its mythologies on these folk beliefs. German Romanticism drew on the folk myth of Melusine to imagine a range of watery temptresses. In poems and paintings, the primordial association of femininity with water fuses with figures of the dying, seduced human male. The female principle serves as a destructive force in the works of many German Romantics. This may be because of these male writers' inability to integrate it into their own consciousness.[12]

Water and its demonic forces overwhelm Adam Mickiewicz's *Ballads and Romances* [his 1822 breakthrough youthful collection of poems]. Soon, rusałki became the favorite topic of Polish Romantic art. The pseudo-scholarly apex of the period's fascination with them occurs in Kazimierz Władysław Wójcicki's *Klechdy, starożytne podania i powieści ludu polskiego i Rusi* [Legends, ancient tales, and stories of the Polish and Russian peoples, 1837]. Its author freely fuses folk references with poetic ones, treating Mickiewicz's ballads such as "Świtezianka" and "Rybka" as primary sources. Wójcicki's aestheticized rusałki "eagerly dance in circles and prance around in large groups by the forest, in the green meadow, then scatter to seduce young girls and farmhands." Wójcicki adduces several examples of the former: Young women can fall victim to rusałki as well.[13] Perhaps, for young people of both genders, rusałki serve as projections of a dream about a happy, free life in the state of nature—a dream surrounded by a deathly taboo. Rusałki love tickling their victims to death. Convulsive laughter—which is not, after all, a sign of pleasure—brings on death. The pleasure of cruelty and the cruelty of pleasure that tickling involves figure among the tortures described in Octave Mirabeau's famous late nineteenth-century sadistic narrative, *The Torture Garden* (1899).

Rusałki "seduce young hunters and peasants with their beautiful cheeks and sweet voices; once captured, they pull their victims into the depths. They often lift their heads above the surface of the water and let loose their long, golden braids; as they do so, a lovely sound resonates around them, as each hair vibrates with its separate tones."[14] Goethe's famous 1778 ballad "The Fisherman" forged this modern topos of fatal attraction to a "watery maiden." The maiden draws in a fisherman with her singing and the vision of an immersive maritime horizon. Goethe's poem enacts this seduction with its onomatopoeic rhythms: *Das Wasser rauscht', das Wasser schwoll—*

> The water rushed, the water swelled,
> It clasped his feet, I wis'
> A thrill went through his yearning heart,
> As when two lovers kiss!
> She spake to him, she sang to him:
> Resistless was her strain;
> Half drew him in, half lured him in;
> He ne'er was seen again.[15]

Being seduced by the far horizon, the unknown, or beauty has fatal consequences. Rusałki's erotic charm—they sing while combing their golden hair, symbolic of the magical charm of femininity—is the charm of death. Heinrich Heine's "The Lorelei" (1824) codifies these motifs and their meanings:

She combs her golden hair,
She combs it with a golden brush
And while she combs she sings;
The tune is both miraculous
And overpowering.
It grips the sailor in the ship
With a wild and aching woe;
His eyes are only looking up,
Not at the rocks below.
I believe that in the end the waves
Devoured ship and boy,
And that is what the Lorelei
Accomplished with her voice.[16]

Inspired by various folkloric and Romantic sources (at a point when Polish culture had absorbed what Bessler calls "that Romantic / pre-Raphaelite triad, femininity, water, and death"), Jacek Malczewski created his own vision of these watery demons. He worked out his understanding of them determinedly and consistently. On January 29, 1891, Malczewski, then in Kraków, sent a letter to Wacław Karczewski, who wanted to compose a novella based on the painter's demonic water fantasies. In the letter, Malczewski lists seven building blocks of his "rusałka narrative":

1. There was once a boy, a young swineherd. . . .
2. This boy glimpsed a woman, his ideal, amid the pastures. . . .
3. Once, in the autumn fog, he saw this woman clearly, as she swayed atop the stems of tall weeds. . . .
4. Having grown up, while catching fish he sees a rusałka and decides that she is the same woman—his ideal—and seeks her out all the more urgently. . . .
5. Another time, as he is rafting timber down the Dunajec River, he sees her on the shore amid the willows.
6. Full of the force of youth, he returns home to his village and looks for her in fields and swamps; out in the wild, he is overcome by rusałki and tickled to death. . . .
7. After his death a fairy tale emerges, and persists, in his home village: A young man looked for an ideal woman and found this woman after his death; after nightfall, the drowned young man can be seen in the embrace of a water maiden amid fog

and smoke. Washerwomen who carry water from the river occasionally spot them around nightfall.[17]

In fragments of the letter I omit here, Malczewski pairs each of these narrative threads with one of his paintings. He summarizes this literary–painterly narrative as follows: "In short, he did not find his ideal because it had always resided within him and emerged from within him; after he dies, this ideal radiates outward and fuses with the young man into something singular and unattainable."[18] Malczewski tightly weaves together the folk legend about rusałki with the notion of pursuing an ideal that emanates from the swineherd's artistic soul. He forges a fairy tale about searching for a kind of beauty that proves fatal and deadly. This trope pervades all of Malczewski's work, informing his unique artistic idiom. In relatively conventional fashion, his aesthetic ideal takes on the form of a distant, unattainable woman. At the same time, it is immanently present within the artist himself—though it might only reveal itself fully after his death. Throughout Malczewski's art, death is art's necessary liberating force. He paints in the face of death and confronts it with a directness that is uncommon in Polish painting.

Critics have often understood Malczewski's narrative explanations as translating his paintings' rusałki into metaphysical terms, which Ławniczakowa, among others, sees as opposed to the paintings' ostensible "sensory concreteness."[19] Puciata-Pawłowska similarly argues that the cycle of paintings titled *Rusałki* used folk culture only "as a pretext for representing allegories of dreams and personifications of personal illusions." She sees it as little more than a "costume" Malczewski dons to convey his own experience, including his sense of conflict with the world around him.[20] Such interpretations seem mistaken to me. The rusałki are not pretexts; through figures like them, Malczewski seeks out the fantastical within the mundane. A more appropriate context for understanding his imaginative engagement with the uncanny—in both its senses, the *Heimlich* and the *Unheimlich*—is provided by Bolesław Leśmian's *Klechdy polskie* [Polish folktales].

Leveling Our World and the Netherworld

In letters Leśmian writes to Zenon Przesmycki between 1913 and 1914, he expresses a desire to reconstruct the world of "real folktales as they spin themselves" in order to do justice to their autotelic function. He believes that his research into Polish folktales has led him to unknown, previously unused aesthetic discoveries: "In the course of my study, I have gathered a thousand marvels which branch out, like rapidly growing weeds, now into a novel, now into a poem." He complains to Przesmycki about his publisher, Jakub Mortkowicz, who does not appreciate the ingenuity of Leśmian's idea and seems to think "that these folktales are simple popular stories." Leśmian describes his endeavor as follows: "I have given these stories artistic depth; they are woven out of folklore and hinge on the mutual leveling of our world and the netherworld." In this procedure lies the innovation of Leśmian's folktales, their "ever more singular, ever more ineluctably necessary form."[21] Mortkowicz's critical perception of the folktales as "too frightening and too sensual" caused Leśmian to abandon his attempts at publishing them, though he had certainly hoped to do so in 1914. Let us note that horror and sensuality are characteristic features of some of Malczewski's depictions of rusałki as well.

In a short essay titled "Z rozmyślań o Bergsonie" [Some reflections on Bergson, 1910], Leśmian lays out an original concept of the fairy tale. Here is how he understands it:

> Never proven, always escaping the bounds of logic, flickering on the peripheries of empirical life—fairy tales nevertheless play an important role in our thinking. They form a rainbow bridge that links us back to nonlogical forms of being, to the steep banks of that mystery whose face has nothing to do with human faces. Fairy tales always come about through intuition or instinct. Logic declares their impulses to be blind because a fairy tale's eyes are of a different color from its own.[22]

According to Leśmian, the fairy tale exists in constant cognitive motion; myth, on the other hand, has been stabilized, immobilized, rendered static. His *Klechdy polskie* were intended as narratives of the former kind. Wacław Lewandowski aptly describes them as "epistemological fairy tales."[23]

A few years before the epistolary exchange cited above, Leśmian's contemporary Edward Porębski published *Pieśni ludowe celtyckie, germańskie, romańskie* [Celtic, German, and Romance folk songs]. Porębski described himself not only as these songs' editor and translator, but as a poet who reperforms them. Leśmian wondered how this mode of creativity relates to creative forgeries such as Macpherson's poems written in the voice of a nonexistent ancient Ossian. Writers like Macpherson, Leśmian writes, shield their "everyday, earthly persona" behind "the magical, mysterious guise of a creative being who inhabits their dreams." They are fascinated by songs others have sung before them. What is their goal? "To estrange their own existence by transposing it into the realm of myths and fairy tales, unreachable by human eyes; this transposition allows them to attain perfect solitude and absolute creative freedom."[24] Folk materials, tales that have already been spun, can serve as such "Ossianic" material as well.

Michał Głowiński aptly names the principle that makes the fantastical elements of *Klechdy polskie* modern. "Leśmian transforms traditional fantasy into modern fantasy by no longer attributing real-life existence to his imagined beings, but—as in ballads—by treating them as media through which the individual communicates with the world beyond her." By highlighting the dramatic uncertainty of human cognition, Leśmian "saturates folk fantasy with things that had been wholly alien and unknown to it; moreover, he ironizes this mode of fantasy, puts it in giant quotation marks, turning traditional folk storytelling into a form of play."[25] The autotelic quality of Leśmian's fairy tales and ballads, which seem to ravel of their own accord, conveys not only self-fulfillment but also exhaustion. They are an end in itself. Their strangely "inward," fantastical nature reveals itself in their refusal of metaphysical resolutions; instead, all we get are ever new forms of irony achieved through self-emptying and self-exhaustion. In Leśmian's poem titled "Stodoła" [The barn], we thus find the following question and answer:

> You can break up the barn in four days.
> But who first barned the barn, made it know what it was?
>
> It must have been Majka, the barn maid,
> A being half from the roadside and half from the field.[26]

Invoking Baudelaire's famous sonnet "Le Gouffre," Głowiński asks what "the abyss" signifies in Leśmian's poetry. He arrives at an unambiguous conclusion: "It makes most sense to state this tautologically: The abyss is an abyss. In general, tautology has always been at the heart of Leśmian's work."[27]

"The leveling of our world and the netherworld" and "estranging one's existence": these two principles of Leśmian's fantastical imaginary apply to Malczewski's as well. Let us briefly observe them at work in Leśmian's folktale about a rusałka named Majka. Majka gives the young man in this story a strange book about the habits of her kind. The knowledge it contains does not go beyond canonical folklore, though it is playfully stated. But Leśmian veers from the folkloric canon as follows: The story of the rusałka's love for a peasant is deeply rooted in everyday reality, even as it is laced with the existential experience of infinity and the absolute. It thereby follows the philosophical–poetic principle of the aestheticized folktale as Leśmian describes it in his letters.

The story's young protagonist is Marcin Dziura. His last name literally means *hole,* signaling an internal void. Dziura painfully experiences himself as lacking something ineffable. His inner emptiness "continues to grow as if fueled by yeast kept warm behind the fireplace."[28] On the first day of Zielone Świątki [Green week, a traditional Slavic holiday that celebrates the coming of spring], he encounters Majka in the wheat field while walking home on a moonlit night.

Majka bears all the attributes of a rusałka or a mermaid. Her braid is long, silky, and golden. At one point, this braid visits Dziura's cottage nightly all on its own. [. . .] Beautiful but dangerous, the narrator compares it to a snake. Majka also carries a marker of alterity: a fish tail, which Dziura finds immensely disturbing. Even when blinded by love, he cannot forgive her this "deformity." During his last meeting with Majka, "Dziura looked her up and down and saw the fishtail where it always was; it lay on the forest floor coiled like a shell.—The sight of the tail sobered him up and helped him regain his common sense.—My own woman is better, he thought to himself with satisfaction; she has legs rather than this eyesore."[29] Even so, intercourse with his "woman" does not give him the pleasure of otherworldly exploration.

At first, when Majka charms him, Dziura sinks into the "infinity of water" and sees the lake differently, through her eyes. She could tickle him to death, but she does not because she falls in love with him. She asks him to come live with her at the bottom of the lake, "alive or dead." Majka seems to want to break the chain of associations between femininity, water, and death; however, that does not lie within her power. Dziura experiences moments of the highest ecstasy with her. The rusałka gives him access to metaphysical feelings of the kind he had longed for. She takes him to the other shore, that of "nonlogical being." "His soul, which had been missing one half, was suddenly complete in this surprising dream." The amorous transgression to which they succumb has Marcin Dziura and Majka "linger in the wheat all night until dawn, gazing at each other in silence, fixed in their places."[30]

This discovery of a new form of being is expressed in colloquial, folksy language. Dziura reproaches himself for having fallen in with the rusałka: "Why the hell did I look at the lake with her eyes and rush into infinity through her unfamiliar body, when my soul does not fit into this infinity at all." All the same, he cannot bear to part with her. "He knew only that he would not turn back from this path, and that his soul was growing and expanding in his chest like a mounting haystack onto which more hay was being heaped with a pitchfork." He felt "subtended by a floating meadow as his uncertain soul flew off into infinity."[31] This folktale, like others in Leśmian's collection, has comic undertones. It ends with a grotesque scene in which Dziura's wife, whom he married to protect himself from Majka's charms, forcibly beats thoughts of her from his head with a tree branch.

Demons and Irony

Malczewski's early paintings construct a similar relationship between our world and the netherworld, fusing the fantastical and the quotidian. Then, "after about ten years," Grzybkowska writes, "the rusałka amid the mullein is replaced by a sophisticated, seductively charming chimera."[32] The word *replaced* is apt. In the same landscapes, alongside the same swineherds, there appear chimeras, harpies, and medusas. Wyka describes Malczewski's "folkloric imagination" as oriented around the deep "structures of folktale narratives" in which our world and the netherworld are leveled with each other. Here, it morphs into a "folkloric–mythological imagination."[33]

In a retrospective essay, Malczewski's son Rafał writes a thought-provoking passage about nonsense and surrealism in his father's painting. It names a principle one discovers in hundreds of Malczewski's compositions: "It's all surrealism and uncanny juxtapositions, rather than symbolism; a vision of the world in which a modest homeliness and a mysterious, otherworldly order touch borders."[34] Within this context, Przesmycki's criticisms of the paintings Malczewski exhibited in Krywulta's salon reveal themselves to be quite misguided. "We

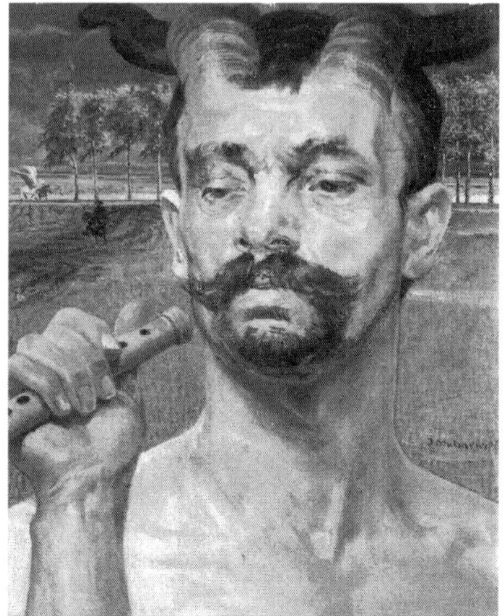

Figure 6. Jacek Malczewski, *Autoportret z faunami* [Self-portrait with fauns, 1906]. The object on Malczewski's head, in the central panel of the triptych, is a springform cake pan. Image courtesy of the Borys Voznytskyi National Art Gallery in L'viv, Ukraine.

value him enormously as an artist who did not satisfy himself with simply copying nature, who worked toward creativity and depth, who did not obey fashions and prejudices. But we must express our reservations about the strange conglomerates into which the elements he creates arrange themselves in almost every painting he composes." Przesmycki describes Malczewski's paintings as "strange, incoherent puzzles" and "dull rebuses." "The staffage almost always ruins the overall effect. Sometimes, we see unaccounted-for, colorless fauns; at other times, strangely naturalistic vacationers or military recruits." According to Przesmycki, Malczewski combines different moods and styles in a way that creates a jarring, brutal effect. "A realistic type" shows up within a "fairy-tale landscape" along with a "'fantastically naked,' coarsely ribald and ugly mythological figure, coming from who knows where."[35]

These are a symbolist's charges against a surrealist. Przesmycki's biggest critique concerns the way Malczewski's strange creatures and objects do not "signify" enough, do not "cohere" on one symbolic plane. (Take, for example, the cheap watch that Malczewski's Nike of the Polish Legions wears on her wrist.) Imprinted with the "seal of symbolism," as Rafał Malczewski puts it, Jacek Malczewski's paintings remained incomprehensible to their viewers, who paid most attention to

their jarring incongruity with reigning poetics and discourses. Leszek Libera reminds us that some clients "begged the master painter to not add any embarrassing accessories to their portraits." Others, "when commissioning a self-portrait or a portrait of a member of their family, asked in advance that the painting not include any fauns, harpies, or tigers, let alone barely clad gentlemen or ladies."[36]

In an important and otherwise interesting monograph on Malczewski's art, Andrzej Jakimowicz focuses on the painter's portraits and self-portraits. He describes the eruption of Malczewski's passion for painting himself as "the mark of a strengthened inward self affirmation," an expression of egotism and the artist's narcissistic tendencies. The eccentric taste Malczewski's self-portraits evince in their choice of garments, accessories, and surroundings signals, to Jakimowicz, that Malczewski "understood all ideas, even those about the afterlife, through the prism of his own personality and of his powerfully distended ego. In terms of his art, [these self-portraits] showcase the accrual of the painter's eccentricities. The latter manifest themselves in his seemingly unreflexive and uncontrolled urge to realize any ideas that come to his mind. This undisciplined unbridling of the artist's imagination (which is not all that rich in content) has caused some scholars to see Malczewski as a supposed precursor of surrealism."[37]

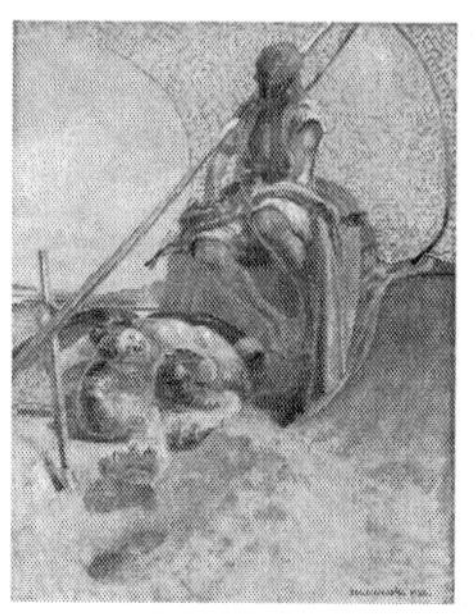

Jakimowicz passes harsh judgment on Malczewski's self-portraiture. But are paintings such as his *Autoportret z faunami* [Self-portrait with fauns, 1906], in which the artist depicts himself with a cake tray on his head, truly expressions of aristocratic dandyism?

It seems useful to shift registers here while remaining within the orbit of Romantic aesthetic categories. The concept of artistic irony—as its legislator, Friedrich Schlegel, understands it—will prove useful. Maria Żmigrodzka, a great expert on the varieties of Romantic irony, calls attention to Schlegel's preoccupation with the idea of ironic free play: the artist establishes a ludic distance toward both his object as well as his own "genius," subverting aesthetic illusions and breaking down aesthetic forms. All this, Żmigrodzka writes, creates a dialectic of "self-creation and self-destruction." Irony's divine aura, its "true, truly transcendent buffoonery," allows one to rise above one's own art or personal genius. The grotesque takes on the guise of contingency and strangeness, coquettishly displaying its unruly impulsivity—yet in this process, the artist's freedom is not "willful," selfish, or egotistical. Indeed, his freedom bears the "highest gravity" of moral and intellectual duty toward his artwork, which takes shape amid tensions between illusion and disillusionment.[38] Malczewski's art could be seen as an expression of his high aesthetic self-knowledge, and the fauns, chimeras, and rusałki that feature in it as signs of the artist's or his model's ironically inhabited embodiment.

In his pointedly titled *Wschodnioeuropejskie rusałki i pokrewne postaci demonologii ludowej a tradycja grecko-rzymska* [Rusałki and similar figures in Eastern European folk demonology in relation to Greco-

Figure 7. Jacek Malczewski, *Mój pogrzeb* [My funeral, 1923]. In this late work, the painter imagines the mythical beings and Polish peasants he spent his life painting mourning him after his death. Image courtesy of the Museum of Jacek Malczewski in Radom, Poland; photograph by Damian Jendrzejczyk.

Roman cultural tradition], Witold Klinger shows that ancient Greek nymphs lie at the origin of our rusałki and other water demons. He derides the Polish Romantics' impression that, by incorporating rusałki into their poems, they were salvaging from oblivion "at least one member of an otherwise forever-lost Slavic Olympus." "This supposed remnant of a Slavic pantheon turns out to be a simple calque from the demonology of the ancient world . . . miraculously preserved amid the destructive currents of subsequent centuries."[39] But Malczewski, like the Polish Romantics and Leśmian, believed that the rusałka was an autochthonic Slavic deity. He made use of this "miraculous" pagan remnant even while submitting it to a singular inversion: Having begun with what he deemed to be Slavic myths, he eventually replaced them with Greek ones. He thus put folklore in the service of "transcendental buffoonery." As Leśmian writes, "A full spiritual relation to the universe needs to embrace all that is human: not only sadness, longing, faith, and doubt, but also laughter, humor, and even jokes. Through a series of evolutionary intensifications, efforts, ecstasies, deformations, overuses, and so forth, laughter slowly morphs into irony, sarcasm, heartfelt mirth, and death. The bridge between laughter and death and that between tears and death is the same bridge."[40]

Laughter and death fuse together in both Leśmian and Malczewski. For the latter, this process begins with death that occurs amid laughter, as rusałki tickle their victims to death; it concludes with the quizzical smiles and guffaws of mourning fauns and chimeras in Malczewski's triptych titled *Mój pogrzeb.* Malczewski's demonism has always been undergirded with irony.

Notes

1. Kazimierz Wyka, *Thanatos i Polska, czyli o Jacku Malczewskim* (Kraków: Wydawnictwo Literackie, 1971), 25.
2. Quoted from Teresa Grzybkowska, *Świat obrazów Jacka Malczewskiego* (Warsaw: Dochnal, Kowalski i s-ka, 1996), 7.
3. All quotations in this paragraph are taken from Jadwiga Puciata-Pawłowska, *Jacek Malczewski* (Wrocław and Warsaw: Zakład Narodowy im. Ossolińskich, 1968), 24, 36.
4. See also Agnieszka Ławniczakowa, *Jacek Malczewski* (Warsaw: Kluszczyński, 1976), 22–23.
5. Puciata-Pawłowska, *Jacek Malczewski*, 85.
6. Grzybkowska, *Świat obrazów Jacka Malczewskiego*, 24.
7. Leonard J. Pełka, *Polska demonologia ludowa* (Warsaw: Iskry, 1987), 101.
8. Quoted in Witold Klinger, *Wschodnioeuropejskie rusałki i pokrewne postaci demonologii ludowej a tradycja grecko-rzymska* (Lublin: Wydawnictwo Polskiego Towarzystwa Ludoznawczego, 1949), 15.
9. Quoted in Pełka, *Polska demonologia ludowa*, 106.
10. Klinger, *Wschodnioeuropejskie rusałki i pokrewne postaci demonologii ludowej a tradycja grecko-rzymska*, 16.
11. Pełka, *Polska demonologia ludowa*, 83.
12. See Anna Maria Stuby, *Liebe, Tod und Wasserfrau: Mythen des Weiblichen in der Literatur* (Opladen: Westdeutscher Verlag, 1992); and Gabriele Bessler, *Von Nixen und Wasserfrauen* (Cologne: DuMont, 1995).
13. Kazimierz Władysław Wójcicki, *Klechdy, starożytne podania i powieści ludu polskiego i Rusi*, ed. Ryszard Wojciechowski (Warsaw: Państwowy Instytut Wydawniczy, 1972), 235, 238.
14. Wójcicki, *Klechdy*, 255.
15. Johann Wolfgang von Goethe, "The Fisherman," in *Goethe: Poetical Works*, trans. John Storer Cobb (Boston: Francis A. Niccolls and Company, 1902), 1:128.
16. Heinrich Heine, "The Lorelei," trans. Anna Leader, *Society of Classical Poets*, January 25, 2020, https://classicalpoets.org/2020/01/25/the-lorelei-by-heinrich-heine.
17. Quoted in Ławniczakowa, *Jacek Malczewski*, 74.
18. Quoted in Ławniczakowa, *Jacek Malczewski*, 74.
19. Ławniczakowa, *Jacek Malczewski*, 74.
20. Puciata-Pawłowska, *Jacek Malczewski*, 64–65.
21. Bolesław Leśmian, *Utwory rozproszone: Listy*, ed. Jerzy Trznadel (Warsaw: Państwowy Instytut Wydawniczy, 1962), 336, 338, 340.
22. Bogusław Leśmian, *Szkice literackie*, ed. Jerzy Trznadel (Warsaw: Państwowy Instytut Wydawniczy, 1959), 31.
23. See Lewandowski's introduction to Bogusław Leśmian, *Klechdy polskie* (Warsaw: PAX, 1959).
24. Leśmian, *Szkice literackie*, 389–90.
25. Michał Głowiński, "Laboratorium wyobraźni," *Twórczość* 2 (1960): 130.

26. Bogusław Leśmian, *Poezje zebrane* (Warsaw: Państwowy Instytut Wydawniczy, 1957), 170.
27. Michał Głowiński, *Zaświat przedstawiony: Szkice o poezji Bogusława Leśmiana* (Warsaw: Państwowy Instytut Wydawniczy, 1981), 302.
28. Bogusław Leśmian, *Klechdy polskie* (Warsaw: PAX, 1959), 50.
29. Leśmian, *Klechdy polskie,* 74, 103–4.
30. Leśmian, *Klechdy polskie,* 71, 76, 54, 55.
31. Leśmian, *Klechdy polskie,* 80, 103, 102.
32. Grzybkowska, *Świat obrazów Jacka Malczewskiego,* 24.
33. Wyka, *Thanatos i Polska, czyli o Jacku Malczewskim,* 27, 126–34.
34. Rafał Malczewski, "Wspomnienie o Ojcu: Część druga," *Kultura* 3 (1955): 18.
35. Zenon Przesmycki, "Sztuki plastyczne: Salon Krywulta," *Chimera* 1, no. 1 (1901): 165.
36. Leszek Libera, *Romantyczność i folklor* (Warsaw: Scientia, 1994), 47.
37. Andrzej Jakimowicz, 55.
38. See Maria Żmigrodzka, "Etos ironii romantycznej—po polsku," in *Problem wiedzy o kulturze: Prace dedykowane Stefanowi Żółkiewskiemu,* ed. Alina Brodzka et al. (Kraków: Zakład Badań Naukowych im. Ossolińskich, 1986).
39. Klinger, *Wschodnioeuropejskie rusałki i pokrewne postaci demonologii ludowej a tradycja grecko-rzymska,* 39.
40. Leśmian, *Utwory rozproszone,* 248–49.

PART II

Socialism, Patriotism, Nationhood

CHAPTER 4

The Patriot-as-Madman

"He is madly in love with his country." It's a cliché, but not a meaningless one.

The "patriot-as-madman," as the Polish Romantic poet Seweryn Goszczyński called him, feels his instincts and blood rise in a great, violent flood when he senses that evil powers have placed the motherland in danger. This patriotic feeling overwhelms his thoughts, attitudes, values, and personality; all other motivations fade into the background. Transgressive and exaggerated, it hovers on the brink of madness; a bystander could diagnose it as a self-aggrandizing psychosis that pushes the patriot toward self-destruction and death.

The patriot-as-madman, whose insanity is both metaphorical and quite real, embodies self-destructive patriotism at its apex. As layers of his personality transform through his fervor, the "madness" that has possessed him loses its quotation marks. In this regard, the patriot-as-madman belongs among mythical and myth-generating beings. He resides in the dark, hidden unconscious of Polish patriotism, the realm where death, madness, and the sacred intermingle. Were this patriotic madness not so instinctive, partly subconscious, and irrational in nature, it would not feel as real. The patriot-madman's loss of touch with rational thinking is precisely what testifies to the strength of his feeling for the motherland: She makes him lose his senses. This condition makes the patriot a danger to himself and turns him into an object of horrified awe for his contemporaries and later generations.

The motherland reveals itself to the patriot-madman as a deity. Polish Romantics first brought about its deification in the face of their country's loss of independent statehood at the end of the eighteenth century. In his classic study of the concept of the holy, Rudolf Otto distinguishes two forms sanctification can take: a "moral" and a "numinous" one. In the former, moral sense, the motherland became holy to

Poles alongside entities such as duty, will, struggle, action, sovereignty, the rule of law—and in this first sense, its sanctification followed the standard patterns of modern European nation-building. But Polish Romantics also sanctified their motherland in the second, numinous sense, which Otto describes as "'the holy' *minus* its moral factor," *sans* rationality or rationalization.[1] In this second guise, as *mysterium tremendum,* the numinous holy inspires confusion, fear, and awe.[2] In this context, the motherland comes to seem like a "dark force," a ruthless, cruel, demonic rival to any of the patriot's other potential love interests. As a deity, it is omnipotent and fearsome. *Thou shalt have no other gods before me.* Someone who imagines his motherland in this fashion can easily lose sight of a more rational understanding of his holy duties, letting himself be possessed by the motherland as by a demon. This demon requires absolute sacrifice: Its follower must even give up his "sanity" and his rational mind, descending into "holy madness." Beckoned by the demon's words and image, the patriot easily loses touch with reality.

Poland's partition gave rise to the first mad patriotic lovers of the Polish motherland, and to these lovers' first suicidal sacrifices on her tombstone. Michał Kleofas Ogiński recounts how Warsaw reacted to the Polish troops' defeat at the Battle of Maciejowice, during which the Polish insurrection leader Tadeusz Kościuszko was multiply wounded and taken prisoner by Russian troops. The news spread through the capital like wildfire:

> Never in my life had I been more devastated than by what I beheld among the people of Warsaw in the days that followed. . . . Though it beggars belief, I can attest to what I saw with my own eyes, alongside many other witnesses: Mothers miscarried upon receiving this news, ailing patients fell into all-consuming fevers, men descended into insanity and did not emerge back from it. As I walked the streets, I encountered men as well as women wringing their hands or hitting their heads against the walls of buildings, repeating "Kosciuszko is gone, the motherland is doomed" in tones of despair.

The memoirist was struck by the extremity of these patriotic ecstasies, which seemed so unbelievable that he felt compelled to underscore the reliability of his and other witnesses' accounts. Ogiński's account is remarkable and unique as a window onto a city fallen into temporary madness, but that is not a reason to disbelieve it. Similar descriptions recur in other memoirs from this era.

In a lecture delivered at the Collège de France on April 12, 1842, Adam Mickiewicz thus describes the lives of Polish intellectuals a generation older than himself: "These writers all died in mourning and despair, forming a long funeral procession as each in turn joined the motherland in the grave." Among these predecessors, Mickiewicz is most touched by Kniaźnin, "driven completely mad by the defeat at Maciejowice. Though he lived for another decade, he did not regain his senses." Others—Naruszewicz, Trembecki, Zabłocki—descended into apathy and inertia. As Mickiewicz puts it, "They were too old to change course and felt that they had failed in their intellectual calling." Whatever one thinks about such diagnoses' medical value, we can see here—in Mickiewicz and in others—a growing conviction that history can cause mental illness: The political strength of the motherland has an immediate impact on the health of its citizens, and the motherland's loss of sovereignty can cause these citizens to lose their minds. Later writers become critical of this "unhealthy," "diseased," "mad" Polish patriotism, but in Mickiewicz's time, the attitudes that will be decried in these terms were only beginning to spread.

The late eighteenth century saw Polish patriots challenge God himself to a duel for having allowed Poland to be partitioned among its neighbors. Niemcewicz recounts how Walewski, the voivode of Sieradz, received a visit from Duke Sanguszko after the last of Poland's three partitions. At the sight of his guest, Walewski rose from his sickbed, had himself brought out to the front porch, and uncorked a bottle of old Hungarian wine. Raising a glass to the sky, he exclaimed, "I raise this toast to you, God. Soon I will meet you face to face as my judge in Heaven. When we meet, I will ask why you have so insistently persecuted Poland and have now caused it to perish. If you don't have good reasons for your actions, I will demand satisfaction." A tipsy Polish nobleman, a member of the great Sarmatian race, might be expected to allow himself such familiarities with his maker. Still, even if we take these statements half ironically, the determination that flickers in them borders on madness.

Within the landscape of Polish collective spirituality, phenomena such as these—amply shared, commented on, enveloped in legend—begin to loom with increasing importance. They create an extraordinarily high benchmark for patriotic despair, an unsurpassable standard of ecstatic love for the motherland. The words "mad" and "madness" acquired, in this context, three oft-contradictory meanings:

1. The patriot was "mad" in a literal sense, having gone insane because of his motherland's defeats and sufferings.
2. The patriot was also "mad" because his political thinking was irresponsible and irrational: He was literally or figuratively drunk or otherwise intoxicated by grief, and his attempts at retaliation were quixotic and futile. Lacking a balanced historical and existential perspective, he reduces politics to morality, confusing reality with a distant ideal.
3. The patriot was "mad," finally, because, carried on the wings of morality and self-sacrifice, he claimed to rise above common sense; rejecting everyday rationality as vulgar and calculating, he refused reason's cold rules in favor of the "true" wisdom of intense feeling and condescendingly insisted that politics without morality leads to crime, and that real life ought to meet the standards of the moral and political ideal.

Mickiewicz articulated this triple vision of Polish patriotic (in)sanity after the failure of yet another anti-Russian insurrection, in an essay he wrote in May 1833 for *Pielgrzym Polski* [The Polish pilgrim], amid the émigré community's various conflicts and intrigues. The essay bears a pointed title: "O ludziach rozsądnych i ludziach szalonych" [Concerning reasonable people and madmen]. Mickiewicz sensed that the crisis caused by Poland's loss of independence had found reflection in the language people used to describe what was essential about their nation's being. This crisis fractured Polish patriotic discourse in a way that persists even today. The second and third meanings of *madness,* mentioned above, make this fracture most readily apparent. Then as well as now, the central political dilemmas of Polish patriotism find expression in debates over what constitutes true madness, "real" and "unreal" patriotic feelings, and what kinds of actions genuinely serve the motherland.

Mickiewicz estimates that the sharp dichotomy between "reasonable, natural diplomats" and simpleminded, uncomplicated patriots emerged around 1772, the year of the first partition of Poland. In the face of the impending partition, the Polish people's collective desire for independence could and ought to have been conveyed through simple, emotional language. But many Poles shied away from such directness, escaping into tangled historically or geographically deterministic pseudo-justifications of their country's existential crisis. Their manipulative rhetoric gave new meanings to the words *reasonable* and *mad*. Instead of invoking God's name, people began to invoke reason; instead of discussing citizens' duties and conscience, they deliberated "circumstances of time and place, difficulties, and hopes." A new, "diplomatic" political discourse arose around the principle that, to save Poland as a whole, one needed to give up some parts of it.

The semantic inversion that the words *mad* and *reasonable* underwent in Poland at this time fascinated Mickiewicz. The common people came to revere as heroes those whom the "reasonable" described as "madmen." This dichotomy became a pattern . . . of which Mickiewicz offers many examples. The members of the antipartition Bar Confederation who helped instigate the 1830 insurrection—Korsak, Dąbrowski, Kniaziewicz—were labeled as "mad" by the diplomatic elites, even as other Polish people admired them. Tadeusz Rejtan [a provincial nobleman who rent his garments in dramatic protest against the Polish Sejm's decision to legalize the first partition of Poland] became the butt of jokes among the elites for his extreme behavior; meanwhile, in other circles, "his name became sacred."

Let us pause over Rejtan. Mickiewicz zeroes in on him to sharpen the distinction between the "old" and "new" discourses of Polish patriotism. "Rejtan," he writes, "spoke the old, plain language of patriotism, swearing on God's wounds that Poland's first partition was a crime against the motherland. Reasonable people called him a fool and a madman; the common people declared his greatness; posterity confirmed the common people's opinion." *But—I ask—was Rejtan merely "declared" mad, or had he* actually *gone insane when he rent his shirt amid a parliamentary vote?* Mickiewicz does not address this question, since his essay focuses on a manipulative discursive practice: The poet exposes the "new discourse" of Polish politics as disingenuous and urges his readers to return to a more direct and truthful "old discourse."

In the opening pages of *Pan Tadeusz* (1834), Mickiewicz's poetic magnum opus, we meet Rejtan again. The poem's hero, Tadeusz, returns home from long years of schooling to find that old, familiar paintings still hang upon the walls of his childhood manor. Next to a portrait of Tadeusz Kościuszko, he recognizes one of Rejtan:

> Next there is Rejtan, dressed
> In old Polish style, aghast now freedom's lost;
> He holds a knife blade to his chest, while *Phaedo*
> Is lying before him, and a life of Cato.[3]

No surviving portraits of Rejtan correspond to this description. Mickiewicz's ekphrasis imagines him a moment before his (historically documented) suicide. Mickiewicz's allusions to Plato's dialogue about the immortality of the soul and Plutarch's *Life of Cato the Elder* imply that Rejtan's suicide was an act not of madness but of stark moral and existential self-possession.

This passage from *Pan Tadeusz* is striking because of how exceptional it is: In the popular imagination, Rejtan gained legendary status as an exemplar not of stoic virtue, but the virtues of madness. Declared "mad" by his fellow parliamentary representatives, he is supposed to have descended into actual insanity. In a poem that glorifies Rejtan as the embodiment of Lithuanian patriotism, Franciszek Kniaźnin captures this paradoxical conflation of virtue with folly as follows:

> So others would recall what virtue was,
> He let its holy fire set his mind ablaze.

In *Pamiątki Soplicy* [Soplica's tales, 1839–41], a collection of fictionalized oral stories from pre-partition Poland, Henryk Rzewuski imagines Rejtan as patriotic, stalwartly and sullenly so, since his childhood. After the Sejm of 1773, during which his memorable protest took place, Rejtan goes back to his family manor. Seweryn Soplica, Rzewuski's magnificent fictional narrator, supposedly knew him as a schoolmate and a fellow soldier. A paroxysm of madness shakes Rejtan when he hears that Poland had been partitioned: "Earlier in life, illness would often make him dizzy, and intense thoughts occasionally kept him up at night, but the quality of his mind remained intact. When he heard that the first partition of the motherland had been unanimously approved by the confederation of the Polish estates, the blow proved too much; the shame he felt on behalf of his country broke his mind into pieces." Rzewuski is not after historical truth here, of course; his Rejtan is the matter of myth and legend, a patriot "whose mind was weakened by his service to the motherland" and whose madness eventually drove him to suicide.

In an essay titled "Rejtan i dylematy pierwszego rozbioru Polski"

[Rejtan and the dilemmas of the first partition of Poland, 1987], Jerzy Michalski describes with a professional historian's characteristic thoroughness Rejtan's quite reasonable motivations and the understandable esteem in which many contemporaries held him. At the time, Polish society could not have actively resisted the partition, but many yearned for some statement of moral opposition to it. Rejtan stepped into that role and played it perfectly. As Michalski puts it, Rejtan expressed a view that ought to have been expressed by Stanisław August, Poland's reigning monarch—but which the king could not have voiced without inviting considerable personal and political danger [in the face of Poland's military weakness relative to the powers partitioning it]. "It would have also been politically dangerous for the whole Sejm or a politically prominent group of its members to take a heroic stand against the partition. Rejtan's protest was obviously ineffective and therefore did not incur broader national risks. At the same time, his actions fulfilled Plutarch's ideal of the solitary public hero who is willing to sacrifice everything for his country." Rejtan's power paradoxically lay in his weakness—in his inefficacy, he embodied the commonly held belief that "the patriot's main duty was to insist that Poles were not *voluntarily* agreeing to the partition of their country." Michalski argues that Mickiewicz still saw Rejtan through this Plutarchian framework and thus immortalized him. That's certainly the case in *Pan Tadeusz,* though Mickiewicz does not consistently maintain the same attitude toward Rejtan throughout his writing. More important, the legend that grew around Rejtan outweighs any factual accounts Mickiewicz or others may have tried to preserve.

The alternative biography of Rejtan that acquired canonical status—the warp onto which the myth of his life was woven—can be summarized as follows: Driven to extreme despair because of the misfortunes that had befallen his country, Rejtan went insane and committed suicide. This baroque accumulation of misery is in bad taste, despite and indeed precisely because of its fantastical exaggerations. All the same, it laid the foundation for Romantic and post-Romantic, writerly and painterly legend. Rejtan personified most fully and expressively the figure of the Polish patriot driven mad by the motherland. Taken to an extreme, love of the country transforms the metaphoric madman into a diagnosable one. Already at the Sejm, where Rejtan made his dramatic stand, his detractors called him a "half-wit" and remarked on the obsessiveness of his political determination.

Rejtan's patriotic madness manifested in word as well as in gesture. He lay down on the doorstep of the parliamentary chamber (by some accounts, he spread-eagled himself) to prevent representatives from leaving; he tore open his shirt and yelled taunts that have come down to us in several versions: "Go on, trample on this blood that I am ready to spill for you, on this chest that I am willing to put between you and those who would take away your dignity and freedom"; "Kill me, trample me, but do not kill the motherland!"; "By God and by the wounds of our Savior, brothers, I implore you, do not dishonor Poland's name!"; "Trample me, wound me, just like you're wounding your motherland!"; "Today I went to confession and ate the body of Christ, who sacrificed himself for you; trample upon me if you wish to tread on Him as well." Emanating horror, these entreaties accuse their addressees of breaking taboos and effectively committing sacrilege.

Mickiewicz saw such dramatic expressions of determination as laudable uses of "old language": They invoke God and invite physical identification with one's humiliated country. (The latter would have particularly appealed to Mickiewicz's Romantic sensibilities.) Jerzy Zawieyski notes that all the statements attributed to Rejtan are "strangely emotional and lyrical," "far removed from the language of diplomacy." He seems to have felt in his body the pains of his country as it was being "riven apart" and "torn into pieces." Mickiewicz borrows the language of Rejtan's apocryphal declarations in his Romantic drama *Dziady* to depict his suffering hero Konrad. Other Romantics described themselves as haunted by a motherland that appeared before them as "a bloody specter" (Konstanty Gaszyński) or by "the ghost of the murdered motherland," "pale, with unmoving eyes, covered in fresh, gory wounds" (Seweryn Goszczyński).

A hitherto unknown parliamentary representative from the town of Nowogródek opened a veritable procession of Polish patriotic madmen and "madmen." To follow Rejtan's example is to act like "a fanatic, a lunatic who sees himself bound by duty to care for every tiniest piece of the motherland" (Zawieyski). Initially compared by his contemporaries to the stoical heroes who kept faith to Roman ideals of virtue, Rejtan rapidly transformed from an ancient statesman to a Romantic character, and into a personification of "Poland" as well as "existence" itself. The legend that enveloped Rejtan renamed madness as clear-sightedness and identified patriotism with self-destructive determination. In the preface to his book of sonnets about the 1830 insurrection against Russia, Hieronim Kajsiewicz writes that "if our generation has not yet sobered from its holy spirit of self-sacrifice, which others consider madness, if despite many failures and sufferings we live and die filled with this madness, imagine the generation that will follow ours—whose persecution and suffering will be even greater." This generation, Kajsiewicz implies, will be even less sober and more maddened, inebriated with "the holy spirit of self-sacrifice." Rejtan marks this attitude's point of origin, the birthplace of a national mental disorder. Because of its mythic significance, each detail of his narrative is pregnant with meaning as a potential model or symbol for others.

Like other horrific events of Rejtan's life, his death by suicide has become the matter of legend. Several different accounts of it are in circulation, each offering a different set of emphases. The poet Julian Ursyn Niemcewicz describes his suicide as follows:

> The day when three foreign royal courts ruled in favor of Poland's first partition marked the last day of Rejtan's life. He could not bear this blow; his mind, previously clear as daylight, fell into confusion. When news of Rejtan's madness reached his brothers, they all came to Lithuania . . . but he did not know who they were and attacked them ragefully, until they had to restrain him. . . . From then on, he no longer recognized anyone, he could not bear to wear clothing, he only received food through the window to the room he was put in. One day, an incautious servant brought Rejtan a drink in a glass vessel; Rejtan snatched it away, broke it, and used the shards to cut himself open. Thus did our immortal compatriot, on par with the great Romans of Cato's time, end his life.

Notably, Niemcewicz does not in any way condemn this suicide as a sin; he frames it within ancient Roman custom and, like Rzewuski, ties it directly to Poland's loss of independence.

Polish Romantics typically discussed patriotically motivated suicide in these categories of Roman civic duty, studiously avoiding Christian injunctions against taking one's own life. But in other contexts, the incompatibility between Christian and Roman ideas of virtue did preoccupy them. Rufin Piotrowski, who claims he had an opportunity to assassinate the tsar but decided against it, belatedly explains in his *Pamiętniki* [Memoirs, 1860–61] that he had faced the choice between remaining "Polish" (i.e., a Christian) and becoming "a Roman." Only the latter would have seen the killing of a tyrant as a noble gesture and had no moral misgivings about it.

Niemcewicz felt certain that Rejtan was not in his right mind when he committed suicide; yet he also saw the insane Rejtan as making a conscious, intentional choice, analogous to Cato's famous refusal to outlive the Roman Republic. Roman Kaleta has collected a number of similarly polyvalent accounts of what supposedly happened on August 8, 1780, the fateful day of Rejtan's suicide. The attitudes of those who describe it obviously color the shapes and meanings of the day's events. I must admit that many of these accounts make a strong impression on me, too: They are memorably, theatrically expressive. One version of the legend, which transposes Rejtan's death into 1790, depicts his extreme despair as part melancholy, part psychotic trance: "The one time someone offered him a drink in a glass vessel, he quickly grabbed it, broke it, and used the shard to cut his own throat." In another version, the insane Rejtan swallows these glass shards; yet another instance depicts them coming from a broken windowpane. The final draft of Mickiewicz's *Pan Tadeusz* shows Rejtan brandishing a knife, symbolically equivalent to Cato's sword. An earlier draft briefly but vividly describes Rejtan as having "torn out his own entrails." Rzewuski words his account somewhat differently; he argues that Rejtan "broke the windowpane in his room and used the glass to rupture his intestines." The choice between the throat and the entrails makes a considerable symbolic difference, of course, especially if one is trying to decide whether Rejtan's death was an act of mere madness or patriotic madness. Kornel Ujejski gives his suicide clear moral meaning by styling him as a courageous gladiator whose dignity contrasts with the dissolute levity of other Polish nobles. "The whole country was like a Roman circus in which a few gladiators perished to collective applause. One of them, Rejtan, tore out his entrails with his own hands." Ujejski, who deemed himself the nation's prosecutor and called out every sin against "the religion of patriotism," saw Rejtan's suicide as a model gesture of courage and protest.

In a remarkable monograph titled *Klasycyzm, czyli prawdziwy koniec Królestwa Polskiego* [Classicism, or the true end of the Kingdom of Poland, 1983], Ryszard Przybylski analyzes the poet Ignacy Krasicki's *Rozmowy zmarłych* [Conversations among the dead]. Krasicki began to write *Rozmowy* in 1798, after all of Poland's territories had been partitioned among its neighbors. They testify to his contemporaries' preoccupation with whether suicide was an appropriate response to their country's loss of independence. "Solon claims that one can and must survive in captivity. Cato counters that such a life is dishonorable and lacks meaning." Polish Romantics continued to debate this antinomy. Rejtan became their hero because of the determination with which he pursued extremes: first in his madness, then in his suicide. I say he "pursued" these extremes because, for the Romantics who admired him, Rejtan's madness was a state not of unconsciousness but of higher consciousness. Far from impulsive, his actions seemed inspired.

Jerzy Zawieyski refers to this Romantic tradition in "Pomiędzy plewą a manną" [Between weeds and manna], an essay published in 1968. Historical sources show that after three days of fame at the Polish Sejm and some subsequent aimless wanderings around Warsaw, Rejtan isolated himself from his family (although one wonders whether, at this point, his family wanted to isolate themselves from him). He moved to a small brick cottage on his brother's estate in Lithuania; in its seclusion, he began to write the story of his political work in the Sejm. Seweryn Rzewuski's sources, from which Zawieyski borrows, describe how Rejtan "saw a Muscovite general through the window of his cottage. The general's soldiers were stationed in Nowogródek, and he had come to pay his respects to Michał, Tadeusz Rejtan's brother. Tadeusz desperately wanted to meet the general but acted threateningly, so the servants locked him up." Rejtan supposedly commits suicide in response to this episode. Zawieyski comments, "Rejtan's suicide becomes another expression of his moral protest against the partitioners of his country; this second protest, unlike the first one, proves fatal."

Soon, imitating Rejtan turned into a trend. "False Rejtans" who merely "aped" him began to pop up. One such false Rejtan, Jan Suchorzewski, who in 1790 opposed the Sejm's decision to adopt a democratic constitution, couched his protests in dramatic, Rejtan-style rhetoric.

In an essay titled "Po obu stronach drzwi" [On both sides of the door], Marian Brandys describes Suchorzewski as a "Rejtan" figure alongside Rejtan himself, but also the twentieth-century writer and activist Jerzy Zawieyski, mentioned above. Like Brandys, I will now make a "dizzying leap from the eighteenth century into the present." Rejtan's persistence into contemporary literature testifies to how many meanings—and how many mysteries—have accumulated around his story over the last two centuries. Zawieyski's twentieth-century retelling of Rejtan's life [. . .] underlines the latter's conflict with Polish King Stanisław August. Unlike many other writers, especially contributors to the popular press, he acknowledges that the king's choices had some moral justification. All the same, his tone deepens when he begins to describe Rejtan, in whose madness and exile he clearly recognizes his own political plight. This is how Zawieyski narrates Rejtan's wanderings around Warsaw after the decisive vote in favor of partition, which may have been spurred by Rejtan's rising paranoia or actual threats of dispossession and banishment: "He must have frequently fled from the inn where he stayed, moving from one inn to another; possessed by fear, he must have wandered all the way to Warsaw's farthest peripheries. After some time, he probably didn't keep any lodgings at all; instead, he walked the streets, sleeping in doorways or in caves and ruins. The memoirs of travelers to eighteenth-century Warsaw attest to how many such caves and ruins he could have found in Poland's capital."

Already at the end of the eighteenth century, writers remarked on the metaphorical and literal similarities between the fates of Rejtan and Poland. "Just as Poland's traitors tore out their country's entrails, so did Rejtan tear out his own and thus end his life." By ripping open his garments at a fateful meeting of the Sejm, Rejtan had indicated that Poland was being ripped apart as well. Like the motherland, he was banished to ruins and into hiding. Poland hadn't been *completely* lost at that point, but Rejtan sensed that it would be. Jan Paweł Woronicz reiterates this parallel in a poem written after Poland's final loss of independence in 1795:

> Strangers to ourselves, wherever we step
> The bloody corpse of the motherland stares up at us.
> Amid strange places and people, everything irks us;
> Even in sleep, which ought to bring us rest, we feel the tug
> Of hearts and senses conjuring up a dream
> That's but a dream, and which must quickly vanish.

Similar feelings must have inspired Zawieyski's outline for a play, which his all-consuming madness did not allow him to finish. The work followed Rejtan's last year of life, spent in despair as he hid in his former property's neighboring forests. "Were one to write a play about Rejtan," Zawieyski writes, "it could take the form of a long monologue. The king's carriage breaks down, like on the day of his assassination.

This happens in the forest. Instead of being pulled by horses, the carriage is pulled by the traitor Adam Poniński, marshal of the Sejm that agreed to Poland's partition. Sitting atop a tall tree, Rejtan speaks down to the king and insults Poniński. He describes the king's misery and the ugliness of the nation's betrayal." What literary convention ought this play to be written in, Zawieyski muses? "Born from the madness of a national hero, it leans more toward the grotesque than toward tragedy. Or maybe it could combine both genres?"

Written in 1980, Jerzy Krzysztoń's *Obłęd* [Madness] strikes such a generic balance. Closely modeled on Rejtan, its protagonist, Krzysztof J., has been driven mad by his love for the motherland. Visions of Poland appear before him, threatening to plunge him into apoplexy. "But it is not clear whether this apoplexy will come from ecstasy at the glory of the Polish Republic and the Virgin Mary as its queen—or from despair at its people's misery, failure, and foolishness." The tragic and the grotesque coexist around this new Rejtan, whom the political disappointments of December 1970 find not in a small cottage, a ruin, or a forest, but in a mental hospital on the outskirts of Warsaw. Krzysztof J. is a true son of his nation, whose past grandeur is hopelessly entangled with despair over its present-day abjection. This entanglement is precisely what drives him mad and makes him a worthy heir of Rejtan and his successors.

"Though this be madness, yet there is method in't." The patriot's insanity carries some of Odysseus's wiles. Outside the mental hospital, reality feels absurd and monstrous. Only within its confines can Krzysztof J. rally people to the cause of true national values; only there can the patriot dream out the nation's ideal version of itself. Jerzy Andrzejewski's *Notatki szpitalne* [Hospital notes, 1983] repeats this trope. Andrzejewski writes them as annotations to a fictional appeal a madman makes to the highest authorities of communist Poland, having been driven insane by its realities. "Under these circumstances, it seems irrelevant whether M intentionally drove himself insane, or whether the reality in which he lived gave rise to his illness and imposed it upon him. His madness is as deeply situated in Polish culture as Orestes's madness was in the social context of ancient Greece or Alyosha Karamazov's in the darkness enveloping nineteenth-century Russia." M's schizophrenia, Andrzejewski insists, does not discredit "the truth of what his visions express: He is surrounded by an overwhelming, nearly all-powerful enemy." His paradoxical statement is not untrue. In Polish culture, schizophrenia and realism are not opposed to each other; psychosis lets one see social reality for what it is. Andrzejewski takes M as an exemplar of a particular national mentality. Does this form of madness exist in other cultures? He doesn't say. For him, insanity always bears a local, national inflection and cannot be uprooted. "Let every nation speak about its own madmen." And so we do!

The Romantic madman wastes away in the fires of self-sacrifice; however, his offering is not always futile. Krzysztoń's novel represents madness as a monstrous initiation ritual: By descending into hell, we are redeemed and purified. "Someone has to do it on our shared behalf," the author, his narrator, and his protagonist all agree. Someone has to test out the particularly Polish concept of liberation through suffering on his own person. Krzysztoń took this task upon himself.

Starting with Rejtan, successive attempts at saving or reclaiming Poland's independence ended in failure. Each of these unsuccessful insurrections had its madmen. We will not try to list them all here, though at some point it might become useful to do so. For now, before we move on to the insurrection of January 1863, let us recall two figures and two literary works inspired by the insurrection of November 1830.

The first of these is Zygmunt Krasiński and his autobiographical *Adam Szaleniec* [Adam the madman, 1831]. When Krasiński found out that the 1830 insurrection had begun, he decided that he would not—could not—take part in it. The shame of this realization drove him to madness, as he confessed in letters to the English journalist and translator Henry Reeve. Insanity would not have possessed him so violently had it not been for his preexisting, carefully fashioned image of himself as a brave knight, a patriot ready to give up his life for the motherland at a moment's notice. . . . Krasiński confesses to his friend that he misled his beloved with the patriotic image he painted of himself: "I lied to her, and now that a hundred thousand other people are up to the task that I lied about, I cannot keep up my false pretenses." The disenchantment of his knightly self-ideal triggers a psychic crisis. "Writing this, I felt feverish, brokenhearted, miserable; my mind was racing." Krasiński enters a fugue state: "To dream, to lie to yourself, and thus to sink ever deeper into madness—that's not even the worst of it." "I write foolish things and let my imagination run wild, blissfully unsure whether my career will peak in madness or in numbness:

Will I end up an escapee from Bedlam, a wild-eyed madman foaming at the mouth, blood dripping from my chest, thoughts tumbling and colliding in my head?" In a letter to his father, Krasiński adds, "I walk around aimlessly, I cry like a child, I awaken with manic intensity." "I wrote many things, some of them reasonable, some immoderate, as my moods shifted. When my soul was riven by madness, I relieved it by writing out my mad thoughts."

Note how Krasiński's mental states blur together: "being as if mad," "being mad," "writing out the mad thoughts." His letters gradually constellate into a prose poem about Adam the madman. In a letter to Reeve dated June 21, 1831, he confesses that he only feels alive "when describing the madness of a man with whom I identify." When Reeve comments that Krasiński's alter ego, Adam, is a "dilettante" and not a real madman, the latter responds with anger: He intends Adam "to be a real Bedlamite." He accuses his friend of dismissing his writing as a finger exercise, even as it is deeply, woundingly existential to him. In this sequence of letters, he makes one of his most famous and significant pronouncements: "I hope you can understand that Adam *is not* me but also *is* me. I took myself as a point of departure, pushing the truth about me to its limits." Nowhere but in Polish literature does one encounter this phenomenon: a study of the poet's patriotic madness, an autopsy of his patriotically induced dishonor. Krasiński will eventually bring this trope to its fullest expression in *Irydion* (1836). [. . .]

I will address a very different example now. Consider Jan Machnicki, a Galician civil servant whose well-documented insanity was supposedly caused by the defeat of the 1830 insurrection. Machnicki, a madman who lived in the ruins of the castle of Oderburg, would have remained a picturesque legend and the stuff of local memoirs, were it not for the novel Seweryn Goszczyński wrote about his life. In a letter sent to his friend Zaleski in 1840, Goszczyński confesses, "I wrote a rather long prose narrative based on my memories of Galicia. Its hero is a patriot-madman, a real person who only died a few years ago. He used to live in the ruins of the castle of Oderburg before they crumbled to dust." Goszczyński turns this patriot-madman into the king of the castle, the guardian of the ruins, a Romantic lunatic driven insane by his love of Poland's past as well as its future. He disagrees that the man's insanity renders him a poor judge of reality, taking Machnicki's side against his coldly reasonable philistine neighbors: "If you had more feeling and more wisdom, Machnicki would not seem mad to you; indeed, you'd be happy to exchange your reason for his madness." *Król zamczyska* [The king of the castle, 1842] systematically performs this highly Romantic inversion: Madness becomes reason, reason becomes madness. In one episode, its protagonist speaks to the ghost of Stańczyk, the famously wise court jester who served three successive fifteenth- and sixteenth-century Polish kings. In their conversation, Machnicki assumes the role of the king as well as the king's jester. Scenes like these place Goszczyński's novel on the brink between tragedy and the grotesque.

Let us now take Rejtan as a lens through which to read the culminating event of Polish patriotic madness: the insurrection of January 1863. I will discuss literature and history in the same breath here, since the two interpenetrated powerfully in this period. The writer Józef Ignacy Kraszewski, who was so sensitive to the moods of his generation, sketches the following group portrait of the insurrectionists: "A handful of people others declared mad, calling them dreamers, ideologues, revolutionaries, demagogues, were left on their own, waving a bloodied, torn, old Polish flag." Many of Kraszewski's contemporaries shared this view, though they might not have expressed it in such lofty terms.

The insurrection left its mark on all the great writers of this generation. Consider Aleksander Głowacki, better known under the pseudonym Bolesław Prus, whose novels crucially shaped nineteenth-century Polish culture. The fate of Aleksander's insurrectionist older brother Leon permanently marked his sensibility. As Krystyna Tokarzówna recounts, Leon served as one of the great instigators and organizers of the insurrection; yet once it started, his nerves rapidly gave in. Sunk into melancholy and depression, he spent several years in a mental hospital in Lublin before coming into the care of his uncle, a pastor, never to recover. His younger brother Aleksander attributes his illness to the immense pressure he was under, which tore his nervous system to pieces: "An exceptionally noble man, as far as I know he didn't believe that the planned military action could succeed, yet he did not back out of co-organizing it." Leon never went into battle; he was not killed in combat; he was not imprisoned or sent to Siberia. "But the ways others perished were preferable to his," Aleksander writes on March 22, 1902, in a letter to Walery Przyborowski. Aleksander Głowacki / Bolesław Prus could never forget his brother. The latter hovered over him as a ghost and a warning. Leon's fate inflected

Aleksander's view of Polish patriotism as singularly "diseased." It frustrated him so much that he considered moving to Saint Petersburg for his university degree.

Prus's other great contemporary, Eliza Orzeszkowa, responds to the insurrection somewhat differently. She inserts hints of a mysterious recent tragedy into her otherwise satirical novel *Pompalińscy* [The Pompaliński family, 1876], which caricatures Poland's weak, corrupt aristocrats. The idyllic house of the Kniks family resounds with a man's footsteps echoing from behind a closed door. "There was something mournful and mysterious about these footsteps. . . . As if a restless ghost was doing penance in that room's quiet enclosure—or a sad prisoner was worrying the albatross around his neck." The novel eventually resolves this mystery, turning it into an Aesopian parable. It turns out the father of the family was driven mad by the defeat of the 1863 insurrection. "His soul entirely consumed by matters of the commonwealth . . . for an entire year, he has remained somber and silent like a gravestone." Showing no interest in his home, wife, or children, he shakes his head "sadly, pitying some invisible being." At one point, he begins to list "various miseries." "Abruptly, he leaped from his chair; his eyes fixed on a distant point, his face as pale as a corpse's. Pressing his palms to the sides of his head, he cried out in a terrible voice, 'The abyss!' and fell to the ground." This must be the same abyss into which Orzeszkowa herself fell, in her own telling, after the defeat of the insurrection. In her novel, the descriptions I just quoted are focalized through the wife of the patriot-madman. The patriot-madman merely repeats, "All is lost," while vividly enacting the breaking of his heart and the unspooling of his senses. Cezary, the only member of the Pompaliński family who stands any chance of redemption, sees him as "a saint who lost his mind out of love for the common people," "driven insane by his love of the people." We are discreetly made to understand that this kind of patriotic lunacy is something to which many Poles succumb.

In a short book about the novelist Maria Dąbrowska, Andrzej Kijowski shows that the nineteenth-century Polish intelligentsia imagined the household as "forever stilled in its traditional shape, idealized, turned into an Arcadian myth." Life in this household "proceeds according to a centuries-old script with unchangeable characters, the stuff of a Sarmatian comedy: a faithful servant, a former insurrectionist gone mad, a prodigal son, an endlessly worried mother, a father who reigns over all of them." Dąbrowska's *Noce i dnie* [Nights and days, 1931–34] accordingly features a character named Klemens Klicki, cousin of the protagonist Bogumił Niechcic, who has been mad since 1863 and believes the insurrection has not yet ended; at night, he frequently hides in the forest. Dąbrowska describes the symptoms of his postinsurrectionist psychosis with clinical precision. Klemens's death in the paroxysms of his final escape attempt plays a prominent role in the opening volume of her novel, setting the stage for the dramas of Polish life that its protagonists will continue to play out.

I have considered three major nineteenth-century novelists—Prus, Orzeszkowa, Dąbrowska—through the lens of Rejtan. From this standpoint, the patriot-as-madman looms larger than, say, the old, faithful servant or another standard comedic type. The patriot-madman as a character exceeds received comedic schemata, revealing the dramas of actual life. The lightning-rod quality of this figure is evident in the intensity with which many writers respond to these patriotic illusions. Commenting on the Romantic generation that came immediately before them, Józef Szujski and Father Franciszek Krupiński echo what the Romantics themselves said in their darkest moments: In elevating madness, they fell headlong into abject failure. Latter-day writers found it easy to dwell on the prior generation's lack of realism and plain common sense, its lack of a firm sense of reality, its trancelike intoxications, its pathological tendencies toward suicide.

The failure of the insurrection of 1863 makes it possible for the language and criteria of patriotism to gradually change. Writing in 1867, Szujski exudes the fervor of an exorcist: "Madness—to think that we just need to *want* to chase away our enemies, to undertake one or two small conspiracies, and we will be free and sovereign again. May this madness leave our soil forever. It brings nothing but endless miseries and failures." Father Krupiński similarly condemns Romanticism's "paroxysms of insanity," its "hallucinated specters," its "raptures that brought the senses near their breaking point," as well as these phenomena's social effects. What kind of person, Krupiński asks, embodies the Romantic ideal? "An obsessive fanatic, a dreamer, half hero and half madman." This ideal amounts to a "caricature of a human being," Father Krupiński proclaims without mincing words. The false hero's belief that he can solve problems through feeling, which reason could not crack, makes him particularly noxious; he terrorizes society with his actions.

And yet, a generation later, General Józef Piłsudski's legionaries will sing "My pierwsza brygada" [We, the first brigade], an anthem that combines Romanticism with madness:

> We have thrown ourselves into the burning pyre,
> The pyre, the pyre. . . .
> They called us mad, refusing to believe
> That what we fought for could be won by force of will!

In *Droga do Ostrej Bramy* [The way to Ostra Brama, 1982], one of the most beautiful books written in Polish in the twentieth century, Jan Erdman returns to these metaphors. Here, he is writing about Maciej Kalenkiewicz, an eminent Polish army colonel. The last commandant of the Home Army anti-Nazi guerilla unit in Nowogródek, Kalenikewicz died on August 21, 1944, compelled by honor to confront an enemy force that outnumbered his own by ten times. Erdman comments, "I was proud to have personally known Rejtan." He adds that Kalenkiewicz's body was buried in a historic forest cemetery on the outskirts of the town of Surkonty, alongside Polish patriots killed during the 1863 insurrection.

Perhaps, as many of us ardently hope, we have now finally managed to exorcise Romanticism from Polish culture. But have we exorcised madness along with it? I don't think so. [. . .]

The understanding of the phantasms that haunt the Polish literary imagination—Rejtan the suicide, Konrad Wallenrod the traitor, various revenge-seeking vampires—as inherently evil stems from Christian ethics, which had been used to rationalize passive acquiescence to Poland's loss of independence. In the guise of religion, philosophy, and ideology, such judgments were brought forth to tame the impulses of the overwrought patriotic imagination, to stop it from crossing over into the taboos of madness and death. Thus repressed, this forbidden imaginative sphere found its expression in art, where even the most controversial desires and doubts, even the most unattainable longings, are given a hearing. Romantic writers and artists devoted themselves to depicting the intense psychic turmoil experienced by their generation. They gave free rein to this turmoil in order to understand it, coconstruct it, tear it apart, and occasionally to bring it relief. Romantic poetry became a theater in which the buried soul of the Polish people took center stage.

Figure 8. Jacek Malczewski, *Melancholia* (1894). In real life, the painting is a huge canvas, approximately 55 × 94 in. It overwhelms the viewer not only with its mass of bodily movement, but also with its sheer size. Image courtesy of the National Museum in Poznań, Poland.

Between 1890 and 1894, Jacek Malczewski slowly produced a painting titled *Melancholia,* a symbolic representation of Poland over the course of the nineteenth century. It depicts a tangled crowd of figures of all ages, from childhood through adulthood into senility, suspended between the floor and ceiling of a large room. Malczewski depicts these figures as effortfully trying to make their way toward a sunlit, open window. Caught mid-gesture, the figures fixate on distant points invisible to us while listening to some inaudible music. Beyond the window stands a woman clad in black. Her back is turned toward them. Perhaps she represents melancholy, or death, or Poland—the three ideas often blur together in Malczewski's paintings. The procession of Polish generations stops just beyond the line of the sun and freedom. They remain trapped in darkness. The tragic irony of their nation's fate marks these figures' faces with sadness, or with morose determination, or with a desperate hesitation, insanity, a longing for death. These specters' paradoxical combination of paralysis and dancelike movement makes their destiny seem inevitable.

Let me end with an aphorism about Poland.

Were she not so abject, people wouldn't fall so madly in love with her.

What am I getting at? That Polish people have a particular proclivity toward misery, that they like to dwell in it, that—suicidal or mad—they want to die for their country but will not live for it?

No. I am trying to say that Polish people are very human in a particularly non-Darwinian way. They belong to a branch of humanity that seems to have fallen out of the confines of evolutionary logic. . . . Polish people refuse to acknowledge that only the fittest can survive and are worthy of praise. They reject the truisms that might makes right, and politics has nothing to do with morality. What else would drive the maddening eternal return of Polish struggles for independence throughout the nineteenth century? Despite all of Poland's partitions, the insurrectionists insist on an insane proposition: Poland fell prey to immoral political machinations and has a moral right to sovereignty. . . . This belief flows from a corner of our shared human sensibility that loves the abject, the weak, the oppressed, and the wounded. Polish people understand that if they stand with the defeated against the sane and the reasonable, they also stand with the irretrievably traumatized who have been driven insane. That is a heavy price to pay for "loving one's country."

Notes

1. Rudolf Otto, *The Idea of the Holy,* trans. John W. Harvey (New York: Oxford University Press, 1958), 6.
2. Otto, *Idea of the Holy,* 12ff.
3. Adam Mickiewicz, *Pan Tadeusz,* trans. Bill Johnston (New York: Archipelago Books, 2018), 3–4.

CHAPTER 5

Socialism as a Prometheism

We are reaching the end of Prometheism as a political formation: In recent times, this view has gained considerable traction. We are told that Prometheism has not just fallen into crisis; it has come to an end. *Utopia u władzy* [Utopia in power] is how Michał Heller and Aleksander Niekricz aptly named their history of the USSR. The Russian Revolution had been inspired by a cult of humankind, progress, science, and technology. The regime to which it gave rise sent Prometheus to the gulag, yet it continued to deploy Promethean discourse. One Prometheus was placed in a concentration camp with another one, a commissar, as his torturer. From Arthur Koestler to Leszek Kołakowski, writers have gradually unveiled this paradox. The figure has consequently come under suspicion. When Andrei Sakharov enjoined his readers to abandon the doctrinal logic that eventually transformed Prometheism into Stalinism, he simply declared that Prometheus needed to be stopped. The heaviest intellectual blow was dealt this political formation by a philosopher who had once been its ardent follower: Leszek Kołakowski. I will return to his *Main Currents of Marxism* (1976) later in this essay.

Romanticism as a historical movement definitively shaped contemporary Polish culture. Since Adam Mickiewicz, through Stefan Żeromski, and into the present, its magic has not waned, and its ideals persist among us. Individual freedom, national independence, revolt against the ugliness of reality, the pursuit of human happiness—these are the beacons Polish culture continues to follow. These Romantic ideals predominated even among Polish socialists and communists: Their debates over this nineteenth-century movement amounted to mere quibbles, such as whether the poet Juliusz Słowacki was more or less of a "democrat" than Mickiewicz. Even now, or at least until recently, Romanticism has grounded all major Polish social movements: The "messianism of the people" or the "messianism of the masses" is how scholars used to describe the public protests that preceded the 1863 Polish insurrection.

Adam Mickiewicz best conveys the potentials and contradictions of Polish Romantic Prometheism. The poet dreamed of writing a play about a Prometheus who was a "Christian" as well. This dream inspired part III of his lyrical play *Dziady* [Forefathers' eve, 1832], which features a conciliatory, Aeschylean version of the Promethean myth. Mickiewicz's version of the titan—unlike, say, that of Percy Shelley—does not hold onto an irreconcilable antagonism against tyrants. But as an artist and thus an ideal human, he carries in him a spark of the divine creative principle. This godlike creativity constitutes one of the most important themes of modern Promethean mythmaking. At the end of the prologue to part III of *Dziady,* which takes place in a prison cell in Lithuania, the prisoner writes down prophecies about death, birth, and what he calls the Great Transformation. An allegorical character, the Spirit, then praises the human being as a Promethean titan:

> Ah, mortal! If thou only knew thy power!
> When but a thought, like a spark in the mist
> Shines in thy mind unseen, great storm clouds lour
> To pour forth gentle rain or savage tempest.
> If but thou knew, that as each thought alights
> There gather round in silence, and stand by
> Like storm-hounds, angels both sooty and bright:
> —Wilt dash to hell, or flash out in the sky?—
> Yet thou, like a steep cloud, fliest on aloof,
> Knowing not where thou art borne, nor what thou do.
> Ah, mortals! Each of you might, imprisoned, alone,
> By thought and faith overturn the stoutest stone![1]

The power of the human spirit is not just limitless, but also unvanquishable. *The spirit can overcome any and all material resistance:* This principle lies at the heart of Polish Romantic Prometheism.

This Romantic image bears some relation to the Prometheus of ancient Greek myth. The titan features in all ancient narratives as humanity's special protector, perhaps even our creator. Humans owe many of their skills, including technological ones, to his generosity; he also teaches them the foundations of social life. Prometheus steals fire from the gods and gives it to mortals. According to some versions of the myth, he also sculpts humans themselves out of clay. In Hesiod, he is a "criminal" who frequently breaks divine laws to defend human beings—and who therefore falls victim to Zeus, the offended tyrant. Chained to the Caucasus, an eagle (or perhaps a vulture) tears at his liver daily. Each night, the liver is miraculously restored for further punishment. [. . .]

What is Prometheus's crime? He takes humans' side against the gods and lifts the limits that the power-hoarding immortals imposed on our mortal condition. In both Hesiod and Aeschylus, the struggle between the gods and the obstinate titan ends in reconciliation. However, the second and third parts of Aeschylus's trilogy in which this reconciliation is represented have been lost. As a result, the European imagination has lingered over the figure Prometheus strikes in the first of these three plays, *Prometheus Bound*. Adamant in his suffering, he challenges the gods amid the pain through which they put him.

In an ode titled "Prometheus" (1774), Goethe creates one of the most significant modern versions of the Promethean myth. The ode synthesizes the many ways this myth was previously reworked in the early modern period; through these reworkings, Goethe tailors the titan's image to his own needs. The young poet [. . .] refuses to reiterate classical versions of this myth; he must modernize it. Goethe's Prometheus creates in revolt against beings higher than himself. He refuses to worship Zeus and asks him with disapproval and mockery:

> I ought to honor you? What for?
> When the heavily laden suffer,
> Do you ever relieve them?
> When the frightened shed tears,
> Do you bring them calm?[2]

The source of the titan's power and of his capacity for transcendence is his *Heilig glühend Herz:* his holy, burning heart, a heart burning with holiness. It stems from his capacity to love and feel for others, neither of which the Olympic gods possess.

Goethe wrote other Promethean poems in this period [. . .], about figures such as Tantalus, Ixion, Sisyphus. Like Prometheus, these figures embody an awareness of suffering and injustice as the foundations of the human condition. As Simone Weil would later put it, "Prometheus suffers because he has loved men too well."[3]

In *From My Life: Poetry and Truth* (1811–33), Goethe recalls what preoccupied him as he was writing his ode to Prometheus. At the time, he was concerned with existential questions: the original sin and its supposed consequences. He was also being accused (as Rousseau was before him) of espousing Pelagianism, a Christian heresy that denies the reality of the original sin. Great consequences stem from this view, which I will briefly describe below.

Prometheus represented, for Goethe, an archetypal human being. Humans, titans, and gods are all rungs on a ladder of being whose every member is wholly divine and partakes of the four heavenly attributes: power, eternity, wisdom, and love. The gods possess one version of these attributes, but so does Prometheus, and his divinity is equal to theirs. Humans alone, among created beings, also partake of them. They are therefore capable of rejecting established authorities and tyrannies if these external powers threaten the morality and sovereignty of the human spirit. By this spirit's lights, infinite progress must be possible, and the effort of creation holds the highest moral value. Karoly Kerenyi is right to point out that Goethe's Prometheus is neither a god nor a titan nor a human being, but an immortal prototype *(Urbild)* of the human as an ancient rebel who accepted his fate: the first inhabitant of earth, an antigod who usurped mastery over it. This Gnostic, rather than Greek, Prometheus belongs to modern spiritual history; he prefigures the ways humanity is conceived by both Nietzsche and the existentialists. [. . .]

The Promethean ethos finds its ground in a conviction that human beings need to be their own creators and saviors. If no one held such beliefs, how could the French Revolution and later democratic and socialist ideations ever have emerged? A faith in humankind's capacity for progress, for redemption without recourse to authorities or outside norms; a refusal to use religion to sanction social injustice; a humanistic cult of the human being as the ultimate value—those are the basic forms these Promethean ideas take.

Without Prometheism of this kind, the Declaration of the Rights of Man and Citizen would not have been written. Born of a revolution that descended into terror, it barely escaped the guillotine. But it is wrong to speak only about the guillotine and not about the Declaration as fruits of the revolution, to derive human rights discourse not from the revolution itself but from mysterious external forces. François Furet insists that we must not describe the French Revolution as a totalitarian movement, fashionable as this critique may have become.[4] [. . .] Instead, we must continue to remind ourselves of its paradoxical, Janus-like quality. We must work against prevailing, ever more popular stereotypes in which a direct line of descent leads from the Prometheism of the French Revolution to twentieth-century crimes against humanity.

The Romantics constructed an image of Prometheus as an eternal rebel against tyrants. Byron worshiped him as a rebel whose "Godlike crime was to be kind."[5] Shelley openly broke with Aeschylus's depictions of him: "I was averse," he says in the preface to *Prometheus Unbound* (1820), "from a catastrophe so feeble as that of reconciling the Champion with the Oppressor of mankind." The titan also looms large in Romantic socialist utopias; in Edgar Quinet's vision of humanity's march toward freedom and happiness, he emblematizes our capacity for progress. "Humanity is its own Prometheus" is how the nineteenth-century historian Jules Michelet later famously put it; Michelet also names him as humanity's first democrat. Literary critics describe the protagonists of Victor Hugo's *Les Misérables* (1862) and *Toilers of the Sea* (1866) as Promethean figures. Nineteenth-century writers frequently portrayed Christ himself as Promethean, alluding to an old tradition of seeing the titan as a prefiguration of his self-sacrifice for the sake of humankind. Raymond Trousson underlines that Prometheus appealed to the Romantics because his rebellion was not self-enclosed and egocentric; the titan was a "philanthrope" who put his heart and knowledge into building a new world. Woven from these new strands, the modern Promethean theme became absorbed by European socialism as its secularized religious underpinning. It is no wonder that the titan has occasionally been described as a "socialist Christ."

Karl Marx partakes of this ideal as well. He knew Goethe's "Prometheus" by heart, as one of his most beloved poems. He describes the titan as "the most eminent saint and martyr in the philosophical calendar." To define his own philosophy, he cites Prometheus's words from Aeschylus's tragedy: "In a word, I hate all the gods." Marx was influenced by the versions of this myth forged by Goethe, Feuerbach, and other Romantics. In his own twist on these retellings, he emphasized self-knowledge and self-awareness as the most important attributes of the Promethean human-being-as-creator, as "man" who is "man's god."

Marx's understanding of Prometheism came under harsh—dare I say libelous—critical interpretation from Eric Voegelin, in an article he wrote in 1959. Describing Marx (alongside Hegel and Nietzsche) as a speculative Gnostic, Voegelin excoriates as intellectually dishonest his attempts to define humans as self-creating beings. Like the Gnostics, he claims, Marx wants to erase material reality as it exists; In its place, he wants to construct an alternative "system" of reality. Prometheus's revolt against the gods serves as his model. Since ancient Roman Gnosticism, Prometheus, Cain, and Eve have symbolized the liberation of humanity from the tyrannical reign of the gods. For Voegelin, the dethronement of the gods, Prometheus's victory, and other revolutionary symbolic inversions express Gnostic aims and ideals. This underpinning of spiritual revolt against the cosmos and the gods was not, he argues, present in the Hellenic version of the Promethean myth. Even for Aeschylus—Voegelin claims—hatred toward the gods amounts to madness.[6]

Marx refuses to recognize Prometheus's revolt as madness, Voegelin argues, and thus converts the intended meanings of Aeschylus's play into their opposites. Therein lies his supposed intellectual dishonesty, and from the latter stem the falsehoods of nationalist socialism. But Voegelin forgets to add that, if Marx's Prometheism was intellectually dishonest, it was not any more dishonest than the work of Goethe and the Romantics—and, indeed, that such acts of reinterpretation are common and natural in the cultural life of myths.

I do not discuss Voegelin's essay so systematically merely to critique its method or errors of factual omission. It helps me articulate what I think Prometheism means to Marx and socialism in general. In this spirit, consider also Kołakowski's understanding of Marx's Prometheism, which differs from Voegelin's. Kołakowski sees Marxian thought as dominated by three motifs: Romanticism, Faustian Prometheism, and rationalism, with an emphasis on the first one. Let us consider how he reaches this conclusion.

Like the Romantics, Kołakowski argues, Marx dreamed of "a return to perfect harmony," a "state in which no middle term intervened between the individual and the community, or the individual and himself." This dream constituted "an attack, expressed or implied, on liberalism and its theoretical basis in the social contract," especially on the assumption that "men's conduct is necessarily governed by selfish motives and that their conflicting interests can only be reconciled by a rational system of laws."[7] Marx faced a choice between two basic convictions: Either human beings are intrinsically hostile toward each other, or they are intrinsically sociable. Marx believed that men turn against each other only because of capitalism. His "Faustian–Promethean" tendencies, as Kołakowski calls them, manifest in a "faith in man's unlimited powers as self-creator," and in a notion of "history as man's self-realization through labor." Human beings are defined by their social existence; their creativity within it knows no bounds. "Salvation, for Marx, is man's salvation of himself; not the work of God or Nature, but that of a collective Prometheus who, in principle, is capable of achieving absolute command over the world he lives in."[8]

Kołakowski sees Marxism as embodying a tendency that periodically resurges within human history: the utopian struggle back to some original unity, to "paradise on earth." Categorically opposed to utopianism, Kołakowski turns against these Marxian dreams; he is especially critical of Marx's faith that the future can be brought into the present, that he and his contemporaries possess the intellectual tools for imagining and constructing a perfect society, free from conflicts and errors. Kołakowski also disputes Marx's conviction that it is possible to know human beings' true nature, and that this "nature" has an essence irreducible to empirical contingencies. These utopian convictions, he implies, were bound to bring only one outcome. "Marx took over the Romantic ideal of social unity, and Communism realized it in the only way feasible in an industrial society, namely, by a despotic system of government."[9]

Kołakowski outlines a trajectory from the deification of humanity to the cult of personality, from Prometheism to Stalinism. He describes *The Main Currents of Marxism* as "not only an historical account but an attempt to analyze the strange fate of an idea that began in Promethean humanism and culminated in the monstrous tyranny of Stalin." Granted, despotic socialism does not embody Marx's *intentions*. Nevertheless, Kołakowski insists, we must ask "how far it represents the logical outcome of his doctrine." On the path toward regaining perfect social unity, Marx's logic compels one to dismantle, one after another, all institutions of social mediation. "And thus Prometheus awakens from his dream of power, as ignominiously as Gregor Samsa in Kafka's *Metamorphosis*."[10] So concludes one of the book's most damning sentences.

Today, we are abandoning Prometheus for a variety of alternative ideals. Gilbert Durant claims that the myth is dying because of a resurgence in Dionysian thinking; Herbert Marcuse provides an interesting version of this argument in *Eros and Civilization.* Marcuse takes Prometheus as a symbol of humanity's capacity to transform nature through labor. He juxtaposes Prometheus, the producer, against Eros, the force of desire—and desire is, for him, the only real creative force. Humans must seek liberation by turning away from the Promethean myth and following Orpheus and Narcissus into erotic and aesthetic activity. Marcuse holds a Dionysian, but not a tragic, vision of the human condition.

Camus opens another non-Promethean alternative, with Sisyphus as his emblematic hero. Sisyphus pushes a rock up the mountain every day, and every day he watches the rock roll back downhill. He walks down and resumes his labor from the beginning. But "at each of those moments when he leaves the heights and gradually sinks toward the lairs of the gods, he is superior to his fate. He is stronger than his rock." Camus idealizes Sisyphus's futile heroism and hard-won clarity of mind. This "desperate wisdom," as Gustaw Herling-Grudziński calls it, rejects religious consolation.

But Kołakowski also opposes the reframing of our human condition "in terms of the static myth of Sisyphus," in the spirit of Camus's pessimism. What better alternative can he offer? "The biblical legend of Nebuchadnezzar, who was degraded to the condition of a beast when he tried to exalt himself to the dignity of God."[11] It's hard to call this image consolatory; it's more of a warning. Indeed, with its calls to penance for our excessively bold dreams and actions, it sounds very much like a church homily. Partly tongue-in-cheek, it gives Kołakowski, the intellectual, a way of expiating himself for not being more helpful.

The paths of the intelligentsia and the people have diverged. No longer does the ethos of Promethean socialism conjoin the "elites" with the "masses." Today, the former tend to share Sisyphus's tragic vision of the human condition; the latter, meanwhile, seek optimism in the Catholic Church and versions of national messianism.

It all comes down to how we understand human nature. Did we commit original sin? Are we always at war with one another? Either of these original conditions would compel us to curb our aspirations to self-making, self-saving, and self-liberation as harmful forms of willfulness. Still, in practice, neither of these concepts of humanity accords sufficient weight to the condition of the oppressed, the suffering, the humiliated, and the persecuted (however much John Paul II might be trying to change this). Empathic attention to the marginalized has always been the domain of Promethean socialism, since it assumes that humans are not intrinsically evil.

Please believe me: I am not trying to use Rousseau to pull us back into totalitarianism. However, though the appeal of Prometheus might be waning, the problem of human suffering is not.

Late in life, Czesław Miłosz unexpectedly turned toward affirming the intrinsic goodness of humankind. One of the epigraphs to his *Nieobjęta ziemia* [Unattainable earth, 1982], is a fragment of Goethe's "On the Divine" (1789), one of the Promethean poems we have been discussing. I will adopt this epigraph as my own essay's ending.

Let man be noble,
Helpful and good;
Because only this
Sets him apart
From all the beings
We know.

Hail to the higher beings
Whom we do not know
But believe in.
May men come to resemble them.
May we learn faith
From their example.[12]

Notes

1. Adam Mickiewicz, *Dziady: Forefathers' Eve,* trans. Charles S. Kraszewski (London: Glagoslav Publications, 2016), 180.
2. [My translation. For an alternative one, see Johann Wolfgang von Goethe, *Selected Poems,* ed. Christopher Middleton (Princeton, N.J.: Princeton University Press, 1994), 29.—Trans.]
3. Simone Weil, *Intimations of Christianity among the Ancient Greeks* (Boston: Beacon Press, 1958), 67.
4. See François Furet, *Interpreting the French Revolution,* trans. Elborg Forster (Cambridge: Cambridge University Press, 1977).
5. Lord Byron, "Prometheus," *Poetry Foundation,* originally published in 1816, https://www.poetryfoundation.org/poems/43843/prometheus-56d222b61d799.
6. Eric Voegelin, *Science, Politics, and Gnosticism* (Chicago: Henry Regnery, 1968), 36ff.

7. Leszek Kołakowski, *Main Currents of Marxism: The Founders, the Golden Age, the Breakdown,* trans. Paul Stephen Falla (New York: Norton, 2005), 335.
8. Kołakowski, *Main Currents of Marxism,* 339.
9. Kołakowski, *Main Currents of Marxism,* 1209.
10. Kołakowski, 8, 343, 344.
11. Leszek Kołakowski, "Can the Devil Be Saved?," *Encounter,* July 1974, 12.
12. [My translation. For an alternative one, see Goethe, *Selected Poems,* 79. —Trans.]

PART III
Aesthetics, History, and Critical Method

CHAPTER 6

The Project of Phantasmatic Critique

The First Enfranchisement of the Imagination

I recently consulted several thick French dictionaries to study the etymology of a word spelled *phantasme* or, alternately, *fantasme*. As it turns out, the word initially carried medical connotations. It referred to the disruption of cognitive faculties, as when a patient sees objects that are not there. But then, this "pathologizing" tendency came under critique. The dictionaries designate these medical uses of *phantasme* as "archaic" or "old-fashioned."

This semantic shift reflects a broader cultural process. The phantasm has ceased to be perceived as the symptom of an illness. On the contrary, scholars underline that every normal, healthy person develops fantasies and phantasms (as I go on to discuss, the two are not always the same thing). Phantasms used to be seen as false and illusory; now, that is no longer the case. These changes dovetail with some shifts in social attitudes toward the imagination. Because of these changes, the term *phantasm* now often refers to *both* visual daydreams *and* pathological hallucinations. In dictionaries, the editors refuse to distinguish between these two meanings.

Romanticism's new theories of the imagination played a crucial role in the demedicalizing and popularizing of the word *phantasm*. One of these theories derived from early modern theosophy, particularly from the writings of Paracelsus, who treats the imagination as a creative, cosmic, spiritual force. Like that Swiss philosopher and alchemist, the Romantics understood the imagination as a manifestation of the divine. They crucially distinguished between (cosmic) "imagination" (the French *imaginaire*) and (noncosmic) "fancy" (the French *imaginal*). The former, *mundus imaginalis,* designates a supernatural realm in which the correspondences between the human and the cosmic become discernible.

Amid these questions of nomenclature, let us not lose sight of the general point: The Romantics celebrated dreams, phantasms, and fantasies to an extent generally unprecedented in the modern world (though not *entirely* without precedent [. . .]). I like to describe the cultural shift they effected as the First Enfranchisement of the Imagination. Let me name a few qualities and contexts of this revolution.

First: Romantics criticized Enlightenment thinkers' understanding of ancient tradition as dogmatic and imaginatively constraining. The latter saw myth as a "fabrication." The former were convinced that myths contained great truths as long as one knew how to decipher them. Romanticism waged war against normative, supposedly universal, formal conventions. It looked to cultures Western Europe had previously dismissed or otherwise disregarded—folk culture, East Asian culture, Scandinavian culture, Slavic culture—drawing attention to the symbolic languages these cultures developed. One might say, paraphrasing Durand, that the Romantics thus also took issue with the iconoclastic attitudes of their contemporary positivists, whose writing aimed to enact the "depreciation of symbols." [. . .]

Second: Romantics stood up for a sphere of reality that had previously not been taken seriously, the inner life. Romantics believed that our inward experience gives us insights into the cosmos itself through noncausal, unpredictable bonds of sympathy and correspondence with the world beyond us. In a letter to Alphonse Toussenel dated January 21, 1856, Charles Baudelaire thus proclaims that "the imagination is the most scientific of the faculties because it is the only one to understand the universal analogy, or that which a mystical religion calls *correspondence*." But the Romantics cared for more than the imagination's cosmic resonances and dimensions. They also fostered the imaginative capacities of the individual, particularly the artist, for their own sake. Reconceived and revalorized, inner life became the domain of free imaginative play. The avant-gardes of the twentieth century described themselves as setting words free. Romanticism could have called itself the Movement for the Emancipation of the Phantasm.

Thus, the Romantics discovered what came to be called the "subconscious" sphere of human experience. They loosened the forces of repression and censure that had previously held this sphere of experience in check. The discovery of these inward realms provoked an existential crisis whose intensity the Romantics often described as madness. They did not, however, see this madness as pathological. Far from it, such crises opened alternative, nonrational means of addressing existential dilemmas. E. T. A. Hoffman represented these discoveries incited by the "subconscious being" inside us through his characters' mysterious, haunting doubles. These Romantic protodiscourses of the unconscious eventually proved useful to Freud as he sought names for its structures and forms. *Conscious* phantasms and daydreams, particularly those of young people, preoccupied the Romantics and their audiences too. (Take the very successful example of Lord Byron.) A new kind of art came into being in this period, centered around dreams, phantasms, visions, and daydreams. This art was frequently accused of being "diseased." Freud belatedly inverted this criticism, insisting that what the Romantics represented was completely normal.

Third: As the Romantics reclassified reality, giving it a new order and nomenclature, they also transposed into art a discourse of self-understanding that had previously been the province of mysticism and religion. They began to speak of "inwardness" and the "soul," and to engage in the nonpsychological probing of the phenomenology of human existence. Paracelsus (and Jung following him) used the term *imaginatio* to describe the inward human being's mystical powers. Many Romantics believed in these mystical powers as well.

An art that focuses on inwardness and the difficulty of conveying inner experience must necessarily assume that there exists more than one reality; indeed, it must suspect that other realities might be higher than the one we ordinarily inhabit. Such an art will therefore also find great interest in altered states of consciousness. Romantics undertook a concerted imaginative effort to fracture our seemingly singular reality and probe its multiplicities. Among others, they sought to enter and redescribe the world of the dead, previously known to European literature only through a few limited, long-standing conventions. Liminal states interested them most of all, especially states of being between life and death: whence the existential seriousness with which they represent in their writings all kinds of otherwise distasteful-seeming, excessively prolix ghosts and revenants. Each new, alternative sphere of being the Romantics uncovered turned out to hold phantoms and phantasms of its own. The land of the dead had a particularly rich fauna: ghouls, vampires, werewolves, all sorts of creatures and realms transposed from folk culture. In these experiments, literary characters' ontological status is often blurry. Critics still debate, for example, whether Gustaw, the main hero of part IV of Adam Mickiewicz's

Romantic drama *Dziady* [Forefathers' eve, 1832], speaks to us as a living person or as a ghost.

Fourth: As the Romantics' liberated inner phantasms blended with fantastical beings they found in folklore, they developed an unprecedented openness toward low culture. By the end of the nineteenth century, the amalgamation of Romanticism with folk culture gave rise to what we call popular culture. Having cocreated the latter, the Romantics went on to draw on it as it sharpened and intensified their shared favorite themes. Naturally, in the process, popular culture also domesticated and tempered many Romantic phantoms, which otherwise would not have easily fit its tastes. Its two central genres, horror and melodrama, both brim with sentimental and sadistic Romantic clichés, which entwine with especial force in the archetypal novelistic and cinematic narrative of the cruelly oppressed beautiful woman whom a hero eventually saves. These fantasies of persecution and rescue, without which mainstream narrative fiction could not sustain itself, come from Romanticism.

Let me pause to consider the relationship between the *phantasm* and *phantasmagoria*. Max Milner, the author of a book on the subject (*La fantasmagorie*, 1982), shows how the latter term, which initially designated an apparatus for optical illusions, became the name of a literary genre. The apparatus and the literary genre shared the same creative principle: They created and inspired phantasms. Conceptually speaking, Milner argues, one might describe the phantasmatic as the work of the unconscious and the phantasmagoric as a consciously applied aesthetic framework. The phantasmagoric gives voice to the phantasm by transforming it into an object of awe, fascination, and aesthetic pleasure. Twentieth-century cinema, which originates in the phantasmagoric magic lantern, maintains a close relation to both.

Fifth: The Romantics invented and elevated the Romantic hero. This hero concentrates within himself the whole charge of their movement's originality and innovation. Among his (*sic!*) distinctive traits are Prometheism and courage in combatting evil. A sense of doom, a demonically marred beauty, radiate from this type of character as well. (One of the Romantic hero's grandchildren, the novel character named Fantômas, carries the double phantasmatic–phantastic principle in his name.) Most readers are amazed by Romantic characters' boldness, their openness to risk, their alertness, the inevitability with which they succeed, even if initially met with failure, and the adequate rewards they always receive for their efforts. Scholars have considered these traits from many different angles; here, what concerns me is this character's aptitude—which cannot be understated—for becoming the object of fantasizing or phantasmatic identification. Romantic heroes persist in popular culture as the inspiration of some of its favorite melodramatic, picaresque, erotic, and magical plot twists. . . .

Sixth: The phantasm originates in the daydream. Put formally, the phantasm is a derivative of the daydream and the latter's signature dualisms and sharp contrasts (which Romanticism also embraces). The Romantic daydream juxtaposes two modes of being and two realities, attaching distinct orders of value to them. The "here and now" is always inferior to that which "lies beyond" it. The Romantic hero is always "somewhere else," never mentally present where he is present physically. This mode of being inevitably creates an identity crisis, one of Romantic literature's favorite subjects. The hero endlessly pursues new disguises, new masks, new costumes; this tendency finds reflection in the incredible, fastidiously arranged bluster of Romantic-era fashion. The histrionic nature of Romantic theater also stems from this dreamy longing to be "somewhere else." Phantasms arise from expressions of such attitudes and feed on them, inspiring a wide range of (real-life and fictional) costumes and disguises that the Romantics don. In what follows, I will reflect on the phantasm as a mask and costume at greater length.

Freud and the Scene of Phantasms

Freud was well-versed in Romanticism; he came of age in a society whose art and consciousness Romanticism had created. However, that's not the whole story: He also witnessed vehement critiques of the Romantics as creators of emotionally unhinged fantasies whose detachment from reality made them exceptionally pernicious. As a result, Freud's inspirations are always twofold: the Enlightenment and positivism on the one hand, Romanticism on the other. Eventually, he manages to reconcile these two poles. Enlightenment thinkers' interest in the imagination was often constrained by their belief that the emotional nature of fantasies made them inferior to cold, objective reason. The Romantics stirred emotions and imagination to their limits; this allowed them to probe aspects of our inner worlds that had previously been passed over in silence. Freud wanted to discover the laws of inner reality. However, he understood that science alone could not convey what Serge Doubrovsky came to call, decades later, the singularity of subjective existence.

Freud wanted his thinking to be accurate; scientific-like precision would allow him to uncover what is truly real. When he encountered the phantasm, early on in his study of hysteria, this phenomenon posed a difficult problem for him. How can one distinguish between "true" and "false," "real" and "imagined" phantasms—and adjust one's treatment of them on this basis?

Jean Laplanche and Jean-Bertrand Pontalis published a remarkable study of Freud's theory of the phantasm in 1964 in *Les Temps modernes.* Reissuing it as a book twenty-one years later, the authors emphasize their faithfulness to Freud and their refusal to commit to Lacan's alternative views of psychoanalysis. Laplanche and Pontalis show that Freud's concept of the phantasm carries some crucial ambivalences and hesitations. Freud could not decide whether the phantasm bears the seed of an actual event or is a completely fictional imaginary construct. He wondered whether there exists a finite number of phantasmatic schemata—"scenes" or "situations," as he called them—or whether the imagination has free rein in constructing them. Following the former hypothesis, Freud coined the term *prephantasm* to designate a putative primary system of phantasms that are inherited phylogenetically. Laplanche and Pontalis draw attention to the opposition that emerges in Freud's early thought between "structures" and the "imagination": between the defined, circumscribed repertoire of what Lévi-Strauss and Lacan will come to call the "symbolic order" and the imaginative creativity that exceeds such strictures.[1] Jean-Paul Valabrega, who also saw himself as continuing Freud's thinking, took this systematic, structuralist treatment of phantasms to a certain extreme. Convinced of their universality, he believed he could reconstruct a complete system of human phantasms, a "phantasmatics" *(la phantasmatique).* Valabrega argued that the phantasm is an "irreducible, structural element" of human consciousness with strong ties to myth.[2]

Freud himself formulated several accounts of the phantasm across his writings. He devoted particular attention to it between 1906 and 1909, in essays such as "Delusion and Dream in Jensen's *Gradiva*" (1907) and "The Creative Writer and Day-Dreaming" (1908). I will not follow the development of Freud's thought chronologically. Instead, I will lay out alongside each other the main types of phantasms Freud differentiates and the methodological problems their study opened for him. In "The Creative Writer and Day-Dreaming," Freud is clearly inspired by literature, particularly by the phantasies and ideas of the German Romantics. At times, it seems that the father of psychoanalysis could not have formulated his scientific insights without these Romantic inspirations. *Gradiva,* a novella by an imitator of Hoffmann named Wilhelm Jensen, and a novel by the Swiss writer Carl Spitteler called *Imago* had a particularly strong impact on his work. Freud devotes considerable attention to the latter in *The Interpretation of Dreams. Imago* is also the name he gives to the first psychoanalytic journal he founds in 1912. The hero of Spitteler's novel once saw a woman with whom he believes himself to have fallen in love. This woman ended up marrying someone else, had children, and appeared to be happy. Having decided that he loves her, and having been disappointed in this longing, he constructs this woman's ideal image. . . . The erasure of reality by the force of ideas: that is exactly how phantasms work.

Phantasm (*fantazm* in Polish, *phantasme* in French, *Phantasie* in German) refers not to our active "capacity to imagine" *(Einbildungskraft),* but to a preexisting imaginary world in which the neurotic as well as the poet often find refuge. (That is how Laplanche and Pontalis define it as well.) Jean Bergeret believes that, for Freud, each phantasm has a double origin, an inward and an outward one. "Psychic reality" is the realm where the two sources meet.[3] Freud used the word *Phantasie* to denote both unconscious phantasms and daydreams. Some of his translators tried to distinguish between them, using the words *fantasy* and *fantasie* in referring to conscious phantasms, and *phantasy* or *phantasmes* to unconscious ones. But these editorial innovations have generally not taken root, in great part because it is hard to sustain these distinctions in Freud's own writing.

The *Dictionnaire de la psychanalyse* [Dictionary of psychoanalysis] distinguishes between Freud's understanding of "phantasms" *(Phantasien)* and "prephantasms" *(Urphantasien).* The definition it gives suggests that the phantasm is an imaginary scenario in which a defined human subject is present. This scenario depicts a person's wish fulfillments, occasionally unconscious ones, in ways that might be deformed by her repressive mental defenses. Phantasms, thus understood, can take many shapes: They can be conscious fantasies (i.e., daydreams), unconscious phantasms, or prephantasms. The latter tend to follow the typical phantasm-generating scenarios observed in children and neurotics (parental intercourse, seduction, castration). Their form is not closely related to the patient's personal experiences. Freud claims that prephantasms' apparent universality stems from the fact that they are inherited via phylogenesis, but this hypothesis has remained unproven.[4] The *Dictionnaire général des sciences humaines* [General dictionary of the human sciences], published in 1975, also describes the question of whether phantasms are purely fictional constructs or they are constructed out of traces of a child's real experiences as unresolved.

As I mentioned above, Freud had great methodological difficulty determining to what realm of existence phantasms belong: Do they have some ties to reality, or are they purely imaginary? He needed new concepts and tools to reckon with them. At the end of *The Interpretation of Dreams* (1900), Freud posits—not without the influence of Romantic humanism—that "*psychic reality* is a special form of existence which must not be confounded with *material reality*."[5] In the twenty-third lecture of his *General Introduction to Psychoanalysis* (1915–17), titled "The Development of the Symptoms" and devoted to phantasms and phantasies, he returns to the difficulty of distinguishing between reality and fantasy in phantasmatic narratives and proposes that the blurring of this distinction is the defining quality of the phantasm. The only way the psychoanalyst can proceed when faced with phantasies is "to neglect for the time being the difference between the real and the imaginary. . . . This is obviously the only correct attitude toward these psychological products because they are, in a sense, real." Freud argues that phantasms are not completely illusory. He defines their reality as "*psychological* reality in contrast to *physical* reality."[6] (Carl Jung also stresses the etiological reality of phantasms: They are real enough to provoke serious somatic disturbances and deep psychic consequences in the patient.)

Freud follows this discussion of phantasms with one of his most momentous statements: "*In the realm of neuroses the psychological reality is the determining factor.*" In case we wanted to suggest that psychic reality only matters within the world of the neurotic, let us recall the earlier statement Freud makes in the same chapter: "You can readily say that we are all sick, or rather neurotic, since the conditions favorable to the development of symptoms are demonstrable also among normal persons."[7] . . . Today, we still speak, somewhat exaggeratedly, about the "fundamental illusions" held by most healthy individuals, among which one might include virtually all the convictions that make up our worldview. Psychologists stress the "normalcy" of phantasms in people who do not suffer from personality disorders.

Freud goes further to say that phantasies are a mental space human beings struggled to "reserve" for necessary moments of respite from reality: "In the activity of the imagination, man enjoys that freedom from external compulsion that he has long since renounced." Freud invokes Theodor Fontane to emphasize this point: "There is no getting along without auxiliary constructions." Let us recall that Freud also cites this statement by Fontane in *Civilization and Its Discontents* when he writes about the necessity of psychic intoxicants and illusions, without which we could not bear the misery of our lives. In the twenty-third lecture of the *General Introduction to Psychoanalysis,* he finds "the nature of imaginative happiness" to lie in "the restoration of the independence of pleasurable gratification from the acquiescence of reality."[8] We need to accept, Freud concludes, that "the twilight-realm of phantasy is upheld by the sanction of humanity and every hungry soul looks here for help and sympathy."[9] No human being exists who is not "hungry" in this fashion. Such is the phantasm's powerful, everyday compensatory function.

Freud and his commentators discuss "phantasms" in strikingly dramatic, literary, narrative terms. They describe a scenario played out in the imagination, usually tied to some longing or drive; they speak of "actors" and the "staging of desires," of the phantasm itself as a theatrical stage. These terms are derived from poetics, from theories of narrative and drama: Freud and his followers see phantasms as novelizations, scenes, dramatizations, episodes, fictions, novels. Pursuing these associations further, one might say that Freud reveals within each of us a constantly ongoing theatrical production—or, better still, an endless film, given that the latter art seems to feed on our phantasms more than any other. This inward "theater of the soul" invites comparison to the very different, sociological "theater of everyday life" described by Erving Goffman. I will not explore this parallel quite yet. Susan Isaacs articulates quite well the mode of being phantasms and their articulation take within psychoanalysis. They are not inherently verbal, though they can occasionally be verbalized. Primitive ones initially take shape as affects; only later do they acquire visual or theatrical representations.[10]

Phantasms exist on the border between medicine and literature. We should pause over the paradox of their status as a "literary" phenomenon. Their literary representations obviously conform to the rules of literature; more strikingly, the phantasms present in our inner lives often appear to have a literary structure as well—or, at the very least, they tend to be articulated in literary terms by those who experience or describe them.

It will not surprise us that Freud understands phantasms through the prism of literature if we recall his 1908 essay on "The Creative Writer and Day-Dreaming." Poetic creativity, Freud argues, can be seen as a kind of play, phantasm, or dream. Freud finds in children the kernels of what could be called literary activity. As she plays, the child creates her "own world" and "a new order" within it. Freud is right that "the opposite of play is not what is serious but what is real," that is, ordinary, everyday reality.[11] Play, as it takes place in this created alternate reality, is deeply serious. Its world is as real as the one that exists beyond it; the two cannot be assimilated to each other.

Continuing this fascinating line of thinking, Freud notes that adulthood does not free us from a burning, childish need for "another reality." "Whoever understands the human mind knows that hardly anything is harder for a man than to give up a pleasure which he has once experienced. Actually, we can never give anything up; we only exchange one thing for another."[12] Daydreaming preserves the child within the adult; it becomes a substitute for children's imaginative play. The fantasies conjured up in daydreams resemble nighttime dreams and seem to be cut from the same cloth. The expression day*dreaming* conveys this intuition.

"I believe that most people construct phantasies at times in their lives," Freud proposes in a provocative, culminating statement. However, in contrast to the relative ease with which children share their daydreams with others, it is very difficult to convince an adult to confess hers to another person. Why is that? "The adult," Freud argues, "is ashamed of his phantasies and hides them from other people. He cherishes his phantasies as his most intimate possessions, and as a rule he would rather confess his misdeeds than tell anyone his phantasies."[13] So great is the reach of our repressive mechanisms, which are strictly managed by a network of censorship and warning that is embodied, above all, in social conventions.

But things the ordinary person cannot own up to can become

fodder for artists. Literature could be seen as the product of phantasms' liberation, and as aiming to free up the phantasms of its readers. Communing with them in literature gives us aesthetic pleasure; we are thus permitted to indulge in them "without guilt or shame." Freud does not worry whether literary phantasms are somehow different and more unique than more commonplace, everyday ones. He does insist that literature is able to name phantasms because it gives them an aesthetic quality. The ordinary person's phantasies could easily be repulsive. By contrast, the writer's "essential *ars poetica* lies in the technique of overcoming the feeling of repulsion in us which is undoubtedly connected with the barriers that rise between each single ego and the others."[14] By tempering the phantasm's inherent selfishness, the literary work can serve a therapeutic function for its readers.

Imaginings, Delusions, Hallucinations

Naming the phantasm as a concept should be counted among Freud's great accomplishments. (Credit should also be given, in this regard, to Melanie Klein and Georg Groddeck, the latter, an analyst of the terrifyingly moralizing, multigenerationally phantasm-spawning *Struwwelpeter.*) After Freud, this concept came to be accepted as a generally useful tool for a humanistic understanding of individuals and their social interactions. The categories and terms Freud coins to describe it have long been liberated from orthodox Freudianism. But without Freud, this very useful term would never have entered our dictionaries; nor would it have been able to fulfill the functions it currently plays in sociology, pedagogy, psychology, and literary and film criticism. None of these fields can do without the notion of the phantasm and the critical toolbox it opens. Thus, critics speak—justifiably so—about erotic phantasms alongside social, political, and religious ones. [. . .]

Literature, especially the writings of authors like James Joyce and the surrealists, played an enormous role in proving phantasms' importance to the humanities. The surrealists, as is well-known, had a subversive relationship to psychoanalysis and were keen to unveil even their most scandalous thoughts, to shock and scandalize the public. Supposedly following Freud's insight that people tend to hide their private phantasms and can only enjoy them with aesthetic detachment, the surrealists depicted theirs with much noise and little distance. Articulating them became one of the main means by which the members of this movement produced their much-desired scandals.

But the surrealists also inspired other artworks that maintained an appropriate artistic distance from the phantasms they represented. Consider Michel Leiris's *Manhood* (1939), that summa of phantasmatic surrealism: an autobiography that consists of an aesthetically structured collection of phantasms. In his innovative book titled *On Autobiography,* Philippe Lejeune comments on Leiris's work to highlight one of the phantasm's most valuable qualities. He writes, of made-up biographies, "The substitution of an obviously made-up story, one unrelated to real life . . . is extremely rare, and the referential character attributed to narrative is thus easily called into question by a survey of literary history. But, disqualified as autobiography, the narrative will retain its full interest as phantasm at the level of its utterance, and the falsehood of the autobiographical pact, as behavior, will still reveal to us, at the level of enunciation, a subject that is, despite everything, intentionally autobiographical."[15] Things that are fraudulent or "made-up" in one order of reality have considerable value in another: They reveal the autobiographer's phantasmatic life.

In the last few decades, the practice of collecting and publishing descriptions of ordinary people's phantasms, especially erotic ones, has become quite popular. Nancy Friday's bestselling book series is one good example. Techniques of steering and satisfying phantasms have developed as well. *Playboy* magazine, founded in 1953, has honed them to tremendous success. Consider also Manuel Puig's wonderful novel *Kiss of the Spider Woman* (1976). Peppered with academic footnotes on various types of homosexuality, it depicts two prisoners who bond by retelling each other films they have seen. The author gives the phantasmatic dimension of his work an uncommon density: The narration consists of the detailed recounting of phantasmatically inflected plots. Puig's novel should be studied more closely from this perspective: It reveals the power cinematic phantasms wield in the spiritual life of our contemporaries. [. . .]

The Black Veil

At its best, the style of thinking the humanities foster revolves around the phantasmatic. To explain what I mean, let me pause for a while (as a counterexample) over the thinking of Ronald David Laing, one of the fathers of antipsychiatry and a polemical critic of psychoanalysis. A practitioner in both fields, Laing followed a phenomenological approach to psychiatry. He focused on the so-called schizophrenogenic family, mechanisms by which a family can incite madness in one of its members. In *Self and Others* (1961), particularly in chapters on "Phantasy and Experience" and "Phantasy and Communication," Laing polemically analyzes our titular concept and comes up with his own, original understanding of it. He underlines that unconscious phantasy is too rarely studied from an existential or a phenomenological point of view; he also insists that no holistic account of interpersonal relations can avoid discussing this phenomenon. The aim of phenomenology as a field is to get to the heart of phantasmatic experiences—and that is also Laing's own aim.

Self and Others reiterates versions of the same thesis: It is impossible to truly understand or reach another person. Families full of veils, shadows, and silences become, for Laing, models for interpersonal relations in general. Like a mummy, every person is wrapped in many layers of phantasies, imaginings, and projections that make it impossible to discern what is "real."[16] We are swathed in cocoons we cannot tear open or demystify. Without knowing it, we submit ourselves to our repressive upbringing as to a form of hypnosis; we wander among shadows, without recognizing them as such. The hypnotic quality of existence imposed on us by our families is only a small version of the larger social mystifications by which people are kept apart from each other. For Laing, the medium and manifestation of this separation is our pervasive theatricality: the artificial, deadened quality of our mutual expression. Writing about the "family nexus," he reconstructs this pattern mercilessly. [. . .]

Self and Others critiques psychoanalysis's deductive mode of reasoning. For Laing, its method makes phantasms cognitively inaccessible to the psychoanalyst: She cannot discern their true (i.e., deceptive) nature. Laing himself continues to unmask the pretenses and poses that emerge in our interactions with others; with considerable irony, he highlights the complicated games of displacement and substitution in which our own and other people's phantasies make us engage. These displacements and substitutions are inner as well as outer, private as well as public, shared with others or not shared with anyone at all, responsive to real and unreal situations. "It is ironical," he notes, "that often what I take to be most public reality turns out to be what others take to be my most private phantasy." Laing is fascinated by our "immersion in social phantasy systems." The contexts in which we place ourselves are doubly deceitful: first, because they are fictitious, and second, because we do not realize this. Laing focuses on the role phantasms play in intragroup communication, particularly within families: "The close-knit groups that occur in families and other groupings are bound together by the need to find pseudo-real experience that can be found only through the modality of phantasy. This means that the family is not experienced as the modality of phantasy but as 'reality.'" A person who finds himself in such a group treats its unconscious phantasms as reality. These collective phantasms are very difficult to unmask. Indeed, "if Paul begins to wake up from the family phantasy system, he can only be classified as mad or bad by the family since to them their phantasy *is* reality, and what is not phantasy is not real."[17]

Based on this understanding of phantasies and reality, Laing conducts captivating analyses of human situations, many of which resemble readings of novels or plays. The works of Iris Murdoch, Fyodor Dostoevsky's *Crime and Punishment,* Jean-Paul Sartre's *No Exit,* and Jean Genet's *Balcony* all come to mind as one reads *Self and Others*—and Laing cites some of them himself. Like Freud, he possesses an acutely literary, humanistic sensibility. His analysis of the letter Raskolnikov's mother writes to him, and of the son's reaction to it, is masterful. Laing frames this analysis in a strikingly original way. To describe the physical effects of psychic stress, as Raskolnikov might be experiencing them, he draws on the reactions of eight psychiatrists to whom he showed this excerpt from Dostoevsky's novel. All eight felt inner tension rise within them upon reading the fictional letter. Two of them felt as if they were suffocating; three others experienced sharp stomach pains.

To explain Raskolnikov's inner life, Laing makes fine distinctions between the imagination, phantasms, dreams, and daydreams. He notes the roles that various illusions play in Raskolnikov's self-understanding, drawing attention to the tension between his phantasies and his imagination. Laing summarizes part of this analysis as follows: "When he finally knows that the old woman will be murdered tomorrow, he feels himself like a man sentenced to death. In the modality of his phantasy, *he* is the victim, whereas 'in imagination' and in 'reality' he is the executioner." As Laing pithily puts it some pages later, Dostoevsky's protagonist is "Napoleon in imagination, a little boy in his dream, an old nag-woman in phantasy, a murderer in fact."[18]

Self and Others opens with an epigram from Confucius: "The way out is via the door. Why is it that no one will use this method?"[19] The aphorism reflects Laing's own stance toward phantasy, which he frequently reiterates throughout the book. He also deploys it in one of his most forceful, recurrent images: The social system of phantasms makes the act of walking out the door seem like ingratitude or cruelty, like an act of murder or suicide.

Laing enjoins us to walk out the door and claims to do so himself. But we should ask ourselves whether it is really possible to leave the world of phantasms. Freud, for one, would disagree.

The striving for transparency, for direct access to essences of things and beings, is omnipresent in Laing's "antipsychiatric" writings, especially *The Divided Self* (1960). Laing wants to reach the real "I" and to transform phantasmatic interpersonal ties into direct relations. He holds up as an ideal the imagined person who can shed all the veils the social world wraps around her. . . . His existential phenomenology thus ultimately becomes a kind of existential utopia.

In this quest for total transparency, might Laing be missing or destroying something important? Are there some human values to which such a pursuit of transparency might blind us? Laing's fight against phantasies' destructive tendencies inadvertently threatens an essential, imaginative part of ourselves. (I say *inadvertently,* because didn't Laing also write the LSD-inspired *Bird of Paradise* [1957])? Can we ever reliably distinguish between "destructive" and "nondestructive" phantasies? Or, for that matter, between "phantasy" and the "imagination"? Creating phantasies constitutes an organic part of our existence. It is not just the province of writers. Were we to aim for Laing's desired transparency and shed all the phantasies that the imaginative part of ourselves has created, we might fall into an even deeper and more dangerous illusion stemming from our lack of self-knowledge, from our incomplete understanding of the conditions of our existence.

Nathaniel Hawthorne's short story titled "The Minister's Black Veil" (1836) takes us to the heart of this dilemma. A gentle minister hides his face behind a black veil that he refuses to take off, even on his deathbed. He frightens his congregation in a way that increases his pastoral influence over them. The minister's self-veiling is an inexplicable, voluntary gesture that he finally addresses as he is dying:

> "Why do you tremble at me alone?" cried he, turning his veiled face round the circle of pale spectators. "Tremble also at each other! Have men avoided me, and women shown no pity, and children screamed and fled, only for my black veil? What, but the mystery which it obscurely typifies, has made this piece of crape so awful? When the friend shows his inmost heart to his friend; the lover to his best beloved; when man does not vainly shrink from the eye of his Creator, loathsomely treasuring up the secret of his sin; then deem me a monster, for the symbol beneath which I have lived, and die! I look around me, and, lo! on every visage a Black Veil!"[20]

The pastor dons the veil as a symbol of the nontransparency and insincerity of human relations. It represents all the walls, boundaries, and falsehoods we interpose between each other. This is the moral lesson the minister intends to teach his community. But could one not also interpret the Black Veil as a revelation of our shared ontological despair, of nontransparency as something to which the conditions of our existence condemn us? Hawthorne's narrator suggests as much when he comments that "good Mr. Hooper's face is dust; but awful is still the thought that it moldered beneath the Black Veil!" His congregation's mutual relations have not changed: The Black Veil is more durable than the face it covers.

"Freud, the Novelists"

Freud forged an image of the human being as infinitely aggressive. He saw civilization as "an agency within [the individual] to watch over [aggression], like a garrison in a conquered city," and rejected any "enthusiastic prejudice" to the contrary.[21] Charles Mauron highlights how much this standpoint offends religious and humanitarian feelings.[22] This seems to be one of the reasons Jung's ideas often have better traction.

Freud was the great demystifier. But he left phantasms untouched: Having revealed their existence, he let them be. Valabrega underlines that Freud not only opened them as a problem for the study of the human being but also showed that we only have one possible, viable way of dealing with them. For all his impulse toward laying things bare and getting them out in the open, when he discovered phantasms' organic existence in the human mind, he did not hurry to destroy or disenchant them. Quite the contrary—he appeared to accept them as a singular kind of mask we all need to wear to keep on existing. Like a mask, the phantasm exists at the crossroads between what is and what seems.

Freud and Laing ultimately espouse two very different understandings of the human. I will exaggerate the contrast between them in the service of the broader distinction they exemplify for me. The conflict between Laing's and Freud's vision of the human is that between utopia and anti-utopia, between Rousseauism and its opposite.

Larvatus prodeo: I go forth masked. Does this statement from Descartes's *Private Notebook* convey the essence of human existence? Or is the opposite true: Must we, and can we, tear off all our masks, including those woven out of phantasms? Are phantasms necessary means of symbolically satisfying our desires by transposing them into the realm of the imagination? Or are they a veil we need to remove to get to the essence of our conscious being?

Freud occasionally compares phantasy to a natural reserve "set up" in an industrializing environment "to preserve the *original state of the country,* protected from the changes brought by civilization."[23] "The national reserves maintain this old condition of things, which otherwise has everywhere been regretfully sacrificed to necessity. Everything may grow and spread there as it will, even that which is useless and harmful."[24] In this domain, the "useless" or the downright "harmful" is allowed to persist; reality has no power over phantasy. Phantasms can be soothing and comforting as well as terrifying. (Consider Freud's notion of the uncanny in this context.) Freud seemed to believe that both soothing and terrifying phantasms can have a liberatory, transgressive, therapeutic effect. Situated midway between myths and stereotypes, they share the qualities of both. Like myths, they often contravene against social norms; but like stereotypes, they are typically forces of reconciliation and conformity.

The humanities must not look away from phantasms, which structure the average person's imagination in a way that is both creative and uncreative. Phantasmatic critique needs to acknowledge this duality. It also needs to study more closely the conflict between the phantasm as an expression of creativity and its function as a reflection of kitsch and stereotype. Pedagogy ought to pay more attention to them as well. A proper education needs to teach young people to exist within both kinds of reality into which they are thrown: everyday life as well as the phantasmatic world.

As an anti-utopian who did not hope to forge direct, unmediated ties between human beings, Freud had a deep intuition about the *inherent theatricality of our existence.* In his passionate attraction to literature, he tends to be drawn to highly theatrical literary plots and situations. He finds in these literary scenarios condensed forms of phantasmatic ideation—and uses them to ground his metapsychological thinking. Wilhelm Jensen's *Gradiva,* a rather mediocre story, opens a window onto Freud's literary method. To heighten the story's fantastical elements, Jensen multiplies them to the point of incoherence. Scholars have noted that Freud ties up some of the loose ends of this story and bridges its narrative gaps. In this sense, Freud's commentary becomes a new short story of its own. As he reconstructs the protagonist's spotty biography to fit his psychoanalytic principles, he openly reflects on the analogy between psychoanalysis and novel writing.

The phantasm that most fascinated Freud was the *Familienroman,* one of the most basic human phantasms which deals with a person's origins and provenance. The name, which means the "novel of the family," already indicates that Freud conceives of its structure in literary terms. Freud devotes much attention to this phantasm in his major works (and, in the process, inspires Otto Rank's *Myth of the Birth of the Hero* [1909]). The phantasm he calls the *Familienroman* emerges under the pressure of the Oedipus complex, as something like its novelization.

As is well-known, Freud was struck by the similarity of children's neurotic inner dramas to the tragic plot of Sophocles's *Oedipus Rex* (as well as William Shakespeare's *Hamlet*). He even renamed what he initially called the "father complex" *(Vaterkomplex)* as the "Oedipus complex." Marthe Robert shows that, in so doing, Freud wanted to "emphasize the share of literature in the theoretical edifice"—with a special focus on the literature of Greek and Roman antiquity.[25] Written toward the end of his life, the book he eventually named *Moses and Monotheism* (1939) initially bore the working title *Der Mann Moses, ein historischer Roman* [Moses the man: A historical novel]. Freud knew himself to be writing another *Familienroman,* woven around the phantasms that surround the provenance of the founder of the Jewish faith.

In the *Familienroman,* Freud also charts out the plot of his own life. He insists that his writing does not merely illuminate pathological cases but reveals our shared human condition. The central burden we carry is the incest taboo: the minimal universal law that, as Lévi-Strauss puts it, separates "nature" and "culture" from each other. Freud's writing took inspiration from his own phantasms, as Robert's (well-titled) *From Oedipus to Moses* persuasively shows. The competencies of the writer and the doctor coincided within him. By his own terms, he studied other people's unconscious as a doctor—and as a writer, he probed his own.

In an essay about Central Europe's great cultural achievements, Milan Kundera lists "Freud, the novelists" in a single breath. The novelists he has in mind include Kafka, Hašek, Musil, Broch, and Gombrowicz. Kundera underlines the difference between the "psychological" and the "phenomenological" novel, but he does not draw a line between novel writers and Freud. Freud and the novelists, Kundera argues, "revalidate what for centuries was ill-known and unknown: rational and demystifying lucidity; a sense of the real; the novel." He praises their "mistrust of History and of the glorification of the future; their modernism, which has nothing to do with the avant-garde's illusions;" their anti-utopian and anti-lyrical tendencies.[26]

The true great novel of Central Europe is the novel of disillusionment that paradoxically also searches for gnosis: for deep, secret modes of understanding. That is the kind of novel Freud, a student of phantasms, wrote as well.

Notes

1. See Jean Laplanche and Jean-Bernard Pontalis, *The Language of Psychoanalysis,* trans. Donald Nicholson-Smith (New York: W. W. Norton, 1974).
2. See Jean-Paul Valabrega, *Phantasme, mythe, corps, et sens* (Paris: Payot, 1992).
3. See Jean Bergeret, *La personnalité normale et pathologique,* 3rd ed. (Paris: DUNOD, 2021).
4. See Elisabeth Roudinesco and Michel Plon, *Dictionnaire de la psychanalyse* (Paris: Fayard, 1997).
5. Sigmund Freud, *The Interpretation of Dreams, trans. A. A. Brill* (New York: Carlton House, 1913), 476.
6. Sigmund Freud, *A General Introduction to Psychoanalysis,* trans. G. Stanley Hall (New York: Liveright, 1920), 320–21.
7. Freud, *General Introduction to Psychoanalysis,* 321, 311.
8. Freud, *General Introduction to Psychoanalysis,* 323–25.
9. Freud, *General Introduction to Psychoanalysis,* 327.

10. See Susan Isaacs, "The Nature and Function of Phantasy," *International Journal of Psychoanalysis* 29 (1948): 73–97.
11. Sigmund Freud, "Creative Writers and Day-Dreaming" (1908), in *The Standard Edition of the Psychological Works of Sigmund Freud,* ed. and trans. James Strachey (London: Hogarth Press, 1981), 9:421.
12. Freud, "Creative Writers and Day-Dreaming," 422.
13. Freud, "Creative Writers and Day-Dreaming," 422.
14. Freud, "Creative Writers and Day-Dreaming," 428.
15. Philippe Lejeune, *On Autobiography,* trans. Katherine Leary (Minneapolis: University of Minnesota Press, 1988), 26.
16. R. D. Laing, *Self and Others: Selected Works of R. D. Laing* (London: Taylor and Francis, 1998), 2:36.
17. Laing, *Self and Others,* 2:22–25.
18. Laing, *Self and Others,* 2:52, 153.
19. Laing, *Self and Others,* 2:xv.
20. Nathaniel Hawthorne, *Twice-Told Tales* (New York: Modern Library Classics, 2001), 37.
21. Sigmund Freud, *Civilization and Its Discontents,* trans. James Strachey (New York: W. W. Norton, 2010), 82, 109.
22. See Charles Mauron, *Des métaphores obsédantes au mythe personnel* (Paris: Libraire J. Corti, 1963).
23. Sigmund Freud, "The Loss of Reality in Neurosis and Psychosis" (1924), in *Standard Edition of the Complete Psychological Works of Sigmund Freud,* 19:187.
24. Freud, *General Introduction to Psychoanalysis,* 324.
25. Marthe Robert, *From Oedipus to Moses: Freud's Jewish Identity,* trans. Ralph Manheim (Garden City, N.Y.: Anchor Books, 1976), 208.
26. Milan Kundera, *Art of the Novel,* trans. Linda Asher (New York: Harper, 1986), 124–25.

CHAPTER 7

The History of Literature and the History of Ideas

The history of literature versus the history of ideas: This important, polysemous juxtaposition can be approached from many well-trodden paths. It has bred a long tradition of scholarly research that hinges on distinctions between "literature" and "philosophy" as well as between "literature" and "ideology." Here, I pursue a rather one-sided approach, which will help me articulate a crucial *difference* between the history of literature and the history of ideas. Scholarship that assumes these two fields exist in harmony has recently borne much fruit: It has yielded many theses, essays, research discoveries, and keywords. We can now afford to acknowledge these fields' equally fundamental antagonism—especially since passing over it in silence works to the detriment of literary history.

When A. O. Lovejoy first named the history of ideas as a separate discipline, he did so by recognizing its separateness from literary history. Lovejoy also argued that literary history is best understood as a means toward the history of ideas, and not as an end in itself. He spoke in support of emergent historians of ideas, but his argument caught on surprisingly well among historians of literature, to the extent that many of them now see themselves as adjutants of the former field. The history of ideas now consequently wields a quasi-imperial power over literary history that cannot be dismissed as a *maladie imaginaire.*

An ongoing new trend in scholarship makes reflecting on these issues additionally pertinent. Across several humanistic fields, the traditional or "classical" method of the history of ideas has fallen into crisis. In a lecture delivered in 1972 at a colloquium organized by the French Society for Literary History, the scholar Jean Erhard, a proponent of the history of ideas, laid out a range of counterarguments against the positivist approach that had hitherto predominated in France. Erhard drew parallels between Lovejoy and the fin de siècle literary sociologist Gustave Lanson, highlighting the methods the two thinkers shared. One of the heaviest charges he brought against these methods was their reductiveness. They fall prey, he argued, to "the double temptation of mechanically reducing that which precedes their main subject and of teleologically deforming that which follows it."[1]

Erhard would not have launched such an attack on the history of ideas had it not been for Michel Foucault's harsh criticism of the field in *The Archaeology of Knowledge* (1969), published three years before Erhard's lecture. Erhard credits Lucien Febvre as his inspiration, but Foucault is the one who reanimated Febvre's arguments and generalized from them. To clear the ground for his concept of the archeology of knowledge, Foucault submitted the history of ideas to devastating critique. "Archaeological description," he writes in his account of how our present-day understanding of the "archive" and "archeology" came into being, "is . . . an abandonment of the history of ideas, a systematic rejection of its policies and procedures, an attempt to practice a quite different history of what men have said."[2]

I will not delve into Foucault's reasoning. However, let me draw attention to the two foundational features of the history of ideas that he most forcefully calls into question. One of these is the field's methodological commitment to creating appearances of historical continuity. ("Genesis, continuity, totalization: these are the great themes of the history of ideas, and that by which it is attached to a certain, now traditional, form of historical analysis.") The second is its assumption that human subjecthood does not change across time. The tenor of this critique is colored by Foucault's fervent rejection of anthropology. He insists that "archeology . . . is neither a psychology, nor a sociology, nor more generally an anthropology of creation." But this does not make his arguments less relevant to the history of ideas. The weaknesses Foucault reveals in both fields are manifold and real. In its present concord with the history of ideas, literary history shares many of these weaknesses. I agree with Foucault that "the history of ideas . . . is the discipline of beginnings and ends, the description of obscure continuities and returns, the reconstitution of developments in the linear form of history."[3]

Let us return to the issue with which I began. The antinomy I stage between the history of literature and the history of ideas is not a mere interpretative heuristic, a means of forcing the problem into a dialectical structure (though in principle, such an argumentative move seems sound to me). No, this antinomy preexists my argument. It inheres in how these two fields understand each other and structures the struggles between them. To use Hans Robert Jauss's terms, at the border that separates them there simmers a conflict between formalism and Marxism, and between these two methods' respective accounts of how history and literature relate to each other. Jauss, the author of "Literary History as a Challenge to Literary Theory" (1970), believes that one can build a bridge between literature and history, overcoming the antinomy between historical and aesthetic understanding. [. . .] For him, the antagonism between the history of literature and the history of ideas originates from a tension between aesthetic and historical approaches to literature. This tension prevents one from instantly perceiving literature as embedded in history in the same way ideas are.

The history of ideas and the history of literature are both historical fields, as their names suggest. But they examine and create *different kinds of histories*. The disparity between them finds recognition among the members of a new French school of historiography, the so-called Annales school. This new movement—to put things very simply—juxtaposes against each other superficial and deep, holistic kinds of history. Its newness stems from its innovative, interdisciplinary methods (combining history with geography, economics, sociology, anthropology, and so forth), as well as from the new archival terrains that it lays open for historical interpretation ("History's virgin territories," as Emmanuel Le Roy Ladurie calls them).[4] Already in the nineteenth century, Jules Michelet had intuited that such interdisciplinary histories might be possible. He called for someone to write a "history of the body" or a "history of hunger." Now, what he asked for has come to pass: Last year saw the publication of Jean-Paul Aron's *The Art of Eating in France* [*Le Mangeur du dix-neuvième siècle*, 1989], to much popular attention and acclaim. This book's popularity revealed how much demand there has been for a history of eating—or, more precisely, for a history of the *mangeur*, the "eater." (The word *mangeur* has no obvious equivalent in Polish, which calls for a historical investigation of its own.) Aron's volume might seem like a far-fetched example. But it shows how unexpected and diverse are the narratives that this new approach to history (which attends, for example, to culinary discourses) allows us to tell.

Inspired by the Annales school, French historians have recently gone one step further. Earlier this year, Jacques Le Goff and Pierre Nora put out a three-part edited volume, *Faire de l'histoire* [Making history], which aims to lay out "a new type of history." The subtitles of this volume's three parts highlight the range of this new method's innovations: it promises "Nouveaux problèmes," or new problems; "Nouvelles approches," or new approaches; and "Nouveaux objets," or new objects. [. . .] These emergent methods have relegated to the past an understanding of history-telling confined to narratives of adult, white, "civilized" European males. Today's historians venture into unknown territories, including those whose appeal lies in their apparent timelessness: climate, the body, myth, the sacred . . . Cultural "mentalities" (Le Goff's term) as objects of study loom large over this new research. He sees them as agents of inertia that confound the linearity of time and narrative as different aspects of a culture's mentality develop at uneven, nonparallel paces. Le Goff sees in the history of mentalities "a new kind of history which, in its search for explanations, dares to look behind the looking-glass."[5] Both the suggestion of newness and the allusion to Lewis Carroll underscore how much distance this new historical method puts between itself and traditional, linear, supposedly one-dimensional history writing. These recent approaches do not do away with historical thinking. But they reframe history within more modest, localized, and particularized spatiotemporal dimensions.

This new critical conversation allows us to rename the difference between the history of literature and the history of ideas as one between their respective *temporalities.* The temporality of literary history and that of the history of ideas are not the same—just as that of literature itself is not the same as that of ideas, let alone ideologies. People have intuited these differences for a long time. I will focus on the way Eugène Ionesco expresses such intuitions in one of his essays. Ionesco articulates a notion of art shared by many of his contemporaries, including the Polish novelist Witold Gombrowicz. He argues that artworks exist beyond ideology and by their nature cannot be reduced to it. Ideology can surround art but cannot penetrate it (except, of course, in the case of explicitly, didactically ideological artworks). The absence of ideology from the artwork does not make art empty of ideas. On the contrary, art is the ground where ideas germinate and take shape. To put this differently, Freud did not inspire Sophocles, but Sophocles inspired Freud through the way his plays represent human existence. Ideology does not lie at the root of art; instead, the artwork lies at the root of ideology and philosophy alike. This is because art is *true,* whereas ideology is merely didactic, giving the moral of the story. Ionesco charges the critic with just one task: She must attend to the artwork, its inner world, and its mythology. She must let the artwork speak to her and silence her own received ideas, ideologies, and preconceived opinions. Art seeks to express realities that are otherwise incommunicable, and it occasionally succeeds in this effort; such is its paradoxical, true nature. Ionesco sees an insurmountable, irremediable contradiction between literature and ideology. By putting "ideas" and "ideologies" in the same category, he suggests that the former form part of the latter. Both can only produce false consciousness or intentional distortions of reality.

A successful interpretation of an artwork—whether it follows a Marxist, Buddhist, Christian, existentialist, or psychoanalytic method—must therefore culminate in affirming the artwork's irreducibility to and separateness from the method at hand. Ideology cannot enter a true work of art from the outside, whether in the guise of an idea that supposedly inspired it or as a concept guiding its supposedly correct understanding. The artwork remains a world unto itself, closed and impenetrable. In this regard, though ideas and literature may seem to have much in common, they are alien—indeed, hostile—to each other. The history of ideas cannot help us understand literature because the truth of art cannot be translated into ideas. The former can inspire the latter but cannot be subordinated to them. To make this point, Ionesco juxtaposes Samuel Beckett against Bertolt Brecht, professing his distaste for the latter as a didactic ideologue. Brecht's characters, firmly embedded in society, lack a metaphysics. And, for Ionesco, "there is no art without metaphysics, and there is no society away from its nonsocial context."[6]

Ionesco's rather extreme pronouncements articulate a contradiction felt by many artists who see art as something sacred, identified with truth and revelation. Literary critics and historians rarely express their views in such an extreme way. (At least in theory, their profession compels them to approach the artwork more critically.) But stating this contradiction so baldly shows it to originate in the belief that art and ideas exist in altogether different realms. Ionesco himself uses the term *realm* to insist on this point: for him, the degree of difference between "literature" and "ideas" merits it. The realms in question are temporal ones: The difference between literature and ideas hinges on whether a given entity exists within time or beyond it. Ideas are temporally and socially embedded; art, at least in some senses, is timeless and independent of its social context. [. . .] This distinction takes us back to the question of the ontology of the artwork, its mode of being, an oft-discussed issue that any ontological account of reality needs to tackle. The artwork appears to exist both within time and beyond it. At its best, its proper sphere of being is eternity. Ideas, especially if we understand them as ideologies, are bound to the progression of history and easily prone to being relativized by it.

The contrasts I am paraphrasing are extreme, and my reader should be wary of their starkness. But this dichotomy marks an important starting point for distinguishing between the temporality of the history of literature and that of the history of ideas. To put things in less extreme terms, the two fields measure time in different units. Ideas exist in what is commonly termed the *longue durée.* In this long view, individual events have a relatively short range of influence. As Fernand Braudel puts it, the event's "delusive smoke fills the minds of its contemporaries, but it does not last, and its flame can scarcely ever be discerned." Braudel, with whom the theory of history as *longue durée* originates, further explains this concept by recalling a night he spent in Bahia watching fireflies. The insects flickered in the night but could not illuminate it. "So it is with events," Braudel explains. "Beyond their glow, darkness prevails."[7] Brief flashes in historical time, individual events do not tell us anything truly significant about it. [. . .] One would be hard-pressed to articulate a clearer distinction between theories that embrace the notion of history as a series of events, and those that reject this notion. Historians of ideas tend to take the latter position.

By contrast, the history of literature tends to be narrated as a sequence of events. It accords the status of an event to literary personalities, works, and masterworks. In this sense, literary history bears close relation to the "inferior," reactionary kind of political history that busies itself with chronicling major political incidents and assembling the biographies of great leaders. Indeed, so fierce is literary history's polemic against eventless narratives of literary history that it typically designates events as the sole possible source of aesthetic innovation.

Of course, literary history can and does occupy itself with the *longue durée.* One should recall that Braudel invokes Ernst Curtius's account of topoi and myths as strikingly analogous to his own thinking. Literary conventions and genres come into view within this extended perspective. Ideas do as well—and we are entitled to be curious about how conventions, genres, and ideas appear and reappear in literary deep time. But such a view of literature should not in itself satisfy us as literary scholars: It goes against the principles of literary aesthetics and thus threatens to deform our vision. When we reduce literary history to a history of the ideas that literature contains, we reduce each period to its intellectual average. Lanson, who embraces these reductions, claims that average literary works are the most representative ones. Lovejoy adds that a period's mediocre writers often give us a clearer sense of its cultural mentalities than the outstanding ones. Yet most literary scholars see literary history as exceptional *precisely* because of the special place that it accords to singular creative events, *precisely* because it devotes itself to studying personalities that give rise to such events and seeks to interpret each literary work on its own terms. Can singular creative events of literary history be integrated into a continuous series like the *longue durée* of the history of ideas? Can they constitute a coherent historical narrative?

To answer this question, we must first reflect on what we mean by *history,* and how we relate it to the "telling of history."

Contemporary critics of the Old Historicism—or rather, not of this method itself, but of its abuses—attribute to it a Hegelian notion of history as an all-encompassing, coherent whole. In "Literary History as a Challenge to Literary Theory," Hans Robert Jauss supports Siegfried Kracauer's critique of such all-encompassing historiography. He writes, "[Kracauer's] study of 'Time and History' challenges the claim of general history that, within the homogeneous medium of chronological time, it can make events of all areas of life comprehensible as a unified process consistent in every historical moment. This understanding of history, still under the influence of Hegel's idea of the 'objective spirit' *(objektiver Geist),* presupposes that everything which happens at one time is determined to the same degree by the meaning of this moment and thus conceals the fact that things which occur at the same time are not really simultaneous." According to Hegel, all events that occur in the same moment are endowed with the same, uniformly distributed, historical significance, by virtue of stemming from the same context and period. Historians such as Jauss and Kracauer want to fracture this uniform sense of significance into multiple "special topics in history," each governed by an internal sense of time. Within this "pluralism of a historical and morphological passage of time," each period contains many temporalities, each associated with a special topic of its own.[8] (Such theories do not automatically presume that these subhistories could not eventually be made to cohere—but that's a separate matter.) In their most serious charge, figures such as Kracauer and Jauss accuse universal history of baselessly unifying the many objects and topics of history and showing indifference to their singularity, privileging a desire to unify, universalize, and create simultaneities among things that are not, in fact, simultaneous and unified. Even if strands of specialized history coexist next to each other, they are not necessarily coeval or synchronous in their internal rhythms. The history of literature is one such special topic of history. It insists on its distinctiveness because it self-defines as a series of events, a succession of individual masterpieces.

However we define the masterpiece, and even if we are critical of the concept of a definable, universal canon, I think we can all agree that calling something a masterpiece designates it as singular and unrepeatable. I think we can also agree that artworks generally aspire to singularity and unrepeatability; we call certain works of art masterpieces, justifiably or not, because they seem to us to fulfill this aspiration particularly well.

Cultural history, especially branches of it devoted to art and literature, thus draws a distinction between masterpieces and pieces of "kitsch." These aesthetic designations delimit the field within which judgments of value can be articulated and negotiated. Again, without going too deep into these terms' complex, much debated definitions or into specific judgments of taste, I want to draw attention to one aspect of the opposition between them, which Paweł Beylin articulates as follows: "A genuine work of art is unique, impossible to imitate or reproduce exactly as a whole. Kitsch, on the other hand, is made to be imitated and repeated. A genuine artwork cannot be disaggregated into removable and replaceable pieces without losing its aesthetic integrity. With kitsch, that can be done quite easily, because it does not have a strong sense of identity." A masterpiece differs from a piece of kitsch, in other words, because unlike the latter, it aspires to a state of singularity. Stanisław Lem speaks in similar terms about the "relativism" of kitsch: "Roger Caillois describes the fantastic as that which carries the irreducible feeling of the supernatural. Its linguistic equivalent is the unmistakable feeling of a text's intrinsic singularity, which guarantees that the text in question is not kitsch. This feeling's unmistakability is the hallmark of the authenticity of the aesthetic features to which it responds. The writer who inspires such a feeling stands apart from those others who declare themselves to be aesthetic relativists, and who produce kitsch because they are unable accurately to give form to their aesthetic intentions."[9] The criteria of authenticity, unmistakability, and singularity that Lem uses to separate true art from kitsch create a web of concepts that one can also use to a different end.

An artwork is defined by its aesthetic or artistic coherence. This definition should lead us to notice that an idea can also bear the qualities of a masterpiece. It should also cause us to accord masterpieces of ideation an analogous degree of respect. It feels entirely unwarranted to distinguish between ideas and literature in this regard. Masterpieces of ideation (think of the ideas of Jesus Christ, Thomas Aquinas, or Karl Marx) are not lesser masterpieces than those of art. But the two kinds of masterpieces do differ from each other. The conflict between historians of ideas and historians of literature revolves around this latter difference. An idea can and often does have an inward aesthetic structure, an autotelic consistency. However, such forms of coherence are ideas' *secondary* rather than *primary* qualities—whereas, in the case of the artwork, they constitute its essence and ground. Recall the distinction that Bachelard draws, in his writings about the phenomenology of poetry, between "thought and 'the poetic image.'" Bachelard underlines (contra Hegel) that "the image comes *before* thought."[10] [. . .] He stands against the conscious or (frequently) unconscious Hegelianism of most historians of ideas, for whom ideas tend to be the primary source of coherence and meaning, the objective unifying force that brings order to the chaos of subjective aesthetic impressions.

The internal coherence of masterpieces of ideation—if you will allow me to use this term—tends to be "loose," "baggy," and "full of holes" by comparison to the inner coherence of the artwork. This is why ideas can easily undergo significant deformations and changes. Literary masterpieces, by contrast, tend to be "rigid" rather than "loose." They are not made to be broken, crumpled, and remolded to the point where they lose their initial structuring features. To say this is not to side with the aestheticist demagogues who claim that the work of any literary scribbler carries greater value than the products of masterful thinking, just because literature's aesthetic structure is more rigid than the structure of an idea. The contrast I draw here does not imply a judgment of value.

As I make these distinctions, I also do not mean to overlook the many literary works that are *not* masterpieces. A masterpiece often seems to explode with newness and scatter newness around itself; but one should not forget that the surrounding environment will have diligently prepared the ground for this explosion. All those who write pretty good, average, and downright bad literature contribute to someone's capturing the "spirit of the times." Moreover, one would be hard-pressed to imagine any field of artistic creation—not just literature—composed entirely of masterpieces. Such a state of affairs would be unbearable to the creators of these masterpieces, and even more so to their audiences. Masterpieces "come into being" out of works that are not masterpieces: The history of literature compels us to accept this conclusion. This is true even if they retroactively impose standards of judgment onto the works that surround and precede them, as their influence cannot be eradicated from the minds of readers, critics, and literary historians.

The methods of historians of ideas infringe on the sovereignty of the artwork. At their best, these methods allow historians of ideas to discover within works of art certain general anthropological or philosophical tendencies. At their worst, these methods turn literary works into mere "illustrations" or specimens of the ideas they are seen to contain, implicitly allowing the history of ideas to assert dominance over literary history. Once literary historians declare their independence, historians of ideas will be forced to admit that theirs is also one of many "special histories." (Though literary historians who insist on this separation also need to remember that their preoccupation with innovation requires a long view of the literary contexts within which it occurs.)

This line of thinking brings us to yet another question of method: What are the proper aims of historical inquiry? The daring writings of Jean-Pierre Faye, editor of the French journal *Change,* have given this question exciting as well as troubling new meanings. Faye shows that it is impossible to "do" history except by *telling it,* and that history can never be "told" in neutral terms. Indeed, the mode of narration historians adopt can have wide-ranging social consequences. (Faye argues that Nazism found acceptance among right-wing activists, and then within German society at large, because its way of narrating history—*le récit nazi*—was extremely persuasive.) The mode of historical narration one adopts also determines the kinds of histories one can tell or call into question.

Literary historians must choose their narrative form and genre with equal care. The most basic, defining choice they face is whether to narrate literary history as a "special topic of history." On this subject, let me repeat the point I made above. When literary history tries to assimilate into the history of ideas, it forfeits its independence; when literary history insists on its distinction from the history of ideas, it relegates both fields to the status of "special topics."

To put things starkly, literary history can be told in a way that either focuses on the *longue durée* or highlights individual events. Its mode of narration can privilege the forces of either cultural inertia or cultural innovation; it can put emphasis on either collectives and collective time or individuals and individual time. But even as the history of ideas typically employs the discourse of the *longue durée* and collective time, literary history will usually focus on singular events and innovations that happen on the individual's timescale. Seeing these fields from such a perspective helps one understand why literary histories that try to imitate histories of ideas are often accused by their detractors of doing archetypal rather than literary criticism. The study of archetypes, like the study of ideas, does not concern itself with what makes an artwork singular or innovative.

Narrating literary history as a series of events requires one to develop a new, separate discourse for each literary work to properly inhabit its inner temporality. In an argument for describing the artwork's discourse as an idiolect, Umberto Eco draws attention to language as the basic structure in which all other aspects of a literary work's organization are grounded. The language of an artwork, he argues, is a

> new code . . . apparently spoken by only one speaker, and understood by a very restricted audience; it is a semiotic *enclave* which society cannot recognize as a social rule acceptable by anyone. . . . The rule governing all deviation at work at every level of a work of art, the unique diagram which makes all deviations mutually functional, is the *aesthetic idiolect*. Insofar as it can be applied by the same author to many of his own works . . . the idiolect becomes a general one governing the entire *corpus* of an author's work, i.e., his *personal style*.[11]

Eco speaks the language of semiotics rather than hermeneutics—but even in this former idiom, he analogously connects art to innovation. [. . .] An artwork's idiolect could also be described as its "point of view." This point of view includes ideas; but the historian of literary idiolects sees these ideas as developed within the artwork, rather than introduced to it from the outside. Herein lies another difference between the historian of literature and the historian of ideas: They disagree on what is "exterior" and "interior" to the work of art. The history of ideas describes ideas as causal forces that enter the artwork from the outside; literary history sees ideas as emergent from its inner structure. By insisting that ideas take shape within the artwork, literary history does not necessarily reject the insights of sociological research methods. But it suggests that a sociological approach to literature is best paired with a psychological or psychoanalytic one.

Alain Besançon, who describes his method as "psychoanalytic history" or as "the psychoanalysis of history," sees works of art and literature as "the second royal road" to the unconscious (the first royal road leads through dreams). He uses literature to distinctly extra-literary ends. All the same, the conclusions to which he comes are of interest to the field of literary study, particularly in his preoccupation with "subjective history," with history and "the experience of the self." Besançon aims to translate into twentieth-century terms the aims that Jules Michelet wrote down in his diary in 1834: "An intimate method: to simplify history, to turn it into biography, as if I were writing about a single man, or about myself."[12] He turns to literature to achieve this end, taking it as an instance of what "subjective history," the "history of the I," might look like.

Wherever the history of literature and the history of ideas touch borders, these fields' practitioners can adopt one of two possible attitudes toward each other. Both attitudes are common, and both deserve some treatment here. I will describe the first one as "subordination" and the second as "confrontation."

When scholars seek to *subordinate* the temporality of literary history to the temporality of the history of ideas, they necessarily subordinate literature itself to conceptual thinking. They take ideas as external means of classifying literary phenomena. This approach erases the particularity of literary works; it reduces them to a gradually evolving continuum of thinking about some concept or group of concepts. Such an approach creates an insurmountable conflict between the writer and the critic. Witold Gombrowicz describes this conflict in the following terms: "An artwork aspires to internal coherence and unity. Criticism, even at its best, creates typologies and classifications that dissolve the artwork into the particulars of its production and into the crowd of other works surrounding it. This goes against the essence of literature as art." The critic is often not unjustified when she deploys the "classifications" Gombrowicz describes here. But as she does so, she must be careful to distinguish the temporality of literary history from the temporality of the individual work of literature, particularly an outstanding masterwork. Seen as a whole, literature contains both the lowbrow and the highbrow; its coherence comes from the temporalities and contexts that groups of works share at their immediate reception. But when a work of literature attains the status of a masterpiece, the temporalities of its reception change, and one must take these changes into account when studying it. Here, the distinction Eco draws between de jure and de facto literary idiolects proves useful. Eco's binary is one among a number of strategies critics have used to set literary masterpieces apart from other pieces of literature. Vossler thus separates *Schöpfung* from *Entwicklung*. Croce distinguishes between poetry and mere literature. Wacław Borowy opposes "literature as a set of true masterpieces" to "literature as a set of cultural phenomena, a social life." For all these critics, it is perfectly legitimate to subordinate literary history to the *longue durée* of the history of ideas, as long as the objects of one's study remain within the bounds of *Entwicklung* and literature's social life.

Interpreting literary masterpieces requires a different approach. This alternative approach does not, of course, involve jettisoning the history of ideas in favor of a "pure" literary history. Quite the contrary, it stages a conflict between the temporalities and idioms of the two fields. As an interpretative tactic, such clashes of temporalities and idioms yield many insights. From the perspective of this essay, one kind of insight is especially crucial: such head-on confrontations estrange the discourses of literary history and the history of ideas from themselves and from each other. The literary work maintains its singularity, but it is also brought into the presence of the "alterity" against which its singularity was defined and developed.

If it manages to maintain such a double focus, the dialogue between the history of literature and the history of ideas comes to serve two further purposes: It becomes a way of understanding the dialogue between the writer and their critics, as well as that between the literary work and its readers.

Notes

1. Jean Erhard, "Histoire des idées et histoire littéraire," in *Problèmes et méthodes de l'histoire littéraire: Colloque 18 novembre 1972* (Paris: Armand Colin, 1974), 72.
2. Michel Foucault, *The Archaeology of Knowledge,* trans. A. M. Sheridan Smith (New York: Vintage Books, 1982), 138.
3. Foucault, *Archaeology of Knowledge,* 137–39.
4. Emmanuel Le Roy Ladurie, "Défricher les terres vierges de l'histoire," *Le Monde,* June 21, 1973.
5. Jacques Le Goff, "Mentalities: A History of Ambiguities," trans. David Denby, in *Constructing the Past: Essays in Historical Methodology,* ed. Jacques Le Goff and Pierre Nora (Cambridge: Cambridge University Press, 1985), 176.
6. Eugène Ionesco, "Brief Notes for Radio," in *Notes and Counter Notes: Writings on the Theatre,* trans. Donald Watson (New York: Grove Press, 1964), 135.
7. Fernand Braudel, *On History,* trans. Sarah Matthews (Chicago: University of Chicago Press, 1980), 27, 10.
8. Hans Robert Jauss, "Literary History As a Challenge to Literary Theory," trans. Elizabeth Benzinger, *New Literary History* 2, no. 1 (1970): 28.
9. Stanisław Lem, "Tzvetana Todorova fantastyczna teoria literatury," *Teksty* 5 (1973): 39.
10. Gaston Bachelard, *The Poetics of Space,* trans. Maria Jolas (Boston: Beacon Press, 1994), xx.
11. Umberto Eco, *A Theory of Semiotics* (Bloomington: Indiana University Press, 1976), 272.
12. Alain Besançon, *Histoire et expérience du moi* (Paris: Flammarion, 1971), 9, 105.

CHAPTER 8

Notes on Horror and Melodrama

Romanticism and Freud's Theory of the Phantasm

Freud wrote a dozen essays about artistic creativity, mostly before World War I. One of them deserves particular attention. It touches on a gamut of still-pertinent cultural issues created by so-called mass culture and the way it weakens normative high-cultural categories of beauty, goodness, and truth. This essay, titled "Creative Writers and Day-Dreaming" (1908), contains Freud's highly original account of "from what sources that strange being, the creative writer, draws his material."[1] It is all the more remarkable for being free of the orthodoxies that otherwise plague many of Freud's works, including *Leonardo da Vinci and a Memory of His Childhood* (1923).

Moreover, the essay is conceptually elastic, adaptable for discussions of a variety of media and genres. Freud could not have imagined the future evolution of cinema when writing in 1908, nor could he have probed its now-considerable archives; nevertheless, the essay illuminates this medium especially well. "Creative Writers and Day-Dreaming" outlines a theory of phantasms as the domain of art—or, at least, of a particular kind of art. In transposing this theory onto contemporary cinema, we must keep in mind Freud's own aesthetic background. As scholars have observed, his sensibility was crucially shaped by classical antiquity, whose cultural heritage he loved and admired, and by the German Romantics, whose writings he knew very well. His concurrent affinity with these two periods betrays an aesthetic ambivalence that colors Freud's thinking about art. In what follows, I will consider this ambivalence at some length.

For now, back to "The Creative Writer and Day-Dreaming." Freud argues that we can consider poetic activity as a game (a kind of play), a phantasm, or a dream. He uncovers the seeds of literary creativity in early childhood. As the child plays, she creates her "own world" and "a new order" within it: a separate, circumscribed, alternative reality.

Freud is therefore entirely right to say that "the opposite of play is not what is serious but what is real," that is, ordinary, everyday reality.[2] The child imbues her play within this imagined reality with immense seriousness. She conjures up a world that seems as real and serious as the "true" one, but that cannot be readily assimilated or absorbed into the latter. [. . .]

Daydreams typically enact our ambitions or erotic desires, or both at once. And it is easier to confess one's crimes than one's phantasies . . . so powerful are the mechanisms of suppression that hide the latter within a branching network of conventions and warnings. Freud underscores that the daydreamer may perceive herself as the only person who has ever daydreamed. She sees her phantasies as something exceptional that needs to be carefully hidden from others, without suspecting that "creations of this kind are widespread among other people."[3] So how can we come to learn people's phantasies? Freud names two possible sources. First, we might hear them expressed by the mentally ill. Their daydreams are not fundamentally different from those of the sane. However, their mental illness and pressure from their psychotherapist combine to loosen the hold of the social prohibition against sharing these secrets with others. The second source is literature, which feeds on phantasies—especially literature of a particular kind.

The genre of literature Freud singles out is born out of its authors' liberated fantasies and aims to free up its readers' phantasms. Freud makes a significant distinction between two kinds of writers. He distinguishes "writers who, like the ancient authors of epics and tragedies, take over their material ready-made"—that is to say, classical writers who let their works be delimited by the bounds of tradition—from "writers who seem to originate their own material." Freud is careful to say that the latter writers only *seem* to be wholly original. He recognizes that social and literary conventions still set limits on the creativity of apparently liberated writers, even if those restrictions are of a different type than those obeyed by tradition-bound ones.

Freud stresses that, in his study of writers who "seem to originate their own materials," he purposefully focuses not on "the writers most highly esteemed by the critics, but the less pretentious authors of novels, romances, and short stories, who nevertheless have the widest and most eager circle of readers of both sexes."[4] Those less ambitious writers do not show much "creative freedom" of the kind literary critics care about: They reiterate literary clichés and stay close enough to social norms and moral conventions that they do not come under attack from public opinion and its guardians. Their revealed phantasms are not particularly original or astonishing, wild or lewd. Were they any of those things, the public would not so widely approve of them. Restrained neither by tradition nor by the pressure to be "highbrow," popular writers toe the line between revealing their daydreams, which they hold in common with vast numbers of other members of society, and exercising moderation in doing so. This intermediate territory between revelation and moderation constitutes the most fertile ground of popular culture as modern democracy called it into being, organized around the commonality and ease of access of social stereotypes.

A few distinctions must be drawn between Freud's perspective and ours. Freud often reaches for third-rate literature (such as Wilhelm Jensen's *Gradiva,* to which he devoted a long essay titled "Delusion and Dream in Jensen's *Gradiva*" [1907]). He tends to treat it as if it were first-rate, despite articulating some differences between first-rate and third-rate writers, as well as between the phantasms of artists and those of ordinary humans. At the end of the day, his criteria are psychoanalytic, practical ones: He is a doctor who aims to disclose phantasms for therapeutic aims. Though this perspective on mass culture cannot be entirely overlooked, here we will not let it dominate over others. Instead, we will devote most of our attention to the question of aesthetic value.

Freud's theory of the phantasm could be productively integrated into theories of literature, popular culture, and cinema. Let us consider each of these possibilities in turn.

Regarding literary theory, here we should focus on modern, Romantic and surrealist literature, since it has elevated the imagination to an unprecedented degree. We might begin our narration with William Blake's famous assertion that "the imagination is not a state: it is the human existence itself." Romanticism freed up dreams and phantasms to an extent unprecedented by prior literature (though it was not entirely without precursors—consider, for example, the work of Hieronymus Bosch). *The First Enfranchisement of the Imagination* is a fitting name for this process. Here, I can only dwell on some of the circumstances that brought this enfranchisement into being.

First: Liberating the imagination required a break with the Enlightenment and its understanding of cultural tradition. Romantics saw this prior generation's interpretation of antiquity as dogmatic, ossified, and imaginatively constraining; they set out to reinterpret antiquity in their own way. They believed that their predecessors conceived of ancient tradition in a narrow, homogenous, one-sided fashion, and sought to replace this view with a concept of antiquity that was heterogeneous, many-sided, and pluralistic. In so doing, the Romantics wove new strands of history into Europeans' understanding of the modern world: folk culture, the cultures of the East and the North—and juxtaposed these traditions against classicist, Mediterranean dogmas. Most important to the process of freeing up fantasies and the imagination, these other cultures were inhabited by specters and monsters quite different from the ones that haunted ancient Greece and Southern Europe. [. . .]

Second: Romanticism embraced a sphere of reality that had previously remained underexplored and unrecognized; it drew on everyday experience and interior life. It did so in spectacular ways, with extreme individualist intimacy, rebelling against prior (frequently ancient) strictures on the number and kind of topics a work of literature could pursue. In so doing, Romanticism *revealed* a new reality, an inward realm in which phantasms were allowed to roam free. Its bluntness, its refusal to stand on ceremony, speaks from this realm to the offense of the movement's predecessors. Romanticism thus discovered the "human unconscious" and began to enunciate things that had previously been kept hidden; things that—if they had ever seen daylight—only saw it under the guise of an ancient myth or motif (e.g., the forbidden, incestuous love of Racine's *Phèdre*). The Romantics did not need pretexts: They felt free to lay bare the phantasms of human beings' inner worlds, particularly the inner worlds of young people. Their movement's breakthrough comes from its freedom of expression: It launched into being a new kind of art, preoccupied with dreams, phantasms, creatures of an imagination that others often decried as diseased but which, from a Freudian perspective, seems absolutely normal and average. Cinema testifies to the normalcy of these phantasms as well, bringing forth the fantasies of the Everyman in an extremely unguarded and direct visual form. We are all able and expected to recognize ourselves in them.

Third: Romanticism evolved a new mode of classifying, ordering, dividing, and naming reality. It translated into aesthetic terms forms of feeling and understanding that were previously the domain of religious discourse. Romanticism proclaimed the existence of some "second," "other," "higher" order of being. It thus proliferated our realities, took liberties with them, and uncovered their preexistent multiplicities. It raised the possibility of exploring the world of the dead, whose representation had previously been restricted to a few canonical tropes. The many new realms that the members of this movement discovered emanated with new phantasms and phantoms. Their underworld bustled with the rich lives of specters, ghosts, vampires, and werewolves, not to mention the many other fantastic creatures that migrated into Romantic literature from folklore—especially Slavic folklore, famous for its copious and diverse demonic sphere.

Fourth: The superimposition of non-Mediterranean "counterculture" (folk culture, Northern culture, Slavic culture) onto newly liberated personal phantasms altered the Romantics' relationship to low culture as compared to their Enlightenment predecessors. Nineteenth-century popular culture emerges from these new imaginative amalgamations. Popular culture grew out of two genres Romanticism created: melodrama and the Gothic novel. Within them, high and low culture came to intermingle in a way that has remained characteristic of many forms of democratic mass entertainment. This is especially true of cinema, the most democratic of the arts, for which melodrama and horror are foundational categories. Naturally, popular culture also strove to *domesticate* these Romantic phantasms, whose fully liberated forms could not have fit into its frameworks. Contemporary cinema moves between these two kinds of phantasms, liberated and domesticated ones; this movement is often discernible within a single film.

Fifth: Romanticism attaches special importance to the figure of the protagonist or hero. Within him (*sic!*), the force of Romanticism's novelty and originality are most fully on display. The Romantic hero is Promethean in his brave, noble struggle against the forces of evil. This chosen figure also radiates a demonic beauty framed by a certain darkness and fatalism. Scholars have written about this hero from many angles. Here, I do not wish to repeat these prior debates but to focus on one question in particular: To what extent does the Romantic hero become the hero of popular culture, the feature film's protagonist? The overlap between the typical male lead and the Romantic hero is considerable, and it is mediated through the popular novel. Romanticism shapes the protagonists of popular novels, who are variously melodramatic, historicized (cloak-and-dagger), adventurous, mysterious, magical. At the turn of the twentieth century, the heroes of popular novels transform into cinematic leads. Sometimes, this happens through the direct transpositions of Romantic plots; at other times, these plots are slightly modified (but still recognizable). Let's name a few influential protagonists of popular novels: Rudolf de Gerolstein from Eugène Sue's *Mysteries of Paris,* Alexandre Dumas's titular *Three Musketeers* and *Count of Monte Cristo,* Feuillade and Bernède's Judex, and Souvestre and Allain's Fantômas. Marc Angenot describes this protagonist as derived from the Romantic type of the "noble bandit." Promethean and ready to attribute providential powers and insights to himself, this character likes to act as an avenger and judge. The line between justice and sadism in his punishments is often murky and frequently crossed. Cinema takes up this character type with enthusiasm and verve.

Sixth: Romanticism's freeing up of phantasms and imaginations stimulates popular writers—popular in both the usual sense and their capacity to reveal shared communal fantasies—toward a freer exploration of eroticism. Popular writers, in turn, open up new cognitive and emotional avenues for their readers. *The Lady of the Camellias* by Alexandre Dumas *fils,* itself a brilliant expression of melodramatic fantasies, conveys the principle of such creative transfers quite overtly when Dumas's narrator compares his love affair to an episode from a novel by Alphonse Karr. In this episode, a man is following a woman with whom he has fallen in love at first sight. He dreams of kissing this woman's hand but barely dares to glance at her shapely foot, which the woman momentarily reveals to him by lifting her skirts to step over some mud. "As he dreams of everything he will do to win this woman, she stops on a street corner and asks him if he wants to come up to her place." Recalling this story saddens the hero of *The Lady of the Camellias.* He fears that his own beloved, who after all is a courtesan, might allow him to seduce her too quickly, bestowing on him too eagerly a love that he would have preferred to gain "through long pursuit or great sacrifice." Dumas punctuates Armand's fearful train of thought with the following aphorism: "That's how we're made, we men, and it's truly fortunate that the imagination bestows this sort of poetry on the senses, and that the passions of the body make this concession to the dreams of the soul."[5]

The American writer Nancy Friday offers an interesting recent continuation of this Romantic eroticism in *My Secret Garden* (1973), which collects a variety of sexual phantasies expressed by women. A delicate subject: not just eroticism per se, but *women's* eroticism. The author [. . .] describes revealing her sexual fantasies to her partner, who had asked what she thought about while she came. In response to her confessions, Friday's partner left her. [. . .] Her burning need to act out certain film roles, literary plots, and life scenarios, and to admit as much, pushed her to place ads in papers calling for women to send her detailed descriptions of their own sexual fantasies. An avalanche of letters ensued that convinced Friday she wasn't alone or diseased in her lusts; the letters also revealed that her correspondents were similarly convinced of their fantasies' uniqueness. It gave both her and her correspondents great satisfaction to discover that other people indulged in fantasies similar to theirs.

Friday's story is remarkable, especially if one also considers the many troubles she encountered when trying to publish her book. Her experience does not merely reinforce Freud's theory of the phantasm. It also reveals how great a role in sustaining, satiating, and fostering these phantasms is played by popular culture, especially popular cinema (to the point where the trope of the "film star" features prominently in both ambitious and erotic daydreams). In a wonderful article published in 1936, Witold Gombrowicz calls attention to the great "power of secret fantasies." Setting official and popular culture in sharp contrast with each other, Gombrowicz names secret dreams and fantasies as the domain of the latter. He also describes the kinds of people who indulge in them, who tend to be young: "Their taste for illusion is typical for young people. The cinema, the potboiler romance, the street ad, an illustration in a newspaper: all this arouses them. With nobody to stop them, they forge private daydreams and keep them secret from others. [. . .] The poet and the literary writer who dream lucidly, within boring official frameworks, cannot imagine what lurks inside the heads of these secretive, conspiratorial dreamers." Gombrowicz describes perspicaciously the urban background where these furtive fantasies take shape. He feels tempted to take on the role of "these secret fantasies' leader." Gombrowicz is ultimately too ironic, too drawn to the gesture of unmasking, to take on such a task disingenuously. All the same, his tendency to "circle around the tacky," his attraction to "middlebrow, passing cultural fads," and to what Bruno Schultz, a brilliant interpreter of popular culture, called "culture's trash heap"—all show that he was deeply sensitive to one of the most important aspects of contemporary culture: urban, democratic, mass cultural production.

Gombrowicz was right to name cinema as secret fantasies' most prominent producer, inspiration, and organizer. In an exciting book titled *Film jest snem* [Film is a dream], Polish film critic Konrad Eberhardt expands on Gombrowicz's thesis by showing how much the logic of film narration imitates the logic of a dream. If cinema has rightly always been described as a "dream factory," that is not merely because its forms imitate nighttime dream-work, but also because they create and recreate *day*dreams. These latter phantasms and fantasies do resemble nighttime dreams. But, by definition, they take place in a state of at least partial consciousness and waking. This is the essential condition of film as well.

One could not imagine cinema without Romanticism. [. . .] The Romantics could not have anticipated cinema as a technology, of course. But their movement foreshadowed this medium and, along with twentieth-century surrealism, prepared us to accept cinema and its heroes as an integral part of reality. Surrealism supplemented Romanticism by incorporating Freudian theory into an enchantment with popular culture on all levels. The "marvelous" nature of twentieth-century urban reality, celebrated by the surrealists, is easily found in their poetic and painterly landscapes and their films. One of the great surrealist auteurs, Luis Buñuel, made a film called *The Phantom of Liberty* (1974). This title recapitulates the role phantoms play in Buñuel's work: It is woven out of fantasies that harmoniously integrate elements of low and high art.

The essay by Freud with which I began these reflections suggests that we place value in other people's fantasies for aesthetic reasons. Freud believes that, if the average daydreamer were to share his fantasies with us, the revelation would not cause us any pleasure; indeed, we would be repulsed by or at best indifferent to him. The writer who successfully incorporates phantasms into his work imbues them with aesthetic pleasure; that allows us to enjoy his fantasies "without guilt or shame." Freud is not implying that writerly phantasms are fundamentally different in content from our everyday, commonplace ones. But he does suggest that the form in which they are articulated, and their aesthetic qualities, determine their reception: "The essential *ars poetica* lies in the technique of overcoming the feeling of repulsion in us which is undoubtedly connected with the barriers that rise between each single ego and the others."[6]

Freud touches on an important issue: It takes an artist to temper the radical selfishness of daydreams and give them an aesthetically satisfying shape. But is that always the case? His aesthetics has come under critique for its wholehearted embrace of the "pleasure principle." Cinema is a realm in which these absolute statements can be called into question. Films frequently transpose perfectly "commonplace" phantasms onto the screen, with hardly any aesthetic tampering. These phantasms do not tend to repulse us. Moreover, by violating our visual sensibilities through an "aesthetic of shock," and by creating intensely cruel phantasms, films inspire mixed feelings in which—to say the least—pleasure is not always dominant. To continue these reflections, let me consider melodrama and the Gothic as literary and cinematic genres.

Melodrama's Psyche and Eros

The Romantic popular novel and the cinematic aesthetic that emerges from it center around a particular character type. Freud, who often takes popular novels as objects of his psychoanalytic research, draws attention to one dominant and recurrent quality that shapes and effectively defines these novels' structure, alongside their characteristic plot and narrative techniques. This central quality, the source of their narrative momentum, is a particular kind of *hero*. The author protects this hero with especial care and always saves him from even the worst difficulties. The author's ego embeds within this character her own imagined and most desired qualities. The most important of these qualities is *untouchability*. "Through this revealing characteristic of invulnerability," writes Freud, "we can immediately recognize His Majesty the Ego, the hero alike of every day-dream and of every story." Film and the popular novel repeat this stereotype of the immortal hero countless times in melodrama, fantasy, and the picaresque. "It is the true heroic feeling, which one of our best writers has expressed in an inimitable phrase: 'Nothing can happen to *me*!'"[7]

Let us consider Fantômas from this perspective. Through a spark of creative brilliance, his name captures both his phantom-like and his phantasm-like qualities. Today, it is difficult to describe the cultural myths surrounding Paris without reference to him—or, indeed, to omit mentioning him when describing the contemporary cultural imagination. Like other surrealists, this character's creator Robert Desnos felt a deep attachment to the mythical image of Paris constructed in the novels of Honoré de Balzac and in that model popular novel, Eugène Sue's *Mysteries of Paris.* He describes these novels as sparking strange memories from his childhood and youth. The paperback covers of the *Fantômas* series, of which there appeared thirty-two before World War II arrested their publication, made a powerful impression on the reader's imagination. [. . .]

The marvelousness of the twentieth century, cherished by the surrealists, became embodied in the myth of the great city. This myth could not do without the centuries-old trope of the omnipotent hero. This hero's outward characteristics had changed, but his essence—as the embodiment of daydreams about untouchability—remained the same. "The man in dark glasses," the phantom-like "emperor of horror, master of preposterous transformations," can never be captured, arrested, or even recognized. His untouchability rises to mythic levels: "A man whom bullets never hit, against whom blades are blunted, a man who swallows poison the way others do milk."[8] Stories and films about Fantômas are all based on this single, unalterable, and unquestionable premise of his immortality.

Freud's thinking explains the popularity of this character type. Throughout popular culture, he embodies the fantasy of immortality; identifying with him, the reader's or the viewer's ego can freely daydream about its own untouchability. For cinema, this is a winning premise. [. . .]

This character type possesses a second phantasmatic quality that concerns his *provenance.* Here, we must recall Freud once more: His essay names a certain type of daydream, the *Familienroman* or family novel, in which children above all (but also some adults) like to indulge. This daydream transmogrifies familial relations by endowing them with an extraordinary status and social dignity, raising the family to a station wholly incommensurate with reality. The daydreamer fantasizes that they are a foundling whose "true" parents are of royal descent, people of the highest standing. One can easily recognize in this fantasy the contours of a certain kind of novel about the development and lineage of the self. [. . .] Indeed, such familial daydreams inform not only our self-created "spontaneous novels" but also "artistic novels." The same is true of film. The "foundling" narrative is an entire narrative genre (think of Henry Fielding's *Tom Jones*). Consider also the Czech filmmaker's Jaromil Jireš's *Valerie and Her Week of Wonders* (1970), a gallery of a child's phantasms about her provenance. In this film, personal daydreams mingle with the conventions and schemata of melodrama and the Gothic. The protagonist imagines herself to be the daughter of a cardinal. She sees his hand, clad in a red glove, reaching out to her from a covered, moving carriage; she runs and kisses it with passion and piety.

Bruno Schulz offers a similar theory of creativity. He sees it above all as the process of "mythologizing reality." He gives great weight to childhood fantasies on family themes, stating repeatedly that "the dark land of early childhood fantasies" constitutes "the cradle of mythical thinking." "Personal, private mythology," as he calls it, gives meaning to the story of one's life. "This shadowy ambiance, filled with presentiment, which condenses around each family story and illuminates it through myth with the force of lightning"—as if this story contained the final mystery of one's blood and bloodline—gives the poet access to the other side of reality, an alternative, deeper version of history. Schulz's *Street of Crocodiles* (1934) and *Sanatorium under the Sign of the Hourglass* (1937) both remain faithful to this artistic credo.

To use Freud's terms, one could describe Schulz's fiction as offering two parallel *Familienromane,* on two distinct planes. On the one hand, we have the story of the Father who undergoes fantastical demonic metamorphoses and moves into a new dimension, into Schulz's "deeper version of history." On the other hand, we have the story of the Son, entangled in the family mythology of the Habsburg monarchy, with its legend of the "benevolent ruler" Franz Josef and the betrayed younger brother Maximilian who is left to die. This myth is supplemented by the typical childish phantasmagoria of a mysterious girl, Bianka, who is "a kidnapped and changed princess." In his film adaptation of Schulz's novel, Wojciech Has remains faithful to both of Schulz's *Familienromane.* His character returns to the mythologies of his childhood because he cannot shape his personality without recourse to some hidden "mysteries of blood and bloodline."

The heroes of popular novels and mainstream films frequently share in the two qualities I have been discussing: untouchability and mysterious origins. The Freudian phantasms of ambition fulfillment they embody are typically erotic in nature. The hero or heroine wants, and is able to, love and be loved. Their whole human existence hinges on this double capacity. We are now entering the sphere of melodrama, which conjoins love with obstacles, intrigues, rogue agents, misery, and sometimes even the death of one of the lovers. Through these motifs, melodrama touches on the problem of evil from a much different perspective and through very different means than does the Gothic narrative.

The history of melodrama as a theatrical genre reveals its most important and persistent qualities and themes. The archive of theatrical melodramas is enormous: Take, for example, the playwright Gilbert de Pixérécourt, who rose to fame in France during the First Empire and the Restoration, and whom theatergoers described as the "Shakespeare of the boulevards." Pixérécourt wrote ninety-four plays, which were performed thirty thousand times during his life. The typology of melodramatic personalities and behaviors is forged in the copious early archive to which his works belong. Among these types emerge the noble but unhappy father; the innocent, beautiful, wronged daughter; the swindling thief who persecutes them; and the knightlike, handsome youth who unmasks the swindler and marries the angelic daughter. In the process, melodrama also develops a peculiar concept of evil.

The types and concepts melodrama creates seep into virtually all of nineteenth-century Western literature. Cinema absorbs them from its very incipience. [. . .] In 1926, Russian formalist Boris Tomashevsky argued that "the social role once played by [the melodramatic novel] bears comparison to the social role currently occupied by cinema, with which [the melodramatic novel] has much in common." While praising this development, Tomashevsky opposed the practice of adapting theatrical melodramas for the screen: Cinema requires its own narratives. In these decades, cinema, as well as the advertisement, definitively enter mass culture. [. . .]

Historians of literature, culture, and especially theater associate the emergence and spread of melodrama with the formation of a new kind of public. Pixérécourt used to say, "I write for those who cannot read." His style therefore had to differ from the styles of those who came before him. "Popular tragedy," as melodrama was initially called, formed the foundation of "the people's theater." As early as at the end of the eighteenth century, the leaders of the French Revolution developed their cultural politics with an awareness of the power melodrama could wield. [. . .] A strong contrast emerged between "imagined" and "real" sufferings. The former derive from classical myths that were, by this point, frequently unknown to modern audiences. The latter come from life itself. One does not need erudition and an education to understand them: only a sensitive heart and an unperverted, ingenuous sensibility.

Melodrama's revolutionary allegiances made it popular among the Romantics. As Musset famously put it, "Vive le melodrame où Margot a pleuré!" [Long live the melodrama that made Margot cry!]. Scholars often describe French Romantic tragedy, particularly the works of Victor Hugo, as directly inspired by melodrama. The Romantics ennobled this popular literary genre, and their contemporaries felt strongly the tie between melodrama and tragedy. One such contemporary said that melodrama awaits its genius, whose task will be to murder tragedy (classical tragedy, that is). Hugo turned out to be that genius. Tomashevsky, a great expert on the transformation of melodrama into Romantic tragedy, highlights their common stylistic strategies and their shared pursuit of so-called strong rhetorical effects. Melodrama was a tragedy for the common people; the Romantics transformed it into a democratic literary genre addressed to all social classes. This sequence of metamorphoses—from tragedy to melodrama and from melodrama to Romantic tragedy—would suggest that many of the convictions about human fate expressed in tragedy passed over into melodrama. That is correct; but in the process, these convictions changed shape. They were no longer embodied in myth, but in the matter of everyday reality; furthermore, melodrama's mass circulation and reproduction turned tragedy's mimetic strategies into stereotypes.

This sequence of events soon made it necessary for writers to emphasize that the stories told by melodrama were based on "real" events. *The Lady of the Camellias* (1848) by Alexandre Dumas *fils*, which eventually became a play, reiterates and stresses that its narrative is not just moving but—above all—*true*. On the novel's last pages, the author reaffirms its veracity as follows: "I returned to Paris, where I wrote this story just as it was told to me. It has only one merit, though this may yet be challenged: that it is true." The story has to be true, even if it is also clearly nonnormative, which Dumas accentuates as well: "The story of Marguerite is an exception, I repeat; had it been a general case, it would not have been worth the trouble of writing down."[9] Melodrama absorbs the life of its contemporaneous society, reshaping it to conform to its generic conventions. Most stage melodramas were adapted from novels, whose relative freedom of sociological commentary and complex, rapidly developing plots were irresistible to theater.

We have gathered several defining features of melodrama: it must be based on a story that is *moving, true,* and *exceptional.* The three features complement one another. Together, they have a powerful effect on melodrama's audiences. The exceptionality of a melodramatic narrative is counterbalanced by its veracity; otherwise, the narrative could be dismissed as "a beautiful illusion." Such an illusion would arouse the audience's suspicion and prevent their identification with the narrative, which is a basic requirement of melodramatic art. Only truth—stories that are both true and exceptional, and could potentially happen to anyone, even if just in daydreams (here a phantasmatic community can form)—can move one to tears.

Classic melodramas *(un bon mélo)* tended to have happy endings. "They were invented to condemn thieves and glorify virtue" is how the Polish *Słownik teatralny* [Theatrical dictionary] of 1824 puts it. To punish crime and save the innocent was necessary if melodramas were to "educate the masses"—as they were, at first, conventionally supposed to do. But this convention changed quickly with the appearance of the melodramatic "unhappy ending," which disrupted the genre's putative contributions to maintaining the social order and the moral norms that guard it.

So, what basic story does melodrama tell in its many variations and forms? *The Lady of the Camellias* summarizes it well: It is the tale of a young woman who "experienced in her life a profound love, . . . she suffered for it, and died of it."[10] This schema can shift somewhat, but its basic principle remains unchanged. [. . .] Love, suffering, and death: those are the recurrent denominators of melodramatic narrative structure in film as well as novels. Let us consider each of them in turn.

The phantasmatic notion of love that grounds melodrama is often described as "romantic love." [. . .] "Romantic love" prescribes a clear role to the woman: She should be sweet, tender, transcendent, and full of devotion, so as to represent the "higher values" that govern the life of a man. Of course—as in Marlene Dietrich melodramas—this female protagonist can initially seem demonic, but soon her true nature comes out: She reveals herself to be capable of genuine, spontaneous, disinterested, passionate love. This inversion is essential; in it lies the otherwise surprising success of *The Lady of the Camellias.* In the melodramatic fusion of the pure "virgin" and the erotically awakened and heightened "vamp," Morin sees a "revolution in the domain of femininity." After centuries of their separation, Psyche and Eros, the soul and eroticism, love and sex, are reunited with each other.

Melodrama asserts the limitless, incomparable power of feeling. "Romantic love" cannot be withstood; it is the greatest force that governs human beings. Sometimes, the gods allow this love to be constructive; otherwise, its passions leave broken, miserable humans in their wake. In both cases, the experience of romantic love constitutes the greatest human value. Melodrama's Eros is not extreme; it reveals itself in pious adoration and exultation, in love rituals built out of small details, fetishes, behaviors, looks, touches, words, and thoughts. Germaine Greer provides an amazing analysis of the role that "the ball" and "the first kiss" play in the mythology of romantic love. They reveal the marvelousness of affective reality: At any given moment, our lives might be invaded by something extraordinary, unforgettable, and transcendent. Love is the most wonderful adventure a person can embark on (this line of thought occurs more often in women's than in men's phantasmagorias). This myth is well instantiated in Jerzy Antczak's 1975 film adaptation of Maria Dąbrowska's novel *Noce i dnie* [The nights and the days, 1931–34], whose unhappily married protagonist, Barbara, reminisces about a phantasmatic version of her would-be lover Józef Toliboski. An intoxicating waltz plays in the background as an impeccably dressed Toliboski bears a bouquet of water lilies toward her. Clad in a white suit and tie, he is a beautiful and salvific angel.

"Romantic love" is a complete, self-sufficient myth. Everyone ought not only to dream of attaining it, but also to believe that its attainment could frame, create, and fill their entire life. *Nothing else would be necessary,* melodrama aims to persuade us. Its new "religion of love" reintegrates fragmented social groups. It supposedly also eliminates "mad love," despite this concept's prior centrality to Romantic, norm-breaking passions. The genre thus trims individualism, through love, to fit the needs of social normativity.

But melodrama would not be tragedy's cousin if it did away entirely with the sphere of suffering and death. Although some melodramas are not wrongly called "fairy tales for adults," wholly removing death and suffering from the genre's sphere would also put it in too obvious contradiction with the lives of its audiences. A truly ambitious melodrama does not hesitate to confront the problem of historical, social, existential evil. Class inequality between lovers, their separation by war, incurable disease—all become the matter of melodrama. But the theme alone does not suffice to give melodrama its expressive force. Its specific, emotionally driven mode of narration intensifies the narrative's emotional content and marginalizes any of its intellectual motivations. Melodrama's commitment to a consistently intense emotional tone flattens its political and existential complications. A uniformly sultry affective atmosphere schematizes, reduces, and ultimately simplifies the realities melodrama represents.

Reshaped into melodramatic form, the mysteries of everyday life reveal themselves. This revelation forms the "philosophical" warp of melodrama as a genre, as it aims to "sell us hope." By representing "absolute" and "total" love as marvelous even in our contemporary world devoid of transcendence, melodrama announces its conviction that love is stronger than death. Melodrama's phantasms of love thereby fold back into the Freudian phantasm of immortality.

Demons, Vampires, Monsters

The surrealist *Lexique succinct de l'érotisme* [Succinct dictionary of the erotic] provides an entry for Count Zaroff, the hero of Ernest Schoedsack's *The Most Dangerous Game* (1932). The lone inhabitant of a deserted island, Zaroff causes shipwrecks in his vicinity in order to hunt human beings, the only pastime that interests him. The entry cites a graphic excerpt from the film's dialogue: "One does not know love's true ecstasy until one has killed."[11] This combination of "love" and "death" (as a result of murder and crime), eroticism and aggression, sexuality, cruelty, and evil, forms a semantic and symbolic nexus for Gothic novels and films. Lewis's early novel *The Monk* (1796) already combines love with crime to reveal the demonic nature of the libido. Its author leans into the old topos that "woman is the Devil" and illustrates this conviction through episodes in which the Devil dons the form of a woman, the more effectively to tempt humans and lead them to their irreversible downfall. . . .

Christianity's fearful insistence that eroticism constitutes a sin gave rise to a great variety of imagined demons. These new, Christian demons joined forces with ones that had already been born of the union of the Greco-Roman concepts of Eros and Thanatos. Fused together, these imaginaries transform desire—which only increases through prohibition and suppression—into a haunting or demonic possession. It comes on us out of nowhere and forcibly takes over. It inspires the self to mad possessiveness and equally powerful, inward-turning hatred of this possessiveness; the combination is ruthlessly destructive. Depictions of love as vampiric unveil the violently erotic bond between the victim and her torturer, the vampire and his prey, who herself becomes a vampire in the process. Lewis's monk Ambrose is drained and tortured by desire; the first character of his kind in European literature, his intensity is matched and visually augmented in erotic thrillers and horror films. These films take up the Gothic novel's typical protagonist: sullen, aggressive, tyrannical, passionate, a "great criminal," immoral, endowed with an ambiguous beauty that bespeaks his evil nature, insane or split in his consciousness. At times—in a peak of phantasmatic creation—this character becomes a demiurge, evil incarnate. One does not encounter such people "in real life"; they are the figments of our imaginations. They make us feel moved and confused by our discovered inner darkness and the monsters that lie within it.

Contemporary cinema sides with this kind of hero much more decisively than Lewis's novel does. This shift in attitude follows the influence of Sade, Lautréamont, Baudelaire, and the surrealists. *The Monk* oscillates between feeling for Ambrose and condemning him; the works of the later writers listed here lose any such ambivalence. Their clarity of mind constructs apologia for desire against social norms and prohibitions, religion and morality, any and all constraints on freedom and passion.

In his film adaptation of *The Monk,* Luis Buñuel takes up Lewis's meandering, antisocial depictions of desire and heightens the devilish nature of the crimes Ambrose commits. He also significantly changes the novel's ending. The original Ambrose is carried away by the Devil, to whom he sold his soul, and dies in terrible pain on the rocks of Sierra Morena. Buñuel's adaptation ostentatiously carries us forward from the eighteenth century into the present—to have us recognize Ambrose's face in that of the pope blessing the populace assembled in Saint Peter's Square. The blasphemous furor of this ending, so typical for Buñuel, reveals the main object of his critique: Underneath the hypocritical mask of church propriety, he highlights an extreme, if intensely repressed, erotic force.

Gothic novels and horror films often offend religious morality and exceed the norms of mainstream popular culture. Melodrama does not pose similar issues. Why? The answer is not hard to find. Melodrama confines itself to the family circle, whose social value it seeks to reinforce; for this reason, its narratives foreclose the possibility of a "mad" love that could threaten the social order. The ending of Helena Mniszek's *Trędowata* [The leper, 1936] provides a typical example of this tendency. When Stefcia Rudecka finally dies, crushed because she has been rejected by the family of her rich, aristocratic fiancé, he and his milieu effortlessly absorb her. "You will remain among us forever," her fiancé exclaims after her death. He hangs her likeness in the gallery of his ancestors' portraits. Its presence amid the ancestors of the twelfth owner of Głębowicze causes consternation; all the same, lifted by her lover's passion, Stefcia posthumously assumes her rightful place. The social conflict is reconciled, even if belatedly; melodrama's "religion of love" furthers ideals of class reconciliation and social integration.

Horror is a different matter. Here, even if "mad love" is not in the picture, "love as a crime" usually is: The extremity of demonic passion takes love to its other extreme. Amid the atmosphere created by horror, Eros becomes deeply alien to everyday reality. Melodrama closes itself off from everyday reality, too, by making love seem miraculous. Still, it carries the possibility—indeed, the imperative—to take love back into the everyday. Melodrama's miraculousness rubs off on the quotidian. Indeed, this might be melodrama's highest aesthetic goal: to aestheticize and elevate daily life. That's not the case with horror, which aims to create a passionate world that exceeds so-called everyday reality, and from which it is not easy to retrace one's steps. It's a long way from a crime of passion back to the white picket fence. From this disparity derives the great difficulty of maintaining a balanced critical attitude to horror's extreme sexual and nonsexual thrills. The range of responses the genre incites is very wide—from arguments that its erotics poses a threat to society's mental well-being, inciting promiscuous or even criminal behavior, to literary critic Walerian Borowczyk's belief that it exorcises pent-up passions.

Horror's *strangeness*—which is also its central aesthetic aim—is dangerous. It threatens to tear apart previously established, sanctioned, and codified norms of reality, even while setting up its own "canon of horror aesthetics." Given these dangers, one might expect that popular culture would decisively embrace melodrama over horror, since the former more adequately fulfills its aims of appeasing and blurring social tensions. Yet that is not at all the case: Waves of popular fascination with horror and melodrama continue to follow on or parallel each other. Scholars of cinema and sociologists occasionally justify these shifting popular predilections through locally emergent historical conditions. For example, researchers claim that horror films became more popular in Germany during periods of high inflation, and in the United States during the Great Depression. Treating cinema as a faithful mirror of social moods, they argue that it registers the rise of widespread unsettledness and danger, as well as people's inability to rationalize these feelings or explain them causally. Imaginary cinematic monsters, vampires, and other existentially unstable beings are, on this interpretation, embodiments of a reality that feels monstrous because it is unpredictable, dangerous, and unclear.

These scholars have a point, but the popular appeal of horror cannot be wholly reduced to contextual explanations. Popular culture, especially cinema, draws at least as much on the world of phantasms as on the real world. Were the film industry to only produce and sell melodramatic dreams, it would cut itself off from an important alternative source of human phantasms: those that are not "prosocial" but "antisocial." In this antisocial sphere of our dreamworlds, which finds its apex in dreams of absolute freedom—freedom from humanity itself—and which necessarily touches borders with criminality, horror finds its deepest and truest ground. Popular culture dips into horror's repository of myths and phantoms carefully, so as not to set fire to its proverbial powder keg of libidinal drives. Cultural depictions of absolute, antisocial freedom therefore tend to culminate in this freedom's taming after a series of adventures. But at the end of the day, the fundamental difference between melodrama and horror lies in their different understandings of evil itself.

Edgar Morin, one of our finest theoreticians of mass culture, uses the terms *projection* and *identification* to differentiate between the perspectives and attitudes that horror and melodrama respectively offer to their viewers. . . . Transposing this discourse of projection and identification into a different conceptual framework, we could say that horror expresses our sadistic phantasms, whereas melodrama expresses masochistic ones. In Europe, this binary division of our emotional and erotic spheres goes back to early modern literature, with its distinction between masochistic sentimentalism and sadistic Gothic literature. Of course, from the very beginning, these themes were never completely separable from each other; they readily coexist together, as they already do in *The Monk.*

The permeability of these binaries in *The Monk* points to a larger principle. The feminine and the masculine, masochism and sadism, everydayness and extremity: the affective spheres of horror and melodrama are not independent of each other. One finds another powerful affirmation of their inseparability in *The Lady of the Camellias,* a masterpiece of melodrama, in which, among the generally highly typical melodramatic episodes, plot patterns, and stylistic choices, there lurks a narrative motif taken straight out of the darkest and most terrifying horror genre: the virginal corpse. Armand Duval needs to behold his beloved's corpse before he can believe she is no longer alive. In a disturbing effort at self-therapy, he thinks that disgust at her decomposing body will assuage the suffering her passing has caused him. And so, a few weeks after her death, he obtains permission to reopen her coffin. "Her eyes were nothing more than two holes, her lips had disappeared, and her white teeth were crowded one against the other. Her long, dry black hair was stuck to her temples, veiling somewhat the green cavities of her cheeks, and yet I could recognize in this visage the white, pink, and joyful face I had so often seen."[12] Thus does melodrama go against its fear of death, time and again.

Morin's distinction between melodrama and horror does hold to the extent that the latter's themes diverge extremely from everyday life. The reader or the audience member is supposed to feel their opposition to the quotidian with particular force. This aesthetic effect stems from a series of stylistic choices that we will describe at some length. But the aesthetics itself is grounded, as I mention above, in a distinct and recognizable concept of evil. In melodrama, evil (like illness, war, or death) is seen as a necessary part of human life, and the genre does not shy away from depicting evil's consequences; however, it also asserts that love holds the power to eradicate evil—and most melodramatic plots inevitably tend toward such an eradication. Not so in horror: Evil comes from outside the human, seeming demonic because the way it possesses its agent or victim is sudden and unpredictable. Evil's power cannot be pleaded with, tamed, or overcome, nor can one become independent of it by patiently succumbing to the suffering it causes (the latter is a frequent melodramatic resolution, since love endows its characters with immortality). Horror depicts evil as active, indivisible, immune to entreaty. . . .

The familiarity of melodrama and the strangeness of horror find direct expression in their preferred color palettes: pink for the former, red and black for the latter. These are not random choices: Wallis's well-known classification describes the former as soft and the latter as sharp colors. The kingdom of melodrama is ruled by "soft" aesthetic values (even if they are occasionally disturbed by aesthetic effects derived from horror); pink, often paired with sky blue, has a way of blurring the contours of reality altogether, suspending us in a uniform, temperate emotional mist (a *mist,* mind you, by no means a *fog*). Horror, by contrast, drowns in "sharp" aesthetic values: its reality is "red," harsh, piercing, distinctive, bulbous, uncomfortable. Violent passions create tensions that do not dissipate even after death. Caught in their thrall, the victim transforms into a vampire. Like melodrama, horror here touches borders with the older genre of tragedy, except one is hard-pressed to find in it any catharsis or release. In this sense, horror exists beyond the "pleasure principle," despite Freud's insistence that pleasure should constitute the aesthetic principle of all artistically created fantasies, if not all our unconscious ones. [. . .]

When asked "Do you believe in ghosts?" the eighteenth-century French socialite Madame du Deffand responded, "No. But I do fear them." This response sums up our modern ambivalence toward the aesthetics of horror. We should understand horror's aim to "scare the audience" within this context. This aim would not make horror films particularly popular, were there not countless people who *want* to be scared by ghosts they do not believe in. There are many ways of explaining this phenomenon. Within the framework I've been setting up in this essay, let us focus on viewers' apparent desire to commune with an "alien" reality.

We all commune with this alien reality, of course, because we all carry it inside ourselves. As it gives rise to dreams and daydreams, it accustoms us to living in two dimensions at once. Gothic literature's connection with dreams is part of what makes it intuitively "cinematic." Film is particularly well suited to depicting ghosts, phantoms, doubles, associations, visions, and nightmares: emanations of the other reality hidden within us and our means for accessing it. In his essay titled "Paris, a Modern Myth," Roger Caillois shows how the duality of our inner life becomes transposed onto the great city, which since

Romanticism bifurcates onto the Real and the Unreal Metropolis. The Unreal Paris is naturally much more capacious than the Real one.

If phantasies and phantasms exist, reality itself might be multiple: Speculative and fantasy fiction flow from this hypothesis. In this sense, Romanticism paved the way for cinema, insofar as fantasy and horror both lie at its aesthetic foundation. In this period, it became legitimate to wonder whether phantasms come from alternate realities or cracks within our own reality. The smooth, coherent linearity of classicism had broken down; in its place appeared a nonuniform, tangled, multidimensional world that eventually also lent philosophical ground to science fiction. Within these "crevices of time," so important to writers such as Bruno Schulz and Jorge Luis Borges, there flourished a genre of fantasy related to memory, devoted to realities that no longer exist or never really existed. Even if a demon or ghoul dies at the end of a horror film or novel, horror reinforces in its audience the conviction that the line between "real" reality and "demonic" reality is very easy to move, cross, destabilize. . . .

All of cinema's well-developed techniques for building suspense effectively go back to this same principle: They disrupt the simplified image of the world that modern technologies proffer. Nicolas Roeg's *Don't Look Now* (1973) constitutes an interesting example of this trend. All that is real undergoes a "shift" in the course of the film, one that is delicate but sufficiently palpable to make its viewer feel confused about where its reality begins and ends. An unreal, ghostly Venice plays a crucial role in establishing this effect: The city itself is the film's mysterious, impenetrable protagonist. Not even Luchino Visconti's *Death in Venice* (1971), with its depictions of a citywide plague, accomplished so powerful an effect.

The two foundational myths of horror—Frankenstein's monster (a.k.a. Golem) and Dracula (a.k.a. Nosferatu)—both have their origins in Romantic literature; they thus confirm that not only the aesthetics of shock and fear but also its main narrative storylines stem from this period. [. . .] Both myths derive from ancient folklore and concern the afterlives of the dead. Dracula, famously rendered in 1897 by Bram Stoker, is the Transylvanian prince of darkness. The blood of countless victims feeds his homeland and lends him an unaccustomed longevity. Frankenstein's monster, made from bits of corpses, reveals the terrifying condition of the "living dead."

Countless sociological and psychological interpretations of these two myths mine them for political and social content. The seductive, magnetic quality of the vampire brings to mind the dangers of fascism and reckless scientific experimentation; Frankenstein further suggests that science could bring into being a monster that humanity would not know how to get rid of. And yet, some qualities of both these myths cannot be reduced to such common political and social denominators. That irreducible part makes them "mythical"—and endlessly interesting. Frankenstein and Dracula take us back to the foundational principles of love and death. At its core, the mythology of the vampire is erotic; it represents love as a crime, an inevitable harbinger and cause of death. Frankenstein symbolizes the simultaneously repulsive and seductive aspects of death. In his aliveness, which transgresses our culture's fundamental taboos, we can recognize our own "beloved" miraculously raised from the dead. The effect of his resurrection is fear and horror intermingled with love, a mingling that resembles the rituals through which we interact with the dead every year on All Saints' Day.

The recent decade has seen a significant shift in how these myths are represented. Consider Roman Polanski's *Fearless Vampire Killers* (1967). Polanski insisted that this film is not a parody of vampire films, but a *comedy* about vampires. . . . The professor who appears to defeat vampires in Polanski's film accomplishes the exact opposite: He spreads their evil across the planet. In the same vein, let us consider Claude Klotz's *A Vampire in Paris* (1974) and Mel Brooks's *Young Frankenstein* (1974). Klotz's novel offers a wonderful parody of the plot and style of Bram Stoker's *Dracula*. Its protagonist, Dracula's son Ferdinand, is found living in 1970s Paris, where he works as a night guard (an appropriate profession for a vampire). Ubiquitous ads for a film titled *Dracula's Lover* fill him with distaste. *Young Frankenstein,* which many critics have described as the best American comedy in recent years, follows the nephew of Dr. Frankenstein himself. In a railway station in Pennsylvania [Janion seems to be referring to Penn Station in New York City], this nephew experiences a vision of *Transylvania*—and soon finds himself transported into James Whale's famous 1931 film, down to the props themselves.

This comic, parodic return to the two central myths of horror tells us much about the current state of the genre. Parodies often flourish when a genre has to fend off threats of degradation or extinction. Should we conclude that horror has outlived its relevance and now awaits a swift demise? Not so: The counterexample of the eighteenth-century preoccupation with the mock-epic would suggest a different interpretation. Under the guise of the mock-epic, the epic was able to persist into, and to transform itself for, modern times: The mock-epic provided a necessary transition point into the romantic epic, the ironic/digressive long poem, and eventually also the essayistic, philosophical novel as written by Thomas Mann and Robert Musil. Horror seems to be undergoing the same transformation: With the emergence of parodic horror films, a new, self-conscious horror genre is in the making, and film as a medium might be redefining itself through it. For the time being, these parodies bring horror back into the fold of the pleasure principle.

Notes

1. Sigmund Freud, "Creative Writers and Day-Dreaming" (1908), in *The Standard Edition of the Psychological Works of Sigmund Freud,* ed. and trans. James Strachey (London: Hogarth Press, 1981), 9:420.
2. Freud, "Creative Writers and Day-Dreaming," 421.
3. Freud, "Creative Writers and Day-Dreaming," 422.
4. Freud, "Creative Writers and Day-Dreaming," 425.
5. Alexandre Dumas *fils, The Lady of the Camellias,* trans. Liesl Schillinger (New York: Penguin Random House, 2013), 45–46.
6. Freud, "Creative Writers and Day-Dreaming," 428.
7. Freud, "Creative Writers and Day-Dreaming," 425–26.
8. Roger Caillois, "Paris, a Modern Myth," in *The Edge of Surrealism,* ed. Claudine Frank, trans. Claudine Frank and Camille Nash (Durham, N.C.: Duke University Press, 2003), 180. [Here and immediately above, Caillois is citing Pierre Véry. —Trans.]
9. Dumas, *Lady of the Camellias,* 206.
10. Dumas, *Lady of the Camellias,* 206.
11. Vincent Gille, ed., *Si vous aimez l'amour . . . : Anthologie amoreuse du surréalisme, suivie du Lexique succinct de l'érotisme* (Paris: Syllepse, 2001), 355.
12. Dumas, *Lady of the Camellias,* 40.

PART IV
The Authority of the Other

CHAPTER 9

Adam Mickiewicz's Jewish Legion

Life Is Elsewhere

In autumn 1855, amid the Crimean War, Adam Mickiewicz traveled eastward from Paris to help create a Polish military unit, which was to fight against Russia on the side of Ottoman Turkey, France, and England. The Polish soldiers "would not be mercenaries, but allies."[1] The poet was accompanied by his secretary, Armand Lévy, "an Israelite devoted to Mickiewicz in body and soul."[2] At the time, Polish émigrés saw the war in Crimea as decisive for their independence movement: "There, by the strait of Bosporus, the fate of Poland was being decided."[3] The Hungarian uprising of 1848–49 during the Springtime of Nations had been squashed by Russia on the orders of Tsar Nicholas I, whom the Poles called the "gendarme of Europe." Despite that disappointment, their hopes for military conflict between Russia and Western Europe, possibly also involving Turkey—a conflict that would crucially weaken Russia—had not faded. Polish (and other) émigrés fomented complicated diplomatic intrigues and extortion efforts to increase tensions between Russia and Western Europe and to involve Turkey in more or less realistic anti-Russian coalitions. The details of their project of "a joint national front, supported by Turkey, fighting against Austria and Russia," because the latter were oppressors of nations striving for independence, frequently changed—but their ideas remained constant. Thus, when the Crimean War began, many émigrés argued that, instead of inciting insurrections within Poland's former territories, independence fighters should constitute a legion in Turkey and combat Russia in the Near East.[4]

After the death of his wife, Mickiewicz often stressed in conversations that "his purpose lies in the East."[5] By that point, he had renounced poetry as ineffective, if beautiful, rhetoric; he had also renounced diplomacy as an art of appearances and covert wheeling and dealing. Drawing on the authority he still held as a poet, he argued that writers like him needed to turn their "inspired songs" into action.[6] Especially after 1848, action was all he cared about; the listless, stuffy atmosphere of Paris annoyed and pained him. Janusz Ruszkowski, who wrote a book about Mickiewicz's millenarian utopianism, highlights that already in 1848, during a visit to Rome, the poet sought to set up a Polish legion that would fight for his nation's independence, having become disillusioned by the passive philosophy preached by his former mentor Andrzej Towiański. To support this thesis, Ruszkowski cites the following entry from the diaries of Juliusz Falkowski, Mickiewicz's younger contemporary and acquaintance: "Mickiewicz wanted to act, to imitate the old military church orders—and not just sit around as Towiański advised him to do. He would get into arguments with Towiański and then remorsefully apologize. When war broke out in Italy, he went there to organize a Polish army unit; he and Towiański argued about it, and Mickiewicz finally decided to stop listening to him."[7] The break between the two men was mostly personal in nature; in many other ways, Mickiewicz remained committed to Towiański's mystical doctrines.

After the failure of the insurrections of 1848, Mickiewicz did not give up his hopes for liberating Poland. But now, the centers of activity he sought out to escape his Parisian stasis were farther east. The Orient fascinated many Romantics, but Mickiewicz's fascination with it deviated from the period's norm. He had begun to dream about the East as a vector for the Polish independence movement many years prior; after 1848, these dreams became focused on military action. In a diary entry dated August 2, 1851, Józef Bohdan Zaleski records an exchange he and Adam had over a beer. The conversation circled around the possibility of restoring Poland to sovereignty, "given that the peasants are being incited to bloody revolt [by the Russians], and the nobles and the aristocracy remain soulless." Because of these internal conditions, Poland's salvation had to come from the outside. "We must create a [military] force somewhere in the West or in the East. Józef Bem's actions in Hungary showed an ideal path toward Poland's liberation."[8]

Bem's biography held great symbolic power for Mickiewicz's generation. General Bem was one of the most famous leaders of the Hungarian revolution of 1848–49. When a Russian military intervention overcame his forces, he was interned in Turkey. Bem recognized Turkey as the only power capable of standing up to Russia, perhaps even of defeating it. In 1849, he and a dozen of his officers converted to Islam and enlisted in the Ottoman army. Their conversion, which was required for entering Ottoman military service, met consternation from other Polish soldiers and émigrés, who felt torn between their country's tradition of Catholicism and an irrepressible desire to fight for its independence. General Bem's own explanation of his decision would have appealed to Mickiewicz: "I did not renounce the religion of my forebears because of ambition; but it seemed like the last possible means of fighting for the independence of our two brotherly nations. I sacrificed the form of my religion but did not change my heart, which remains faithful to Him."[9] Bem believed that "a war between Turkey and Russia" had to come about, "in the course of which it would be possible to liberate Poland. Turkey's forces will suffice to crush Russia's power." Unfortunately, Bem died toward the end of 1850. Rumor had it that he had been poisoned by an Austrian secret agent. He was buried with his head turned toward Mecca, but also with a little bag of Polish soil by his side.[10]

Military action in the East remained one of Mickiewicz's main topics of discussion and rumination. As he confessed to Ludwik Zwierkowski, "I have been wondering how I can support the efforts of those who are eager to take action. Sadyk, Zamoyski, Wysocki: Because they want to do something, they are worth more than all the encyclopedists in dressing gowns put together."[11] The men Mickiewicz names here are Sadyk Pasha, formerly general Mikołaj Czajkowski, who became a Turkish military leader after converting to Islam in 1850 and who created an Ottoman Cossack legion; General Władysław Zamoyski, sent to Turkey by Poland's informal émigré "secretary of foreign affairs," Prince Adam J. Czartoryski, who was seeking to create a second Ottoman Cossack legion; and General Józef Wysocki, commander of a Polish legion that fought in Hungary in 1848 whom many saw as the prospective head of the Polish division of the Turkish army. Though these three men were all preparing the ground for a future military victory over Russia (which mattered most to Mickiewicz), their politics were otherwise quite disparate and often opposed to one another. Jadwiga Maurer accurately lays out why Prince Czartoryski paid attention to "that Turkish convert," Sadyk Pasha: The latter was "the only Polish man in the entire world who still commanded armed soldiers."[12] Armand Lévy wished for himself and all present that "we may change the ending of 'Jeszcze Polska'[13] and cry out, 'March, march, Sadyk, from Turkish lands back to Poland.'"[14]

The speeches Mickiewicz gave when he visited Sadyk Pasha / Czajkowski's military encampment in Burgas overflowed with admiration for the soldiers' heroism. Dobrosława Świerczyńska has recovered a previously lost speech that includes the following exclamations: "Glory to you! Glory to you, officers of the first regiment! Only those who carry arms, and who endure suffering like you, are true, righteous Poles! Long live sons like you, as well as these sons' mother [i.e., Poland]!"[15]

We have here one of the classic stereotypes of male homosociality: The male collective's coherence and morality is reinforced and reassured by the dignity of its shared mother.[16] Mickiewicz's praise of the armed, taut, uniformed soldierly collective contrasts against his contempt for "encyclopedists in dressing gowns."

We should not be surprised by the value system Mickiewicz espouses here. He often speaks contemptuously about writers and scholars, and even more severely about lighthearted leisure travelers and salongoers. By contrast, those who are "eager for action"—military action, that is—accrue his boundless praise. This action ought to be directed against the barbarisms committed by Russia. Its initial defeats in the Crimean War "seemed to foreshadow a series of further losses. Émigré communities wished that Moscow may be crushed and erased from maps of Europe." So writes Władysław Mickiewicz, though his biography of his father emphasizes that "the pagan desire for vengeance was alien to him; he wished that Poland's liberation may also morally uplift its enemy."[17]

Mickiewicz's time in the East was not without its annoyances. He went to Turkey on the orders of Prince Czartoryski, to mediate the intensifying conflict between Zamoyski and Czajkowski. The two military leaders' worldviews differed radically—the former was a Catholic monarchist, the latter a democrat converted to Islam—as did their military interests, since Zamoyski was hoping to fund his Cossack regiment through British sources rather than Turkish ones. These tensions continued to deepen. Jerzy W. Borejsza, a historian who wrote a monograph on Armand Lévy, comments that "it pained Mickiewicz to see that the nascent Polish army was already fragmenting. During his time in Burgas, he realized that Czartoryski and the Hotel Lambert milieu had sent him there to cover up for Zamoyski's political maneuvering."[18] Mickiewicz's unbending ethical stance and his conviction that Poland's freedom was a sacred goal made these realizations hard to bear. Some have said that this disappointment drove him to his grave.

Mickiewicz let himself be ruled in all things by the patriotic moral imperative. His decision to travel to the Near East was supposed to set an ethical example. Let young people see that "though my hair is white, I go where my heart and mind urge me to go . . . even though I am the father of six orphaned children."[19] Mickiewicz was not exaggerating; he was a broken man. Many who saw him at work as a librarian at the Parisian Bibliothèque d'Arsenal remarked that he seemed prematurely aged and embittered.

On the ship traveling to Constantinople, Mickiewicz felt refreshed and brought back to health. As if preparing himself for the military life he dreamed of, he slept on the deck wrapped in his overcoat. Armand Lévy wrote down in his diary that "one of our fellow travelers, Sir Seymour, asked me, 'What does an old man like him [Mickiewicz was fifty-seven at the time] want to find in the East?' The question chilled me. Meanwhile, Mr. Adam is doing well; if anything, he seems to be getting younger."[20] As we all know, Mickiewicz's second youth was short-lived. Indisputably, the hardships and scarcities of a military, quasinomadic lifestyle contributed to his impending death.

The poet did not live to see the failure of his great hopes; and great as they were, they did not inspire in him the fervor of 1848. Mickiewicz died on November 26 in Constantinople. Like his life, his death took place elsewhere, neither in Poland nor in France. The great dreams and plans of would-be Polish legionaries perished in this elsewhere as well. Mickiewicz's messianic convictions attached themselves to both Napoleon I and his later incarnation, Napoleon III. Yet the latter did little to promote the Polish cause during the Crimean War. The allies attained their goal and defeated Russia, but their victory did not affect the former Polish territories. At the peace congress held in Paris in 1856, Russian diplomats ensured that Poland was not mentioned at all.

Israel's Primogeniture

Mickiewicz had held a long-standing interest in creating a Polish army. In his note from June 17, 1855, he mentions "the famed Polish legions led by General Dąbrowski," as well as "other cadres and regiments that had joined forces under the Polish flag in earlier periods: in Germany in 1833, in Piedmont in 1834 and again in 1848, in Hungary, in the Great Duchy of Poznań, in Sicily, in the Duchy of Baden, all led by our own generals." Polish culture traditionally envelops words such as *legion* and *league* in a powerful, if sometimes ambivalent, aura. Mickiewicz knows this and deploys them precisely because of their cult-like meanings. He had previously, heroically, tried to create a Polish legion in Italy in 1848. As he reminds Michał Czajkowski in 1855 in Turkey, "I went to Italy on foot, not even on horseback; both then and now, I felt that Poland could be regained, and that even if I were to perish in the process, good people would take care of my orphaned children, knowing that I had died for Poland: to save and to awaken it."[21] This effort to revive, awaken, and reconquer Poland lay at the heart of what he thought of as his calling, as it did for many other Romantics. He shaped the legion he tried to create in Italy "into a circle, following the master's [i.e., Towiański's] principles," hoping that it would be "the seed of a whole regiment."[22]

The mysticism with which Mickiewicz surrounded his Italian legion suggested that the poet intended his "crusaders" to renew Poland spiritually as well. In his "Memorandum for Napoleon III," written sometime between December 1852 and 1855, Mickiewicz underlines, in Ruszkowski's paraphrase, that "by analogy to the Crusades, the aim of the coming war was to save Poland from the hands of nineteenth-century 'infidels.'" Mickiewicz took part in the revolutions of 1848 with similar aims: "He intended for his legionaries to become Poland's elite, and for the legion's own elite to come from his fellow Parisian 'crusaders,' admirers of Towiański's mysticism."[23] Mickiewicz hoped to create a unit as coherent as a military church order. This hope lay at the heart of his idea of the Polish legion. His "crusaders" were to fight their way to a new promised land, a new Jerusalem—Poland, that is. . . .

"I plan to go to Florence, Milan, Czechia, Kraków" is how Mickiewicz announced his mystical–moral–military mission to Juliusz Łacki, another follower of Towiański, from Rome on April 2, 1848.[24] He wrote this letter on the back of a copy of *Skład zasad* [Statement of principles] that he composed on March 29, 1848, which has come to be called "Mickiewicz's Constitution." Alongside postulates of civil freedoms of all kinds, its tenth principle states the following: "To Israel, our elder brother, we owe respect, brotherhood, support of its heavenly and earthly well-being. Equal rights in all regards." Translating his *Skład zasad* into Italian, Mickiewicz restates this final point as offering Israel "equality in all political and civil rights."[25]

Mickiewicz's designation of Israel as an "older brother" shocked his contemporaries. The poet Cyprian Kamil Norwid roundly criticized *Skład zasad* as nonorthodox "nonsense" in a letter to Józef Bohdan Zaleski. "This manifesto aims to thoroughly demolish the church's religious dogmas and weaken its spirituality. Given the prominent place it gives to 'our older brother,' Israel, it is ultimately headed—to put it bluntly—to the *synagogue*. The logic that lets him see Israel as our 'elder' confirms my point: Christ *abolished* time; meanwhile, he speaks of Israel chronologically, returning to linear time, to blood ties . . .—in short, to the Old Testament!"[26] Mickiewicz's son Władysław adroitly masks his father's supposed Jewish heresy by rephrasing the tenth principle of his *Skład zasad* as "To Israel, our brother" in *Legion Mickiewicza: Rok 1848* [Mickiewicz's legion in 1848], strategically omitting the word "elder." Abraham G. Duker, an astute and erudite scholar of Mickiewicz's attitudes toward Judaism, notes this omission.[27]

To understand what Mickiewicz means by "older brother," we need to probe the messianic, Towiański-inspired course his thinking had taken. "Israel is the name of the oldest family of spirits," the poet asserted in one of his speeches to Koło Sprawy Bożej [Circle of divine purpose] in 1845.[28] "The Hebrew leaders fulfilled their spiritual destiny by lifting up not just one caste, but an entire nation, toward an understanding of the oneness and omnipresence of God" is how he elsewhere explains the "spirit of the Hebrew revelation."[29] Israel owes its spiritual primogeniture to the destiny it was called to fulfill—and to the way the Israelites never doubted Providence. Being the eldest, the spirits of the Israelites can inhabit a variety of "bodies," not only Jewish ones. This principle allowed Mickiewicz to assert, in 1847, that "there are great and powerful spirits living in Poland, both among the Jews and among our peasants; they are Israelites."[30]

Such statements about the primacy of Israel were difficult to digest for Polish émigrés. On July 15, 1842, Zaleski wrote to Goszczyński that "Mickiewicz's messianism is something else. It's an apotheosis of Judaism, a hard principle for earnestly Christian Slavs to embrace. . . . It will be a while before Polish people, or Slavic people in general, accept that the Jews are spiritually superior to them." Like Norwid, Zaleski recoiled from what he saw as a return to the Old Testament.

He asserted that Mickiewicz's ideas threatened Christianity but also Poland's national sense of identity, listing the "personal and national" difficulties that prevented him from embracing the poet's views.[31]

Some of the reluctance with which Mickiewicz's ideas were met stemmed from nationalist prejudice. Right before World War II, a Polish nationalist magazine accused him of biological as well as spiritual Semitism: "It would be pointless to argue that Mickiewicz's messianism—or should we say his 'messianic Zionism' *[mesjonizm]* is not a Jewish worldview." The work of this "messianic Zionist" might bring comfort to Jewish hearts and minds; but real Poles recoil from "anything that smells of Habakkuk, Jeremiah, Ezekiel, and other inspired Judeans."[32]

Mickiewicz had no time for such nationalist antipathies in his thinking about the spiritual superiority of Israel. However, he was drawn not just to an unshakeable faith in a monotheistic God, but also to a path of religious and moral perfection that followed the footsteps of Jesus Christ. From this perspective, in 1844, he contemplated what he saw as "Israel's error": "The Israelites refused the grace Christ brought them. In spite of his coming, they wanted to find a different way to perfection—and what they found were circles of centuries-long suffering." Earlier, on May 3, 1843, during a solemn gathering of Towarzystwo Literackie [Literary Society], Mickiewicz had proclaimed that "the Jews were not reborn because they merely wished to repair their old church, and Christ had come to build a new one."[33] These criticisms did not invoke the common stereotype according to which the Jews had been "punished" for crucifying Christ. Similarly, Zaleski thus summarizes a conversation he had with Mickiewicz in 1851 about "Palestine and the Jews. He was curious about my trip to the Holy Land and asked for details. We discussed the spirituality of the Jewish people and the magnitude of the spiritual mission they had been given and failed to fulfill."[34] The last part seems to be Zaleski's own commentary. Mickiewicz espoused Towiański's goal "not to disband preexisting orders but to complete them, to build a third story in the house of the church without destroying the stories below—indeed, while reinforcing them."[35] "The third story in the house of the church," built atop the Old and the New Order, is a new era of Christianity in which the causes of Poland's downfall have been eradicated "and all the different races and religions have been united into brotherly harmony."[36] Mickiewicz worked to assemble a Slavic–Polish legion in Rome in 1848. In 1855, there came time for the poet to assemble another Slavic–*Jewish* legion that would march toward Poland in a "millenarian crusade," "an eschatological journey toward a new, better world."[37]

"Fate Had Bound Together Two Mutually Alien Nations"

Mickiewicz saw Poland as a singular, mystical haven for the Jewish people. He shared this view with Andrzej Towiański, who wrote that, in Poland, "Israel can be truer to itself than amid other nations." "One readily senses," Towiański argued,

> how crucial it is for Poland to follow God's will in uniting the two parts of its nation, raised alongside each other and sharing an unparalleled degree of spiritual sympathy, despite their different earthly paths and roles. . . . May our love for these brothers, who were once our guests and have become our countrymen, who are spiritually destined to become one with the rest of Poland, express itself in our affection and sacrifices for their sake. May we thereby repay into the coffers of divine and human love the debt we incurred by the way we first treated our Jewish brethren when they came to this soil which God intended them to live on [i.e., Poland], even as He also intended us lovingly to care for it.[38]

Alongside statements such as these, Towiański usually lists Israel's supposed sins and errors. The latter did not preoccupy Mickiewicz to the same extent; especially while he was trying to organize a Polish–Jewish legion, he cared most about the presumed spiritual affinity between these two nations. In his 1843 lectures at the Collège de France, Mickiewicz mentions the "millions" of Jewish people living in Slavic countries, expressing a wish to speak on their behalf as well.[39]

Eastern European Jews had not assimilated to Polish culture and had no desire to do so. Rejecting universalist Enlightenment ideas about humanity, they remained committed to their faith. Gershom Scholem has argued that followers of heretical Jewish sects such as Sabbateanism and Frankism, many of whom came from Eastern Europe, were often inspired by deep, if inarticulable, desires for a moral and national renaissance that far exceeded the typical aspirations of middle-class Western European Jews.[40] Mickiewicz also felt alienated from, indeed actively hostile to, the limitations of a bourgeois mindset. He must have been drawn to Eastern European Jews' intense spirituality, which intensified as the teaching of the Talmud became democratized. Describing this democratizing process as bringing "intellectual emancipation to the people," Abraham Joshua Herschel recounts how nineteenth-century Jewish inhabitants of Eastern Europe "indulged in the enjoyment of studying revered books," adding that "an old book saved from the countless libraries recently burned in Europe, now at the Yivo Library in New York, bears the stamp, 'The Society of Wood-Choppers for the Study of Mishnah in Berditshev.'"[41] In *The Earth Is the Lord's: The Inner World of the Jew in East Europe,* Herschel rightly observes that even in the face of extreme poverty, nineteenth-century Eastern European Jews felt like spiritual kings. The Polish Romantics saw this, too: not just Mickiewicz, but also Słowacki, whose *Ksiądz Marek* (Father Marek) features the amazing character of Judyta, an inspired Jewish woman who embodies Israel's powerful spirit. As Herschel puts it, the nineteenth century was a golden period of Jewish spiritual history.

Mickiewicz believed that "fate had bound together two mutually alien nations" cohabitating on Polish soil. "Our country," he proclaimed in his Paris lectures, "is the principal seat of the oldest and most mysterious of all nations, the nation of Israel."[42] Abraham G. Duker argues that Mickiewicz thus performed a new theosophical synthesis, combining Towiański's ideas about Israel's future in Poland with Jacob Frank's. Inspired by Frankism, Mickiewicz had become convinced that Providence had congregated Jewish people in Poland for mysterious, messianic ends.[43] Traveling to Turkey, he still believed in the two nations' mystical union based on their shared messianic spiritual *misterium;* this union entitled Poland to speak on behalf of, and as, Israel. Lévy underlines that "it must be known that Adam Mickiewicz died without having abandoned the ideas for whose sake he lived. He died without having recanted anything, though some might want to believe the opposite. In conversations, he reiterated what he had in prior years. He died believing what he had proclaimed at the Collège de France."[44]

Mickiewicz also knew how to translate his ideas into a more practical idiom. When he found out that Michał Czajkowski had made ribald jokes (as a Polish nobleman would) about "the Israelites' *interests,*" the poet called Czajkowski out for this in a letter written about two weeks before his death. He insisted that serious matters must not be made light of, "since our opponents are not joking either." He explained his reasoning with down-to-earth pragmatism. "The matter of the Israelites has been on many people's minds for the last dozen years. Back in Poland, they support our national cause and are seen as a powerful force. If this military formation were to succeed, the French government would certainly support you."[45]

Politics and Mystical Illumination

Czajkowski *vel* Sadyk Pasha led the first regiment of Ottoman Cossacks in the Turkish army. In his army encampment in Burgas there also appeared to have resided some two hundred Jews, most of them war prisoners. [. . .] Given the large numbers of Jewish war prisoners and deserters from the Russian army, and given also other possible means of recruiting Jewish soldiers who were generally eager to fight against Russia, Prince Czartoryski's political milieu had explored means of enlisting them into Polish military forces since 1854. Duker notes that "the *Univers Israélite* reported in March 1854 that the Istanbul rabbi 'formed a legion of Israelites which he presented to the Sultan,'" and that "Israelite notables of most cities are furnishing the necessary funds to support it." Going against what Władysław Mickiewicz or Stanisław Pigoń have argued, he adds that "it is inconceivable that Lévy was unacquainted with these rumors, or that he did not discuss them with the poet. Moreover, it is most unlikely that Mickiewicz was not told, in connection with his mission, about the significant successes achieved by the Poles in recruiting Jewish volunteers in England, France, North Africa, and among the Russian war prisoners, for emergent Cossack military units."[46]

Their pragmatism notwithstanding, Mickiewicz's and Lévy's fervor to create a Jewish legion also bore the marks of a mystical illumination. Lévy describes the fateful moment when the idea occurred to them in a letter to Emilian Bednarczyk, cited by Roman Brandstaetter:

> The matter began in a pure, disinterested, uncalculated fashion. That much is beyond debate. The project came into being under the tents of the encampment in Burgas. He [Mickiewicz] was inspired by the sight of Jewish soldiers serving under the banner of the Ottoman Cossacks. I began to speak, and Mickiewicz, Sadyk, and I instantly recognized we were all having the same

> thought; we were expressing each other's desires. This is how great things come into being. That is all. We became convinced that Providence had a hand in this revelation. We were tools prepared in advance to accomplish this goal. Mickiewicz would later often repeat this injunction: Trust in the providential nature of our endeavor. The proof: So many nonrational circumstances meet and connect here, tending toward a single goal, without any premeditation on our part.[47]

It is difficult to question the authenticity of Mickiewicz's statement, as Lévy sets it down here. [. . .] Mickiewicz repeats his Parisian lectures' insistence that the connection between Israel and Poland is providential and "uncalculated." He tries to intuit the deep meanings of historical events, great and small; he sees himself and the two other men as mediums of God's revelation obeying divine command. Again, he suggests that the two nations would not have met in the same territory were it not for the hand of Providence—and argues that the same Providence pulled Mickiewicz's, Lévy's, and Czajkowski's minds into unison. [. . .]

The Flag of the Maccabees

Why call this army unit a "Jewish legion"? [. . .] Lévy describes it as "a third regiment made up of Israelites. The point was not to create a separate army unit, but to make room for Israelites within the preexisting Polish formation and to guarantee that the Jews would be able to observe their religious rites to the extent that wartime conditions allowed."[48] Let me draw attention to that last phrase. Lévy goes on to describe Jewish volunteers as part of the "Polish legion." In a letter dated January 30, 1856, Ludwika Śniadecka underscores that "Mickiewicz's final thoughts went to the formation of Israeli *regiments* commanded by Sadyk, new reinforcements for the Turkish army, and a great new force for Poland."[49]

How should we explain the care taken here with nomenclature: Why a "regiment" and not a "legion"? When he describes the Polish forces, Mickiewicz uses terms such as *host, league, legion,* and *legions* interchangeably. Czajkowski spoke of a "Polish–Jewish corporation." In his valuable 1922 volume on Mickiewicz, Stanisław Szpotański speaks of a "Jewish league," noting that "organizing it was Mickiewicz's main project" in Turkey.[50] Ksenia Kostenicz, a preeminent specialist on this period of Mickiewicz's life, also uses the term *Jewish legion*.[51] The poet himself may have been surprised by the number of Jewish volunteers who presented themselves, and he may have struggled to find a suitable organizational form for it.

It seems appropriate to describe this legion or regiment as "Jewish" or "Israeli" to mark its members' different religious rites and customs. But should we trust Stanisław Pigoń's assertion that, in 1855, "no one around Mickiewicz would have dreamed of there being a separate Jewish language, let alone a separate Jewish banner"?[52] I'm not so sure. Members of Mickiewicz's milieu did speak of a "Maccabean flag." Czajkowski also reports that, upon seeing officer Moshko Horenstein and his friend dressed in a prototype of the "uniform of the Israeli hussars" designed by the head of the regiment, Mickiewicz supposedly joked, "O Goliaths, Samsons, Holofierneses! Beware lest a Judith or a Delilah step into your path, break your ranks, and march you off to make deals with the banker!"[53] Mickiewicz could not and perhaps did not want to resist occasionally making such stereotypical Jewish jokes, which were common in nineteenth-century Polish culture. In this case, as he contrasts brave soldiers against easily frightened civilians, he may have wanted to remind his listeners of the Jews' long history of military heroism. Czajkowski describes Mahmoud Freund, a talented Jewish officer who converted to Islam alongside him, as resembling colonel Berek Joselewicz, the Polish-Jewish hero of the Kościuszko uprising. He picked out Freund as the head of the whole one-thousand-strong Jewish legion.[54]

Roman Brandstaetter underlines that both Mickiewicz and Lévy described this armed Jewish formation in distinctly nationalistic terms. In a letter to Alphonse, Baron of Rothschild, Lévy expressed his wish that "the idea of the Jewish legion be based on old, national Jewish traditions." Like Mickiewicz, he feared that assimilation might bring about "the annihilation of the Jewish people's singular character." Armed action was supposed to rehabilitate Jews as *soldiers*. After Mickiewicz's death, Czajkowski echoed this view when he described the poet's project of building a Jewish legion as a "great" one. It would have enabled "the military resurrection of a great nation—which had suffered so much under the sword and deserved to regain its old good fortune by the sword."[55] This aspiration toward lifting the Jewish race through its proven military valor and its embrace of the saber was one of the principal components of the concept of a Jewish legion. Participation in armed combat was treated as a means of Jewish emancipation. Courage, bravery, and manliness in battle—these were values the Jewish people needed to reembrace so that they could regain their seriousness and significance. As Duker writes, there was a "growing conviction among Jews in the Balkan area that Jewish emancipation could be won only by the sword."[56] Ludwika Śniadecka writes in the letter mentioned above that "a young Jewish Frenchman, Armand Lévy, came along with Mickiewicz; he has committed his whole soul to the project, wishing to lift his abased nation and restore it to much-needed military fame."[57] More recent historical events motivated Lévy and his fellow soldiers as well. In a letter to Władysław Mickiewicz, Lévy describes how he enlisted in Sadyk Pasha's Cossack legion immediately upon arriving in Burgas. He was "moved by the spirit of the great deceased members of your legion and our great army [i.e., the Napoleonic army]."[58] The wish to return Israel to its former glory was cited by many as a reason to enlist.

Lévy's view of action, and especially of that highest form of action—patriotic acts performed on Poland's behalf—was clearly influenced by Mickiewicz. In a letter he writes to Władysław Mickiewicz on September 27, 1855, while traveling eastward, Lévy praises Antoni Iliński, now Iskander Pasha. "[Seventeenth-century chronicler Jan Chryzostom] Pasek would recognize contemporary Poles as his own kind. Though many vices have endured throughout the centuries, so has the highest Polish virtue: indomitable military mettle." Elsewhere, Lévy describes how his encounters "illuminate the mystery of how true, great action can kindle a cleansing inward fire in a person, until light beams through every pore of their being."[59] This mystical sanctification of heroes, this "religion of action," had been central to Mickiewicz.[60] It became so for Lévy as well.

Far from desiring Jewish assimilation, let alone Jews' conversion to Christianity, Mickiewicz trusted "in the superreligious salvific truth that all religions of the Bible carry within themselves" while also protecting the separateness of the Jewish religion.[61] Czajkowski writes that "a Jewish synagogue was built in the Cossack encampment—under Adam Mickiewicz's protection."[62] One must keep in mind that, in 1853, Jews were subject to compulsory military service in the Russian army, within which they were not allowed to follow their religious customs and which they consequently often deserted. Under Czajkowski, they had the chance to preserve their religious difference.

In the encampment in Burgas, Sadyk Pasha issued the order that "Fridays are for the Muslims, Saturdays are for the Jews, and Sundays are for the Catholic and Orthodox Christians to celebrate according to their rites." The same order mentioned the most severe punishments that would befall "whoever tries to convert others through threats or violence, or mocks their faith." Mickiewicz and Lévy rejoiced that the Jews of the Ottoman regiment had been allowed to celebrate the Sabbath. Lévy reports to Czajkowski that "Mr. Adam told me this is the first such occurrence since the Jews had been forced to leave Israel, and one should attribute great significance to it."[63] Clearly, a new era was approaching.

Will the Israelites Leave Poland?

The Jewish legion was to take part in the struggle for Poland's freedom. Lévy took notes about it elatedly; he envisioned joyous transformations that would transpire throughout Polish territories under the aegis of fighting "for your freedom and ours." "The day seemed imminent when the Maccabean flag would fly and the Israelite fighting for Poland would make the great step forward that is his calling, without which his miseries will not end. In opening his heart to the suffering of others, he would earn the right to be treated like a brother by them."[64] These visions resonate with the fraternal ideas of the Springtime of Nations; though those latter uprisings had failed, they remained close to the heart of a "revolutionary Romantic republican" like Armand Lévy.[65] Mickiewicz responded to these prophecies as follows: "If, having come to Polish soil, the Jewish legion attracts Jewish volunteers from even one synagogue, other synagogues will follow. By proving their devotion to Poland and their bravery, the Jews will elevate their race in the eyes of the Poles and in their own."[66]

These statements might not seem to differ from common Romantic ideas about oppressed nations' shared struggle for freedom—and about military heroism as the measure of a nation's greatness. But a new shade of meaning appears in Mickiewicz's thinking, a mystical sense that a special spiritual bond conjoins Poland and Israel. In Lévy's letters to Bednarczyk, we find that Mickiewicz underlined how

"Poland cannot be recreated without the liberation of the Jews and the development of their spirit. Were it to reemerge without liberating the Jews—which I do not believe could happen—it would not be able to sustain itself."[67] Certainly, what Mickiewicz has in mind here recalls point ten of his *Skład zasad* in 1848. He wants to accord Poland's Jews equal civil rights, which, as he argues in 1855, would "fraternize the different races and religions of our homeland." And that is not all: a "development of the spirit," Polish as well as Jewish, is necessary for Poland's sake.

Mickiewicz worried that, once liberated, the Jews—whom he thought as a necessary part of Polish society—might want to go back to Palestine. He expressed these fears after a visit to a synagogue in Smyrna, coming to the conclusion that "a people who prays with such unshakeable faith will manage to sway God."[68] He desired the following: "I do not want the Israelites to leave Poland; just like the union between Lithuania and Poland, two different races and religions, gave our Commonwealth its political and military greatness, so do I believe that a union between Poland and Israel would increase our physical and spiritual powers."[69] Every step of the way, Mickiewicz's thinking about the Jews is diametrically opposed to his contemporary Zygmunt Krasiński's ideas about their "elimination." I have written about the latter's anti-Semitism in a different essay.

Mickiewicz expressed a fear that Israelites might leave Poland after Lévy's conversation with the rabbi at the synagogue in Smyrna. As Lévy describes it, "I happened to mention to one of the rabbis that I thought the time was near when we would return to Jerusalem. 'What are the signs?' he asked me. There are three signs, I told him: the imminent fall of the papacy; Turkey's agony; the destruction of Russia."[70] It is worth making a comparison here: Moses Hess wrote a book called *Rom und Jerusalem, die letzte Nationalitätsfrage* [Rome and Jerusalem: The Last Question of Nationhood, 1862], which lays out a pre-Zionist project for establishing a Jewish state in Palestine. Hess names Lévy as a friend who foretold the Jews' return from exile. As Hess describes it, Lévy commented as follows about his travels through the duchies around the Danube after Mickiewicz's death:

> My friend Armond [*sic*] L., who traveled for several years through the Danube Principalities, told me that the Jews were moved to tears when he announced to them the end of their suffering with the words "the time of the return approaches." The more fortu-

> nate Occidental Jews do not know with what longing the Jewish masses of the East await their redemption from two thousand years of exile. . . . "They asked me," continued my friend, "what are the indications that the end of exile is approaching?" "They are," I answered, "that the Turkish and papal powers are on the point of collapse."[71]

These are two of the three signs Lévy named in front of Mickiewicz in Smyrna. Pigoń may believe that it is very risky to see Mickiewicz as inspiring such ideas, especially ones that go against the earthly authority of the papacy. He forgets the force with which Mickiewicz criticizes the "official church" as he works to build a "spiritual" one. For instance, in a meeting of the Koło Sprawy Bożej [Circle of God's plan] on March 5, 1847, Mickiewicz said that "today's church preserves nothing but form: It has lost the spirit and the life of Christ. The pope has become a housekeeper, a lawyer, a diplomat."[72] He repeated this accusation that the "official church" led by the pope had lost its spirit many times. In a letter to Władysław Mickiewicz dated September 29, 1855, Lévy follows Mickiewicz's spirit when he pushes back against the accusations made against Sadyk Pasha for converting to Islam. "Others condemn him for changing his faith. But people like him did not leave the church; they and their homeland were abandoned by it. Truly, the hero and martyr Bem is closer to God than those who accuse him and his brothers in arms. If the church wants people to return to it, it must take up the rights of the nations and inspire them—especially a faithful and martyred nation like this one."[73] This bitter lesson stems from the church's actions during the Springtime of Nations, when—as Mickiewicz writes—Pius IX proved "willing to sacrifice everything to preserve the current state of what he calls the church: its personnel, its possessions, the clergy's privileges."[74] The poet had absorbed this lesson, as had Lévy. The "official church" could not, in their opinion, serve the ideals of national independence; indeed, it brought harm to them.

A Modern-Day Moses

For all these reasons, I do not hesitate to take up Brandstaetter's idea that Lévy began to dream of the resurrection of a free Jewish state in Palestine "under the influence of Mickiewicz's ideology."[75] Duker sees Lévy as an early Zionist. We can attribute such politics to his employer only indirectly.[76] But it is not without Mickiewicz's inspiration that Lévy negotiated with the Rothschilds to see if they would lend the cause financial support. Czajkowski noted some of the rumors that spread around this negotiation: "Zwierkowski wrote that the Rothschilds wanted to enter into financial relations with the Turkish government, to legally own Jerusalem and a perimeter around it, and thus become the sultan's vassals, bearing the title of dukes."[77] The Rothschilds' fortune, combined with what Hess described as the "great mass of Jews in Eastern Europe," frightened both Turkey and Western European states. It was feared that the Jews would gradually strive to separate Palestine from Turkey and create an independent Jewish state.

The idea of a Jewish legion ended with Mickiewicz's death and the Crimean War. Duker writes that "a reticence over mentioning Mickiewicz's last major interest is symptomatic of Polish historians, but it seems to have been the general rule among his contemporaries as well. All followed versions of opinions voiced by scholars like Marceli Handelsman, who opined that the Jewish legion was not the focal point of Mickiewicz's political activities in the East."[78] Jadwiga Maurer shares Duker's disagreement with Handelsman and launches an extensive polemic against him. "The Jewish legion," she writes, "is an embarrassing objective for mainstream studies of Mickiewicz as a bard and a national poet to attribute to him; in this national context, it is therefore consistently marginalized and erased. Yet this objective mattered a lot to the poet's own spiritual life. We need not consider this question in the abstract; contemporary witnesses simply do not corroborate Handelsman's opinion about how unimportant the Jewish legion was for the poet. Instead, these witnesses all agree that Mickiewicz was possessed by this idea."[79]

Mickiewicz's son Władysław played a not-insignificant role in what Brandstaetter calls the "stylizing" of his father's work—and what I would describe as an attempt to erase parts of it. Władysław Mickiewicz mocks Michał Czajkowski's short book on this subject, stressing that the author's treatment of it was "novelistic rather than historical in nature" and summarizing it as the narrative of how "Mickiewicz and Rothschild enlisted in the Cossack army."[80] The book in question is a manuscript titled *Adam Mickiewicz w obozie kozackim / W obozie w Burgas* [Adam Mickiewicz in the Cossack encampment / In the encampment in Burgas, 1881]. Brandstaetter takes it seriously as a primary source. In the same context, let us mention the polemic that took place in 1898 in the pages of the periodical *Przewodnik Naukowy i Literacki*. Rawita Gawroński published excerpts from Sadyk Pasha's writings; Władysław Mickiewicz vehemently retorted that Czajkowski / Sadyk Pasha's recollections were false and full of fantasizing. The Rothschilds, he insisted, had nothing to do with the Jewish legion. Gawroński responded that Władysław Mickiewicz's criticisms are just "personal opinions" and noted that the poet's son offers no evidence to support them. Gawroński himself had only "made public the letters and recollections of [Mickiewicz's] contemporaries; the authenticity of these documents is beyond doubt."[81] The people Władysław Mickiewicz least wanted to be mentioned in this context were certainly the Rothschilds. Yet we do know that negotiations had taken place between the Rothschilds' representatives and those of the Jewish legion, and the argument that the Jews' involvement in military action would contribute to their emancipation loomed large in these negotiations.[82] Until the end of his long life, Władysław Mickiewicz continued to insist that his father's milieu had never contemplated an independent Jewish legion or legions. It is hard to escape the impression that, as Maurer puts it, Władysław "chose to lie about the legion."[83] Seeking to garner support within Galicia's clerical and aristocratic milieus, he may have wanted to forge a popular and national ideal of his father as a Polish Catholic who was full of evangelizing affection toward the Jews, but who had nothing in common with them in practice.

Even so, the legend of the Jewish legion persisted. Consider the following, very interesting piece of evidence. Leo Belmont's popular "novel-essay" about Theodor Herzl titled *Mojżesz współczesny* [A modern-day Moses, 1931] includes a chapter called "The Wilted Rose of Constantinople." In this chapter, a prophetic conversation that takes place in 1895 reveals the secrets of Theodor's father, Jacob. Tormented by the anti-Semitic slurs and insults he constantly faced in Germany, Jacob had made plans to travel to Jordan. He finally decided against it, drawn back by the comforts of bourgeois life. But he retained some souvenirs of this near emigration, including a letter from Armand Lévy dated forty years back and a dried-up flower, "a rose of Constantinople taken from the wreath Armand Lévy had placed on the coffin of the man who was supposedly the greatest bard of all Slavdom, before his body was placed on a ship to Paris." This "Polish bard whom patriotic suffering had pushed onto the path of mystical intuitions" had recognized the similarity of the fates of the Jewish and the Polish nations. His "sympathy [toward the Jews], Lévy supposedly wrote in his letter, stemmed not only from spiritual inspiration, but also from the poet's bloodline," as his mother was purportedly descended from the Frankists. Theodor Herzl's father recites to his son point ten of Mickiewicz's *Skład zasad,* which Belmont's narrator retranslates literally from a Hebrew rendition; he also describes Mickiewicz's visit to a Parisian synagogue. Mickiewicz spoke to the Paris rabbi as a representative of "all the synagogues," describing legions he was organizing in Turkey that would "enlist Jewish people . . . to help the Polish cause." The poet died of cholera before attaining these aims. Armand, Belmont's narrator speculates, was "the sole witness to his passing; a caring Jewish hand closed the dead man's eyes."[84] In Belmont's novel, Lévy's letter, with its descriptions of Mickiewicz's words and actions, is passed on from father to son—and the son, Theodor Herzl, becomes the creator of Zionism. Before Herzl writes *The Jewish State,* this "modern-day Moses" of Belmont's novel receives Mickiewicz's legacy. In this context, the farewell that the father and the son bid each other—"Next year in Jerusalem!"—acquires a rather unconventional meaning.

Precursor and Successor

Roman Brandstaetter was right to argue that Władysław Mickiewicz forcibly reinterpreted his father's Jewish legion as "an expression of philanthropic philo-Semitism whose aim was ultimately to give the Jews an understanding of Christianity, beginning with its foundational principle of sacrificing oneself for others."[85] Still, Rafał Blüth follows Władysław Mickiewicz in describing the Jewish legion as an expression of "an illogical concept of Christian Zionism whose paradoxical mysticism is deeply strange." He, too, sees in the legion "a natural first step toward a tragic process of Christianizing Judaism" by "introducing Jews to the idea of bloody self-sacrifice, to a determined search for one's own freedom by means of fighting for the freedom of another, twin nation." Mickiewicz supposedly cast this idea of self-sacrifice into the world in reactive protest against assimilated, Europeanized Jews.[86] Wiktor Weintraub and Jadwiga Maurer insist that no actual evidence bears out these claims. Indeed, they directly contradict what Lévy writes about the legion's guaranteed freedom of Jewish religious ritual.[87]

Władysław Mickiewicz—born from the union of the great Polish poet with a foreign woman, as Mateusz Mieses describes him—fought anti-Semitism as it intensified throughout Western Europe and Poland in the late nineteenth and early twentieth centuries. However, he did so in a highly peculiar fashion: He claimed that "anti-Semitism calls up the old sins of the Israelites without taking into account how many Jews have more or less succumbed to the influence of Christianity."[88] Mickiewicz's son reiterates stereotypes of Christian anti-Semitism that describe Jews as selfish and incapable of sacrificing themselves for the sake of others. As he sees it, the Zionist movement of 1912 does not stand a chance. The only Jews who might escape oppression are the ones who accept Christianity: That is the ultimate message of this "son of Adam." One can hardly describe him as following in his father's footsteps.

Early in 1939, the well-known Polish–Jewish writer Mieczysław Braun published in *Nasz Przegląd* an article titled "Adam Mickiewicz's Zionism." In it, he boldly declares, "It is not paradoxical for me to say that Adam Mickiewicz, that Polish genius, was a Zionist." A poet no less gifted than some of the Hebrew prophets, he set up a Jewish legion whose aim was not only to fight Russia for the cause of Polish independence, but also "to resolve the problem of the diaspora." Creating a Jewish armed force was one of the poet's great projects, and no mere Romantic daydream. "Besides, an idea devoid of a certain Romanticism becomes merely a business matter—and we Jews know how quickly business relations fracture and how long ideas can last by comparison."[89] The hope to which Mickiewicz devoted the last years of his life did in fact prove unexpectedly long-lasting.

Let us recall that having felt a spiritual connection to the "millions" of Eastern European Jews, Mickiewicz no longer wanted to convert them to Christianity, rejecting assimilation as only an illusory path toward freedom that renders the assimilated indifferent to religion and traditional customs. He believed in the irreducible singularity of Jewish religious and national identity and wanted to create a military force that would express it. The poet would thus have rejected the way the Polish revolutionary National Assembly of 1789 put the matter: "Jews as individuals among others—yes! Jews as their own collective—no!"[90]

For all these reasons, it is possible to interpret some aspects of Mickiewicz's views as belonging to, or inspiring, proto-Zionism. In a polemical article dated 1932, written against Boy-Żeleński, Brandstaetter insists that "the idea of a Jewish national revival could not have yet attracted mass Jewish support—anything but a small group of supporters—in Mickiewicz's time." He shows in detail that the Jewish legion failed to solidify not only for technical reasons, but also because "of Balkan Jews' relative lack of familiarity with the idea of a nation." As it never managed to crystallize, Mickiewicz's last great idea remained as general in its form as "the first calls for a Jewish national renaissance made by Moses Hess, a friend of Armand Lévy and one of the precursors of Theodor Herzl's Zionist thought." These Zionist convictions, Brandstaetter argues, "continued to strain against assimilationist resistance and indifference, as well as against the antipathy shown toward the Jews in certain corners of Christianity—until they finally achieved a clear articulation at the historic congress in Basil."[91] Mickiewicz's idea flared up and died down fast, but it only appeared to have been forgotten.

Gershom Scholem (someone should do a comparative study of the parallels between Scholem and Mickiewicz) wrote in his 1953 account of the Sabbatean movement that Frankism was the logical conclusion of Sabbateanism. Recalling the famous, if mysterious, article published in 1838 in *Allgemeine Zeitung des Judentums,* which described Mickiewicz as a Frankist and a member of the Jewish nation, Scholem speculates that this greatest Polish poet and messianic prophet was a descendant of Frankist Jews on his mother's side. He ends by concluding that Mickiewicz may have preserved part of the Sabbatean movement's intellectual legacy, including its unfulfilled dream of liberating Israel alongside all other nations. If Scholem is right, Mickiewicz's idea belongs to an intellectual lineage that extends not only into the future, but also into the history of Jewish thought.[92] But for Mickiewicz, one problem and one paradox always remained unresolved: How are the Jews going to reconquer Jerusalem if it is also imperative that they remain in Poland?

Notes

1. As quoted in Michał Czajkowski, *Kozaczyzna w Turcji: Dzieło w trzech częściach przez X. K. O.* (Paris, 1857), 242.
2. Franciszek Rawita Gawroński, *Adam Mickiewicz na Wschodzie (1855)* (L'viv, 1899), 11.

3. Władysław Mickiewicz, *Żywot Adama Mickiewicza* (Poznań: Dziennik Poznański, 1894), 4:402.
4. Adam Lewak, *Dzieje emigracji polskiej w Turcji, 1831–1878* (Warsaw: Instytut Wschodni, 1935), 92, 99.
5. Mickiewicz, *Żywot Adama Mickiewicza,* 4:401.
6. Czajkowski, *Kozaczyzna w Turcji,* 246.
7. Janusz Ruszkowski, *Adam Mickiewicz i ostatnia krucjata: Studium romantycznego milenaryzmu* (Wrocław: Fundacja na Rzecz Nauki Polskiej, 1996), 193.
8. Mickiewicz, *Żywot Adama Mickiewicza,* 4:xxxvi.
9. Quoted in Lewak, *Dzieje emigracji polskiej w Turcji,* 88.
10. Lewak, *Dzieje emigracji polskiej w Turcji,* 88, 91.
11. Mickiewicz, *Żywot Adama Mickiewicza,* 4:401.
12. Jadwiga Maurer, "'Jak mnie nie stanie, nikt tego nie zrozumie': O legionie żydowskim Adama Mickiewicza," in *Polonistyka po amerykańsku: Badania nad literatura polska w Ameryce Północnej, 1990 2005,* ed. Halina Filipowicz, Andrzej Karcz, and Tamara Trojanowska (Warsaw: PAN, 2005), 115.
13. [A patriotic song that became Poland's national anthem.—Trans.]
14. [Instead of "March, march, Dąbrowski, from Italian lands back to Poland," as in the 1797 original written to incite General Dąbrowski and his troops, then serving Napoleon's Italian campaign, to intervene and stop the third partition of Poland.—Trans.] Mickiewicz, *Żywot Adama Mickiewicza,* 4:lxxxvi.
15. Dobrosława Świerczyńska, "Zapomniane relacje o pobycie Mickiewicza w Burgas," *Pamiętnik Literacki* 4 (1990): 221.
16. Kazimiera Szczuka describes this dynamic at Burgas in "Matki, płaczki, wdowy: Żałoba po Mickiewiczu," in *Śmierć Mickiewicza: Teksty i rozmowy w Roku Mickiewiczowskim 2005,* ed. Katarzyna Czeczot and Marta Zielińska (Warsaw: Instytut Badań Literackich PAN, 2008).
17. Mickiewicz, *Żywot Adama Mickiewicza,* 4:409.
18. Jerzy W. Borejsza, *Sekretarz Adama Mickewicza: Armand Lévy i jego czasy, 1827–1891,* 3rd ed. (Gdańsk: Słowo/obraz terytoria, 2005), 129.
19. Mickiewicz, *Żywot Adama Mickiewicza,* 4:401.
20. Mickiewicz, *Zywot Adama Mickiewicza,* 4:426.
21. Czajkowski, *Kozaczyzna w Turcji,* 241–42, 255.
22. Adam Mickiewicz, *Dzieła,* anniversary ed. (Warsaw: Państwowy Instytut Literacki, 1955), 16:186.
23. Ruszkowski, *Adam Mickiewicz i ostatnia krucjata,* 241, 230.
24. Mickiewicz, *Dzieła,* 16:186.
25. Mickiewicz, *Dzieła,* 12:331.
26. Cyprian Kamil Norwid, *Pisma Wszystkie,* ed. J. W. Gomulicki (Warsaw: Państwowy Instytut Naukowy, 1971), 8:62.
27. See Abraham G. Duker's discussion of this omission in "Mickiewicz and the Jewish Problem," in *Adam Mickiewicz, Poet of Poland: A Symposium,* ed. Manfred Kridl (New York: Columbia University Press, 1951), 117.

28. Adam Mickiewicz, *Dzieła wszystkie* (Warsaw: Państwowy Instytut Wydawniczy, 1933), 11:335.
29. Mickiewicz, *Dzieła,* 11:264.
30. Mickiewicz, *Dzieła wszystkie,* 11:438.
31. J. B. Zaleski, *Korespondencja* (L'viv, 1900), 1:245.
32. See Gniewomir, "Mesjonista Adam Mickiewicz," *Zadruga,* nos. 4–5 (April–May 1939): 16–17.
33. Mickiewicz, *Dzieła wszystkie,* 11:270, 499.
34. Mickiewicz, *Żywot Adama Mickiewicza,* 4:xxxv.
35. Mickiewicz, *Dzieła,* 15:520.
36. Stanisław Pigoń, ed., *Adama Mickiewicza wspomnienia i myśli* (Warsaw: Państwowy Instytut Wydawniczy, 1958), 263. [Janion's original essay includes extensive polemics against Pigoń's (anti-Semitic) perspectives on Mickiewicz; since Pigoń and his work are relatively unknown abroad, I have excised most of these polemics to facilitate the flow of Janion's argument.—Trans.]
37. Ruszkowski, *Adam Mickiewicz i ostatnia krucjata,* 246–48.
38. Andrzej Towiański, *Pisma wybrane,* ed. Andrzej Boleski (Kraków: Wydawnictwo J. Mortkowicza, 1920), 2:99, 103.
39. Mickiewicz, *Dzieła,* 11:343.
40. See Gershom Scholem, "La redemption par le péché," in *Le messianisme juif: Essais sur la spiritualité du judaisme* (Paris: Les Belles Lettres, 1974), 147.
41. Abraham Joshua Herschel, *The Earth Is the Lord's: The Inner World of the Jew in East Europe* (New York,: Henry Schuman, 1950), 40, 45–47.
42. Mickiewicz, *Dzieła,* 11:458.
43. See Abraham G. Duker, "Jewish Volunteers in the Ottoman–Polish Cossack Units during the Crimean War," *Jewish Social Studies* 14 (1954): 352, 354.
44. Mickiewicz, *Dzieła wszystkie,* 16:431.
45. Mickiewicz, *Dzieła,* 16:634.
46. Duker, "Mickiewicz and the Jewish Problem," 110–11.
47. Roman Brandstaetter, *Legion żydowski Adama Mickiewicza* (Warsaw: OSTOJA, 1932), 4.
48. Mickiewicz, *Dzieła wszystkie,* 16:417. See also Ksenia Kostenicz's elaboration on this fragment in "Ostatnie lata Mickiewicza: Styczeń 1850–26 listopada 1855," in *Kronika życia i twórczości Mickiewicza* (Warsaw: Instytut Badań Literackich PAN, 1978), 479.
49. See Franciszek Rawita Gawroński, "Sadyk Pasza i Adam Mickiewicz," *Przewodnik Naukowy i Literacki* 9 (1898): 946.
50. Stanisław Szpotański, *Adam Mickiewicz i jego epoka* (Warsaw: Wydawnictwo J. Mortkowicza, 1922), 3:107.
51. See Kostenicz, "Ostatnie lata Mickiewicza," 479.
52. Stanisław Pigoń, "Z ostatnich chwil Adama Mickiewicza," *Myśl Narodowa* 45 (1932): 641.
53. As cited in Brandstaetter, *Legion żydowski Adama Mickiewicza,* 35–36.
54. Duker, "Jewish Volunteers in the Ottoman–Polish Cossack Units," 358.

55. Brandstaetter, *Legion żydowski Adama Mickiewicza,* 25, 15, 38.
56. Duker, "Jewish Volunteers in the Ottoman–Polish Cossack Units," 216.
57. Gawroński, "Sadyk Pasza i Adam Mickiewicz," 946.
58. See Borejsza, *Sekretarz Adama Mickewicza,* 130.
59. Mickiewicz, *Żywot Adama Mickiewicza,* 4:lxxiv.
60. Mickiewicz, *Dzieła,* 16:431.
61. I am adopting a phrase Jan Doktór uses to describe the teaching of the Sabbatians. See his *Śladami mesjasza-Apostaty: Żydowskie ruchy mesjańskie w XVII I XVIII wieku a problem konwersji* (Wrocław: Fundacja na Rzecz Nauki Polskiej, 1998), 245.
62. See Brandstaetter, *Legion żydowski Adama Mickiewicza,* 11.
63. Brandstaetter, *Legion żydowski Adama Mickiewicza,* 11–12.
64. Mickiewicz, *Dzieła,* 16:417–18.
65. Brandstaetter, *Legion żydowski Adama Mickiewicza,* 5.
66. Mickiewicz, *Dzieła,* 16:418.
67. Brandstaetter, *Legion żydowski Adama Mickiewicza,* 5.
68. Mickiewicz, *Żywot Adama Mickiewicza,* 4:426.
69. Mickiewicz, *Dzieła,* 16:428.
70. Mickiewicz, *Dzieła,* 16:428.
71. Moses Hess, *Rome and Jerusalem: A Study in Jewish Nationalism,* trans. Meyer Waxman (New York: Bloch Publishing Company, 1918), 150–51n9
72. Mickiewicz, *Dzieła,* 11:436.
73. Mickiewicz, *Dzieła,* 4:lxxxix.
74. Mickiewicz, *Dzieła wszystkie,* 12:260.
75. Brandstaetter, *Legion żydowski Adama Mickiewicza,* 7.
76. See Duker, "Jewish Volunteers in the Ottoman–Polish Cossack Units," 368.
77. Brandstaetter, *Legion żydowski Adama Mickiewicza,* 25.
78. Duker, "Jewish Volunteers in the Ottoman–Polish Cossack Units," 368.
79. Maurer, "'Jak mnie nie stanie, nikt tego nie zrozumie,'" 120–21.
80. Mickiewicz, *Żywot Adama Mickiewicza,* 4:434.
81. This exchange took place in volume 10 of *Przewodnik Naukowy i Literacki* (1898), 1116–18.
82. See Duker, "Jewish Volunteers in the Ottoman–Polish Cossack Units," 354, 358
83. Maurer, "'Jak mnie nie stanie, nikt tego nie zrozumie,'" 119.
84. Leo Belmont, *Mojżesz współczesny: Powieść-studium* (Warsaw: Dom Książki Polskiej, 1931), 100–104.
85. Brandstaetter, *Legion żydowski Adama Mickiewicza,* 69.
86. Rafał Blüth, "Konstantynopolitańska katastrofa" (1932), in *Pisma literackie,* ed. P. Nowaczyński (Kraków: Znak, 1987), 101–3.
87. See Wiktor Weintraub, "Studia literackie Rafała Marcelego Blütha," in *O współczesnych i o sobie: Wspomnienia, sylwetki, szkice literackie,* ed. Stanisław Barańczak (Kraków: Znak, 1994), 310; and Maurer, "'Jak mnie nie stanie, nikt tego nie zrozumie,'" 95.
88. As quoted in Mateusz Mieses, *Polacy: Chrześcijanie pochodzenia żydowskiego* (Warsaw: Wydawnictwo M. Fruchtmana, 1938), 2:136.

89. Mieczysław Braun, "Syjonizm Adama Mickiewicza," *Nasz Przegląd* 14, no. 1 (Warsaw, 1939).
90. As quoted in Ewa Bieńkowska, "Wybór i tożsamość," *Aneks*, nos. 51–52 (1988): 125.
91. Roman Brandstaetter, "Cholera, trucizna—i Legion żydowski Mickiewicza," *Nowy Dziennik*, August 28, 1932.
92. Gershom Scholem, "Le mouvement sabbataïste en Pologne," *Revue de l'histoire des religions* 143 (1953): 77.

CHAPTER 10

Fragments from a Lover's Discourse

The In-Between

Early in 1993, the *Neue Zürcher Zeitung* ran an article about a fascinating new generation of women writers. Born in the sixties, these Swiss–German writers embody a novel political attitude. They are neither activists nor ardent feminists, nor do they ostentatiously pursue self-fulfillment and self-realization. Their writing is coolly, ironically nonconformist; it tends toward the grotesque and the absurd. Among these emergent writers, the Swiss newspaper names Milena Moser, Andrea Simmen, and—of particular interest to us here—Nicole Müller. The author of the article, Beatrice von Matt, describes Müller as a writer of subtle aesthetic ambitions, which she cannot express as freely as the two others. That is because Müller belongs to a minority and is highly conscious of it. Naturally, von Matt admits, *all* women writers constitute a minority in the publishing world, compared to male authors; Müller, however, is not only a woman, but also a lesbian—and seeks to give voice to her experience as one. . . .

Nicole Müller's *Denn das ist das Schreckliche an der Liebe* [Because that's the terrible thing about love, 1992] consists of 498 numbered fragments. Some readers recoil from its nonnarrative, protocolar quality. But that is the price Müller pays in her search for a new language. Her novel is a battlefield in which writing struggles to catch up with the pace of life, in an atmosphere of absolute seriousness. "192. One must write the way one breathes." "193. I write for my life. Let no one harbor illusions about this."[1] Müller's narrator does not shy away from grand statements. Writing becomes an organic function, thereby revealing how difficult it is to capture life on the page. Everything that matters always takes place in liminal, "in-between" spaces.

Toward the beginning of the novel, the narrator describes herself as follows: "In-between. I am between two genders. Between two countries. Between two languages. Three, actually. German, Swiss-German,

French." In the narrator's eyes, being "in-between" has no advantages. It makes life discontinuous. Yet Müller shows that this discontinuity can become a space of discovery. Like in Roland Barthes's *A Lover's Discourse: Fragments* (1977), the fragment becomes the building block of a new literary discourse.

Müller's "fragments from a lover's discourse," like Barthes's, speak the language of sexuality. Sexuality, for her, is a discourse of power, mastery, and hierarchy. The West is grounded in the mythology of *Logos,* the Word. It conceives of reality as a system of hierarchized binary opposites, including an irreducible gender binary in which anything coded male is inevitably privileged. Women who write can criticize this system but cannot leave it. Movements like *écriture féminine* try to move women's writing out of these binaries, but that is not Müller's enterprise; she notes that women writers who criticize the West and *Logos* are also victimized by them. Her novel continually asks: How can one write (*can* one ever write?) beyond discourses of power? And, second, can writing ever take place beyond normative social discourses?

Consider a few of the fragments devoted to the subject of homosexuality:

> 268. Few understand that being homosexual is catastrophic, above all, for the homosexual herself. No one becomes homosexual willingly.
> 269. It takes great courage to break rules without perishing in the process. . . .
> 434. Suffer, but quietly. Cry out with pain, but kindly mind our ears. Be homosexual if you must, but in the confines of your home.[2]

The sequence shows that social catastrophe threatens the homosexual: Society demands that sexual taboos be veiled in secrecy. Müller's narrator speaks of homosexuality with fatalism; it is not something anyone wants to happen to them. She sketches out a tragic conflict in which she must fall because of a fatal necessity she did not wish upon herself. This vision of homosexuality is far from, say, Jean Genet's. The latter's prose works on a different plane in which these tragic contradictions do not occur. His is a pure genital poetics that recognizes nothing as divided or forbidden. No wonder Hélène Cixous sees Genet as a proponent of *écriture féminine.*

Müller thinks differently. You have not perished, and so you write; you do not perish so that you can write. Her brand of homosexuality finds fulfillment without progeny, yet keeps them in mind: It is to "children" that her novel is dedicated. For Müller, this is not a matter of metaphor, of seeing writing as a form of procreation. "475. I am the mother of my texts. But they are not my children."[3] This is another instance of the paradoxical liminality that constitutes the main existential theme of Müller's novel.

The plot is easy to summarize, as the author herself does in the brief statement titled "The Story" that precedes the 498 fragments. However, Müller warns us, "what's most important is between the lines." The novel obsessively reiterates such statements; meanwhile, conventional forms of literary mimesis fail its narrator. "272. . . . What existed between her and me cannot be conveyed through anecdotes, boiled down to dialogue. It's also pointless to list the physical pleasures. Everything that we had was between the lines." The work of memory and mourning over the loss of her lover takes place beyond language. Facing the departure of a loved one makes Müller's narrator crave a new, different kind of idiom. "382. . . . To find a language that speaks between the lines. A language that conveys life's wonders and its wounds, and does not leave one with the nauseating aftertaste of emptiness, of things left unsaid and those that can never be said."[4] *Eine Sprache zu finden, zwischen den Zeilen, die das Wunder und die Wunden des Lebens erfassen könnte* is how Müller puts the key part of this passage in German. The poetic assonances underline the magical powers that her novel attributes to, and wants to extract from, words.

Flayed

What's most important must stay between the lines. Yet the novel goes on, in a montage of fragments and short passages. Barthes, whose *Lover's Discourse* I mentioned above, makes an appearance when the narrator receives his collected works as a gift from her lover. [. . .]

When Barthes published *A Lover's Discourse* in 1977, he explained "the necessity for this book" as follows:

> The lover's discourse is today of an *extreme solitude*. This discourse is spoken, perhaps, by thousands of subjects (who knows?), but warranted by no one; it is completely forsaken by the surrounding

> languages: ignored, disparaged, or derided by them, severed not only from authority but also from the mechanisms of authority (sciences, techniques, arts). Once a discourse is thus driven by its own momentum into the backwater of the "unreal," exiled from all gregarity, it has no recourse but to become the site, however exiguous, of an *affirmation*. That affirmation is, in short, the subject of the book which begins here . . .[5]

Barthes believes that even the stubborn, recalcitrant, aggravating tones of the lover's voice deserve a hearing. He chooses to *enact* this voice rather than merely describe it. He gives the lover's discourse back to the lover himself to "stage an utterance, not an analysis." The lover's portrait Barthes creates is structural rather than psychological in nature: "the site of someone speaking within himself, amorously, confronting the other (the loved object) who does not speak."[6]

Barthes creates a dictionary of the lover's discourse, arranged in alphabetical order. Some of the entries copy out fragments from canonical literary works about love, such as Goethe's *Sorrows of Young Werther* or Plato's *Symposium*. Alongside them, Barthes cites fragments from Zen scriptures, the writings of psychoanalysts, mystics, Friedrich Nietzsche, the composers of German lieder. "Some come from conversations with friends. And there are some which come from my own life."[7]

A Lover's Discourse is one of the strangest annotated anthologies I have encountered. It does, as Barthes announces, confront us with the fragments of a lover's discourse at its most solitary and abandoned, most ostentatiously centered around the speaking self. Those adjectives all characterize Müller's novel, too, as her narrator struggles to make sense of the one dedication her lover ever addressed to her: "Oui, les mots pour LE dire" (Yes, the words to say IT).[8]

Müller's narrator contemplates several ways she could tell the story of her exceptional passion:

> 272. Having completed 271 of these short episodes, each no more than a few lines long, I was overcome by the desire to speak the way pub goers do as they hold their tall beer mugs. Their eyes turned glassy, their gestures chaotic, they embark on their life stories. They are not sure if anyone is listening. The bar is full of smoke, they prop up their heads on their elbows against the table; when they try to put out their cigarettes,

> they miss the ashtray. Speaking into the void, they reveal their fates scrap by scrap. I'd like to sit like that, taking comfort in a beer bottle, and talk about the love of a century—to myself, to nobody in particular, for whom would I tell it to?[9]

Does the narrator then embark on a long, rambling, beer-infused tale addressed to no one in particular? No, of course not . . .

Müller might be giving us a more sincere hint in fragment 351, part of which describes how one should peel a shrimp. "I buy shrimp. My guest, a young man, has never had them. 'Pardon me,' he asks. 'How do I do this?' I raise the cooked animal between my fingers. 'Start by tearing off the head, then break the shell open with your nails, starting at the stomach. Peel it off. Take the tail between your fingers, press down, and pop! The shrimp is out.'" Soon afterward, the narrator adds that "writing involves pounding at things until they reveal their innards."[10]

"The shrimp is out." It has been excavated; one could also say it has been flayed. The passage brings to mind famous representations of *l'écorché,* the flayed human body. *L'écorché* began its life in anatomy, as a depiction of the muscular system. But from the start, as Roger Caillois observes, there was something baroquely fantastical about these images. Eventually, they came to emblematize a certain narrative style, along the lines of Michel Tournier's philosophical novels. I suspect that Müller's story about the shrimp is also a story about the act of flaying. *A Lover's Discourse* contains an entry on *l'écorché* too. Parodying Plato's Socratic dialogues, Barthes stresses that the lover is not, as Plato would have it, covered in feathers, but stripped of his skin. He has a point.

Müller aims to get inside reality, to lay facts not just bare but *open.* A metaphoric connection emerges here between the body and the writing process. As Michel Tournier puts it, citing Paul Valery, "La verité est nue, mais, sous le nu, il y a l'écorché" (The truth is naked, but beneath the naked, there is also the flayed).

Homosexual Romantic Love

The feeling Müller's novel depicts is best described as *romantic love.* In many respects, romantic love goes against the conventions of patriarchal society—as does homosexual love between women. Some critics, such as Bożena Chołuj, see the novel's love plot as conventionally and constrainingly heterosexual, a trivial version of the love triangle. I disagree: Müller represents homosexual romantic love as a means of breaking free from the social order and creating a love discourse that is free from its conventional continuities, following the spirit of Barthes's fragments.

In *Immortality,* a book that is part novel, part essay, Milan Kundera contemplates the relationship between love and sexual intercourse. He argues that European culture separates romantic love from copulation. "All the great European love stories," Kundera writes, "take place in an extracoital setting." Among these great love stories, Kundera names novels such as *La Princesse de Clèves* and *The Sorrows of Young Werther.* "The twentieth century, which boasts that it liberated morals and likes to laugh at romantic feelings, was not capable of filling the concept of love with any new content" beyond the old, romantic one. Kundera sees this incapacity as one of the twentieth century's main failures: It came up with nothing new in the domain of love. He criticizes those who succumb to romantic feelings; for him, it is a form of false consciousness. The two lovers *Immortality* describes live under the influence of precoital amorous thinking, which tends to associate love with the Absolute. "Love, in order to prove itself true, wishes to escape the sensible, wishes to reject moderation, doesn't wish to seem probable; . . . in other words, wishes to be mad!"[11] Against this background, Kundera undertakes a critique of romantic love through the example of Bettina von Arnim's relationship to Goethe.

The purpose and object of Bettina's love, claims Kundera, was not Goethe but love itself. He mockingly recounts what *die wahre Liebe,* true love, meant for Bettina. But his argument distorts and falsifies her characteristic attitude toward death and immortality, as she conveys it in both her correspondence with Goethe and her book about Günderrode. Kundera does not notice that what Bettina enacts in her books, which are based on actual exchanges of letters but are also a form of recasting, of *reécriture, . . .* is *the work of mourning.* Her melancholic style stems from the double phantasmatic conviction that the beloved cannot be completely let go of but cannot be eternally held on to either. This double belief results in a paradoxical strategy: Bettina's writerly "I" protects the deceased but also seeks to destroy him. Her writing attempts to preserve the discourse of the other—Goethe's or Günderrode's—but also to extinguish it by absorbing it into her own voice. Bettina von Arnim performs an impossible task. She is not merely, as Kundera suggests, trying to hitch her wagon to Goethe's and pass into immortality along with him. Even as she remains faithful to the dead, she wants to let go of them through an idiosyncratic process of mourning. Müller's novel undertakes an analogous labor, as its narrator speaks from the perspective of an irretrievable loss.

All of the classics of European literature represent romantic love as one that is lost or otherwise doomed to loss or failure. One of Müller's fragments consists of a famous quotation from Cesare Pavese: "102. 'The thing most feared in secret always happens.'"[12] This is a form of fatalism. Her discourse strives to make sense of a state that Barthes also lists among his dictionary entries: "I am crazy." "It frequently occurs to the amorous subject that he is or is going mad," Barthes specifies. What does that mean? "I am mad to be in love, I am not mad to be able to say so, I double my image: insane in my own eyes (I know my delirium), simply unreasonable in the eyes of someone else, to whom I quite sanely describe my madness: conscious of this madness, sustaining a discourse about it."[13] At bottom, to say, "I am crazy," is to say that I have become doubled. Love has driven me mad, but I can still talk about it.

Romantic love reveals itself in books and acts through them. Accordingly, *The Sorrows of Young Werther* and several sonnets by Adam Mickiewicz will help me lay out some of its principal qualities.

Romantic love resembles a dangerous, violent predator in how it acts on us. Its descriptions are reminiscent of ancient and biblical stories about divine beings who possess a chosen human being. Through it, the *violence of the absolute* takes physical form. Werther thus describes the effects of spending an extended amount of time with his lover: "My imagination beholds no figure but hers; and I see the things of the world about me only in relation to her. . . . When I have been with her for two or three hours, entranced by her ways and the divine expressiveness of her words, my senses gradually become excited, my sight grows dim. I can hardly hear a thing. I have difficulty breathing, as if a murderer held me by the throat."[14]

A blinding, deafening, amorous trance can only result in an ever-festering injury. Müller compares returning memories to dumdum bullets that, upon encountering resistance in the body they enter, "begin to spin and carve out terrible wounds." Mickiewicz's *Sonety krymskie* [Crimean sonnets, 1826] compare them to a hydra that "sleeps when times are hard and passions are high. But once the heart has calmed, out come its claws."[15] The heart only ever *seems* calm; dumdum bullets and the claws of hydras, or a murderer reaching for one's throat, are always just around the corner.

Müller describes books as "our love's milestones." Books inspire and guide romantic love; they are sites where lovers can attain absolute understanding and their feelings can be fixed into stillness. Committing one's passions to paper can involve great intellectual and emotional difficulties. Love loses its original form and quality in the process; immobilized by being written down, it can die. But writing also brings recognition, remembrance, and mourning, romantic's love essential components. With tears in his eyes, Werther names Klopstock and Ossian to Lotta—and no further amorous tirades are necessary to get his point across. Müller's narrator lists several books that serve a similar purpose for her, including *La Princesse de Clèves* by Madame de Lafayette. The narrator's beloved reads this novel out loud to her. The narrator comments that "all the books she gave me told stories about love that ends in resignation."[16] "Resignation" as a form of loss lies in the province of romantic love as well. Alongside absolute forms of feeling, it is the subject of *La Princesse de Clèves,* even if the concept of romantic love had not yet developed in seventeenth-century Europe. The husband of the princess dies because of how much he loves her. She then refuses to marry Monsieur de Nemours, her longtime admirer whom she loves to distraction, because she fears that marriage might endanger their mutual feeling and wishes to preserve its current form. "Dare I put myself in a position whence I shall be obliged to witness the death of a love in which lies all my joy? There was perhaps one man and one man only capable of being in love with his wife, and that was M. de Clèves."[17] M. de Clèves was the "only" one who could have done it; now, there is no one, and there might not be for centuries. In this sense, her passion does not end merely in resignation but in an attempt to preserve love as an absolute value by arresting it. Nietzsche, too, observes how often we kill what we love so that the object of our feelings can never change. In Goethe's *Elective Affinities,* Ottilie and Eduard die of love; theirs is an ideal bond of feeling whose further development has been forever checked. Romantic love necessarily touches borders with death; a love of death, it easily becomes death itself.

Müller's narrative "I" accordingly performs a dress rehearsal for her suicide: "378. It is amazing how many practical problems one must overcome to commit suicide. I used a carpet cutter to open up one of my arteries, just slightly, no more than half an inch, to make sure that when the time came, I would find the right spot for the incision. The lesion was bloody, gelatinous, generally strange-looking, but I had aimed correctly: *The blood pulsed out in rhythm with my beating heart.*" The nearly trivial naturalism of this gory suicide attempt brings to mind the martyrdom of young Werther. The lover-suicide pays us a visit: Is he or she still alive, or already a phantom? Romantic poetry brims with varieties of this trope, in which it is also typically unclear whether the lover-suicide's beloved is alive or dead. In part IV of Adam Mickiewicz's *Dziady* [Forefathers' eve, 1832], the priest tells Gustaw: "But isn't the beloved you mourn alive?" The latter replies with irony:

> Alive? That would be something to thank God for!
> Alive? How? What illusions do you harbor?
> I swear to you, I kneel, I make a cross with my fingers,
> She has died, and she cannot be brought back to life.

Gustaw thinks for a moment and then adds, "Granted, death takes many forms." His beloved is technically alive, but she is dead to him, having become a philistine. He recalls trying to explain the misery that befell him to a crowd. "One of them calls me a liar. Another nudges me and cries, 'Look, madman, there she is!'" Gustaw believes they are all wrong: His beloved is no more.

Müller's novel begins with announcements of death: "51. I straighten my arm on the bedsheet. Even then, we carried death inside us."[18] Some pages later, the narrator speculates whether her lover has died already, and nobody has told her. A Romantic duality emerges here: Perhaps the beloved has died, which would be a reason to despair; however, maybe her death would not be a bad thing. Jean-Jacques Rousseau's *Nouvelle Héloïse* well conveys this emotional ambivalence: "Would that she were dead! I dared cry that out in a fit of rage; yes, I should be less happy if she were. . . . But she lives; she is happy! . . . She lives, her life is my death, and her happiness is my torment. After having torn her from me, Heaven has taken from me even the pleasure of regretting her loss!"[19] Müller's fragment 410 sounds like a consciously self-trivializing, furious paraphrase of this passage from Rousseau. "Things are horrible, horrible, horrible. She is beautiful, she is laughing, she is happy, she has free time, she eats, she works, she plays with children, she fucks; in short, she exists without me."[20] It may have been better, the narrator implies, if her beloved had died: She would have been halted for good, and the work of mourning could have gone on more peacefully.

The Work of Mourning and Salvation

In a sequence of three early fragments, Müller sets up a mysterious connection between homosexuality and writing:

> 17. What I find unbearable about my homosexuality is the way it compels me always to think about death.
> 18. The thing you refuse to understand, V. told me, is that the child emerges from the body of the mother.
> 19. The thought that, for the rest of my life, I will give birth to nothing but sharp-edged, dry objects, horrifies me.[21]

Thoughts of death connect here with those of childlessness. "The child emerges from the body of the mother," says Müller, who dedicates her book to "children." Yet the narrator "will give birth to nothing but sharp-edged, dry objects." This "sharp-edged, dry object" might be the brick the narrator discusses later; it might also be the book we are holding. Is homosexuality tantamount to parenting only book-children?

The narrator backs away from this metaphoric connection. In fragment 147, she writes that "describing one's book as if it were a child, with the concomitant vocabularies, as something one births, something that causes birth pains, and so forth, is highly distasteful to me. Instantly, the following though comes into my head: The child is something else entirely."[22] The metaphor of books as children comes from male writers, aspiring creators who need to compensate for their inability to bear real-life progeny. For Müller, the writer is the mother, the father, and the child of her act of creation.

Homosexuality is not to blame for the failure of one's attempts at creation. The narrator describes writing as an internal spiritual sediment. "206. For years, a mental image pursued me. Writing lay like a brick within my chest. If I had tried to spit it out all at once, I would have ripped my throat open. But meanwhile, its sharp edges painfully jostled against my ribs with every step. Now I am finally spitting it up, pulverized into small, homeopathic doses." The brick, the unwritten manuscript, comes out the throat as brick powder. Otherwise, it would kill the narrator. Her experience is impossible to externalize in its entirety. As the narrator writes toward the end of the novel, in fragment 494, "Words always come too late. Words always appear later. First, you live."[23] Life cannot write itself, which is why she has taken on the task of doing so—but she has not done justice to it. In this sense, the novel documents not an amorous but an artistic failure. With painful self-recognition, the narrator admits that she did not capture the truth of her life the way she hoped to. Perhaps that had always been an impossible task. Writing exists beyond the breath of life, and possibly it might be lethal, even though Müller's narrator enjoins herself to "write the way one breathes."

At the very end of the novel, literature becomes the narrator's salvation. Until then, she has carried on the work of mourning in a state of timelessness, without allowing herself to imagine a future. The past had become an eternity. "272. The terrible thing about love is the way the beloved enters you, becomes part of you, and you cannot tear her out without renouncing a part of yourself." The beloved becomes incorporated into the "I." That is the paradoxical work of mourning: It reanimates the deceased person without actually being able to bring her back to life. The beloved continues to exist within the lover, both dead and alive. Then, the following happens in fragment 487: "I felt my love break open the ice on whose surface it lay. Making a long, gentle sound, it sank into the depths, to remain anchored here forever."[24] When fate inexplicably decrees that one's mourning is complete, the lost love can fall to the bottom of the abyss. Along with part of oneself, it remains buried there. A dead piece of the self has been parted with.

The narrator cites a salvific phrase from Hélène Cixous: "Flee, don't turn back, it's not worth it: There is nothing behind you, and everything before you."[25] The narrator feels rescued from the condition of only existing in the past. She saves herself from an impending catastrophe; though she still carries her lost love within her, she has allowed it to sink into the abyss. She carries its weight but is walking into the future. Cixous speaks to her, and her words tear the narrator out of the past.

Roland Barthes is Müller's beloved writer. Marguerite Duras had once described him wryly as "a writer who has never known women."[26] [. . .] For Duras, one cannot write about love without having known them.

Müller is not as bothered by Barthes's limitations, and worships Duras alongside Barthes for their ability to tie *Logos,* the Word, back to life itself—a task that Müller sees as one of the most important aims of contemporary literature.

Yet it is neither Barthes nor Duras, but Cixous, who brings Müller's narrator salvation. Though Müller does not engage in *écriture féminine,* she takes up its verve, the courage of its rebellion against the Word. Lonely and banished, not unlike Cixous, she hears this other woman's voice calling her from the other side. Müller's narrator had previously secreted away this sentence like a precious treasure. Now she displays it, letting Cixous exhort all mourners: *Do not turn back.*

Notes

1. Nicole Müller, *Denn das ist das Schreckliche an der Liebe* (Zurich: Nagel and Kimche, 1992), 63–64.
2. Müller, *Denn das ist das Schreckliche an der Liebe,* 83, 144–145.
3. Müller, *Denn das ist das Schreckliche an der Liebe,* 157.
4. Müller, *Denn das ist das Schreckliche an der Liebe,* 8, 86, 120–21.
5. Roland Barthes, *A Lover's Discourse: Fragments,* trans. Richard Howard (New York: Wiley, 1978), 1.
6. Barthes, *Lover's Discourse,* 4, 3.
7. Barthes, *Lover's Discourse,* 8.
8. Müller, *Denn das ist das Schreckliche an der Liebe,* 65.
9. Müller, *Denn das ist das Schreckliche an der Liebe,* 84–85.
10. Müller, *Denn das ist das Schreckliche an der Liebe,* 109–10, 114.
11. Milan Kundera, *Immortality,* trans. Peter Kussi (New York: Grove Weidenfeld, 1991), 196, 197, 298.
12. Müller, *Denn das ist das Schreckliche an der Liebe,* 38.
13. Barthes, *Lover's Discourse,* 121.
14. Johann Wolfgang von Goethe, *The Sorrows of Young Werther,* trans. Michael Hulse (New York: Penguin Classics, 1989), 67
15. Adam Mickiewicz, *Dzieła poetyckie* (Warsaw: Czytelnik, 1979), 210.
16. Müller, *Denn das ist das Schreckliche an der Liebe,* 309.
17. Madame de Lafayette, *La Princesse de Clèves,* trans. Robin Buss (New York: Penguin Classics, 1962), 188.
18. Müller, *Denn das ist das Schreckliche an der Liebe,* 22.
19. Jean-Jacques Rousseau, *La Nouvelle Héloïse: Julie, or the New Eloise,* trans. Judith H. McDowell (University Park: Pennsylvania State University Press, 1986), 364.
20. Müller, *Denn das ist das Schreckliche an der Liebe,* 132.
21. Müller, *Denn das ist das Schreckliche an der Liebe,* 13–14.
22. Müller, *Denn das ist das Schreckliche an der Liebe,* 50–51.

23. Müller, *Denn das ist das Schreckliche an der Liebe,* 67, 172.
24. Müller, *Denn das ist das Schreckliche an der Liebe,* 85, 168.
25. Müller, *Denn das ist das Schreckliche an der Liebe,* 174.
26. Marguerite Duras, "Je vous regarde, ou Le 1er juillet 82," in *Œuvres complètes,* ed. Gilles Philippe (Paris: Gallimard, 2014): 1275.

CHAPTER 11

The Bad Child

INTERVIEWS

The Germans, the Russians, the Jews

KAZIMIERA SZCZUKA: *Your reading habits amount to a biblio-bulimia. How can you explain them?*

MARIA JANION: Reading puts me in a trance; I've always been that way. It may have helped me survive the German and Soviet occupations: I led a phantasmatic literary life in parallel with what was happening around me. The little diary I kept in the forties brims with terror. For example, in entries from June 14 and 15, 1941, I express dread over the mass resettlements of Polish people by the occupant Soviet army: "Today, the Bolsheviks shipped away crowds of Poles; they have been shipping Poles away in endless throngs!" Then, Jews began to be persecuted, sometimes by Lithuanian locals, but mostly by Germans. My entry from July 21, 1941, reads as follows: "Today, they burned all the books from the synagogue and made the Jews strip naked and walk around the fire. Barbarism!" At the time, my mother, my brother, and I were living on Końska Street, right by the Vilnius ghetto. A young Jewish woman, a friend of the family, visited my mother under the supervision of an armed policeman shortly before the mass murder of the Jews in Ponar. She came inside, saw me immersed in my reading, and cried out, "How I wish I could read books and go to school!" I recognized the abyss between our fates. To this day I cannot forget this moment, and I still feel survivor's guilt about it.

In an interview Katarzyna Bielas once conducted with you, you describe watching the Jews of Vilnius being led away to Ponary. The image you draw is shocking, and I have returned to it many times in my own writing. The Jews are rushed into the forest. There you stand, barely a teenager; you look on and promise that you will avenge them. The scene allegorizes the ethical duties of the witness. When did this happen?

I can't recall, 1942 or 1943. I recently looked up the timeline of the genocide in a book on Ponary. People were led out of the ghetto and into the forest several times, in broad daylight. The crowd I saw was huge and luggage-laden. Everyone, including women and children, was carrying knapsacks; they believed they were merely being resettled. In the moment, I didn't know what was going to happen to them. But people had a bad feeling about it. They whispered that it didn't look good, not good at all: This forced march signaled something far worse than resettlement.

News of the genocide reached Vilnius quickly. The distance from the ghetto to the Ponary forest was less than a dozen miles. The crowd moved on foot, with armed German soldiers on either side; I didn't see any dogs. The soldiers hurried the people along with military brusqueness. All my life, I've had this image before me, as well as stories about how soldiers poured quicklime over the corpses. I heard—and I'm sure it's true—that someone remained alive under the dead bodies of others, crawled out, and ran back to the city to report what had happened. This story was told all around Vilnius: One man made it out of the quicklime, ran back to town, and described the site of the genocide. The Jews of Vilnius were not being resettled or moved to concentration camps; they were all being killed on the spot. The bodies were buried rather than burned. Among those killed there were some Gentiles, Poles as well as Lithuanians. But other Lithuanians—the Lithuanian Riflemen's Union [Lietuvos šaulių sąjunga] a special unit trained to exterminate enemy populations, helped conduct the mass shootings. Tens of thousands of Jews, all of the Jews of Vilnius, were annihilated in Ponary. To shoot so many people, it's slow, up-close work.

Were there other survivors?

A few people managed to find secret shelters. A Jewish woman, a good friend of my mother's, survived the war by hiding in the house we lived in. This woman's husband, a Polish Gentile, gave her cover. With their son, they occupied one of our spare bedrooms. I knew who they were, of course, and visited them often. This woman's sisters were massacred in Ponary. She lived in constant terror. But the gestapo never came for her. At the time, those were the only survivors I knew.

After the massacre in Ponary, the city fell silent.

It wasn't just silence; it was fear. The ghetto was completely deserted. It had been a poor neighborhood to begin with; the Jews of Vilnius owned little wealth. After they had all disappeared, I once walked through the ghetto. It terrified me. The houses were emptied out, searched through, and plundered, the doors and windows left wide open. No one in sight. I barely made it through the block without turning back and fleeing.

And what about your promise?

Seeing the Jews being rushed to Ponary made me want to do something. Exactly what I could or should do, I didn't know. The words of the ancient Carthaginian general Hannibal, as Cornelius Nepos reports them, inspired me. *Jusjurandum patri datum usque ad hanc aetatem ita conservavi:* To this day, I have kept the promise I made to my father. The books I read helped me make sense of it all. As did my Latin lessons.

Did you cry?

I don't remember. Eventually, maybe; I really don't know.

How did you keep your promise?

I tried to do so in several ways. Some were inspired by the friendships I made after the war with young Holocaust survivors: Aniela Brodzka, Aniela Kott (Jan Kott's sister), and Samuel Sandler. My dear friend Maryna Żmigrodzka and I were especially close to Samuel. He was a committed communist, but after the anti-Semitic purges of March 1968, he left for Israel. Eventually, he ended up in the United States. During those same March purges, Maryna and I lost our jobs at the University of Gdańsk. We were deemed, as they said, "Jewish in spirit." It's true I taught my students that anti-Semitism is a disgrace to humanity. But I only made real progress on fulfilling my childhood promise recently, as a much older woman. First, in *Do Europy tak, ale razem z naszymi umarłymi* [Let us join Europe, but bring our dead along with us, 2000], I wrote an extensive treatment of Judaism in the work and life of Adam Mickiewicz, Poland's greatest Romantic poet. Then, Jolanta Żyndul, an eminent expert on Judaism in Poland, invited me to give a series of lectures at the University of Warsaw that were eventually collected as *Bohater, spisek, śmierć: Wykłady żydowskie* [*Hero, Conspiracy, Death: The Jewish Lectures,* 2002]. Taken together, these two books convey all I have to say about this history.

Are there any other stories you can tell me?

Yes, eventually. We're diving deep into the past.

And in the past, the war rages on. We are in Vilnius. Do you want to kill the Germans?

I did feel rage and hatred toward them, though I didn't express these feelings in the poems I wrote at the time. In occupied Vilnius, we focused on imagining potential escape paths. Perhaps, we wondered, the British or the French will come to save us. The fall of France was a terrible blow; before then, we trusted in the fixity of the Maginot Line and thought it could never yield to the Nazis. But then, the Germans marched right across Belgium, and the Maginot myth proved hollow. So, instead, we told each other stories about British power.

How were the British supposed to save Vilnius?

In warplanes, of course. I awaited their coming eagerly. I remember how shocked I was to learn of General Sikorski's death in summer 1943. I had just graduated from junior high school. The news that reached Vilnius from the West remained terrible. We began to talk about a different boundary: the Curzon Line, established during the First World War. It marked Poland's initial, 1918 eastern border, excluding Vilnius from its territory. The possibility of this exclusion terrified me most. Soviet Russia and Nazi Germany had Vilnius in a vice; I was aware of that. News continued to trickle in. Will the British abandon us? Or won't they?

Did you want to become a soldier?

A conspirator. A runner. I wanted to go on secret missions. The partisans did allow me to help out with minor tasks, since I had been a girl scout, but not often. Mostly, they kept the youth in a state of patriotic fervor, a constant state of emergency. I took classes in the underground education system, where I formed intense friendships that were qualitatively different from anything I'd previously experienced. Both during coursework and outside it, we felt a deep connectedness, a group identity. The classes were segregated by gender, so these friend circles were all female.

Did these friendships survive?

Not really, they fell apart after we were repatriated. Or, as Krystyna Kersten used to put it, after we were expatriated. The former suggests being brought back to the homeland; the latter, being taken away from it. I felt the latter. After the German occupation ended, the Soviet army took over Vilnius in an imperious way. We did feel a brief sense of relief after the Germans departed, but Soviet resettlements began soon afterward. An officer of the NKVD moved into our home along with his wife. They requisitioned the apartment, taking up a lot of space, restricting our living quarters. I did become friends with his batman, Fied'ka. He was a lovely, older man; he liked me and occasionally brought me Soviet army soup rations. Excellent soup.

Did he make a pass at you?

No, not at all. Before the war, he worked as an accountant at a collective farm. As a young man, he had once issued an illegal grain permit. He got caught and was sent to Siberia, where he spent much of his adult life. One day, officials came to visit. "Do you want to be released?" they asked. "Yes!" everyone shouted. "Join the army and march to the front; you'll find your freedom there." Fied'ka signed up. He walked all the way from Siberia to Vilnius. He and the officer he served occupied our house for some time before marching onward to Berlin. They boasted that they would conquer Berlin, and so they did. Then came another wave of Soviet soldiers and a second wave of resettlements, worse than the first one. So many people. Each morning, we woke up to news of thousands having been taken away. Some were sent to the coal mines in Donbas. When people asked Red Army soldiers what the coal mines were like, they replied, "Zhit' budyesh, nojebat' nie zakhotshiesh" [You'll live, but you won't feel like fucking anymore]. Somehow, my family didn't get taken away. But we did have our apartment searched, by the order of the officer who roomed with us.

Why?

He felt like it; he was a cruel man.

And Fied'ka couldn't warn you?

There wasn't anything he could do. He did sometimes whisper to us that his commanding officer was a bad man—but that nothing could be done about it. I remember that house search: They made me open my book chest, looking for anti-Soviet literature. My family left Vilnius in 1945. Otherwise, we would have been forcibly resettled—or so we told ourselves. My high school classmates left as well; we all preferred to go to Poland rather than move east. So, in the spring of 1945, my mother, brother, and I packed our bags and boarded a freight train. The train took us ever farther west; we weren't sure where it was going, or how we would find shelter at the destination. We made a brief stop on the outskirts of Poznań. People went out to relieve themselves; then we heard gunshots. Jesus and Holy Mary! Some of us fell to the ground, others started to crawl back toward the train; everyone panicked. Then the conductor appeared, walking alongside the train and shouting, "People, people, the war is over!" I remember this moment very well. Somebody once told me they were jealous of this story.

It's straight out of a movie.

Yes! The war is over; people are shooting their guns into the air to celebrate. But we don't all rush to embrace each other because nobody believes the news is true. The nightmare had gone on for too long.

Where does your journey end?

In Bydgoszcz. That's where the train finally took us. We did not move to Łódź until later. . . .

Why Łódź?

It was my idea. While we still lived in Bydgoszcz, I finished high school as an extramural student. To graduate officially, I had to take a series of final exams administered in Toruń. I was admitted to take these exams based on my underground teachers' written assessment of my prior course of study with them. I passed and could apply to go to university. I reached out to my former Latin teacher, Helena Kruszyńska, for advice; she told me to seek out a spot at the University of Łódź. She had bought an apartment in Łódź, on Kiliński Street: My mother ended up staying in that same apartment for the rest of her life. Ms. Kruszyńska had to leave behind much valuable property when fleeing Vilnius, but she'd been able to salvage some money; I don't know what currency it was in. I think she bought the apartment on Kiliński Street from a Jewish family migrating to Palestine. She lived there alone with an elderly servant; her husband had enlisted in General Anders's army and was fighting abroad. Ms. Kruszyńska bought me a ticket to Łódź and put me up at her apartment; then she helped my mother and my brother Mirek move to Łódź and allowed them to stay with her as well. Sometime later, she crossed the border into Germany to join her husband alongside General Anders and left the apartment to us. She and her husband eventually moved to the UK. For a while, we exchanged letters. Once I started attending university in Łódź, I discovered Bratnia Pomoc [the Brotherly Aid Society, a charity for university students with insufficient financial means]. They gave us fried potatoes, hardboiled eggs bathed in a frightful white sauce, and cod liver oil. I used the oil to fry more potatoes; how terrible they tasted. Meanwhile, a new era of my life had begun. I was a university student.

"They Just Stood There and Talked"

Student life was not all work, I hope.

We quickly formed a literary society, which eventually published a collection of poems. *Idąc razem* [Fellow travelers] is what we called this volume, to indicate our unity amid our ideological differences. Andrzej Braun was among the contributors. That year, my first year at the university, I met Maryna—Maria Żmigrodzka.

What was that like?

I saw *une jolie rousse,* a lovely redhead, as Apollinaire puts it in his poem. This lovely redhead was smarter and better-read than anyone else. I was starstruck.

Was she smarter than you? Is that possible?

Of course. She had already done university-level coursework during the war, at the underground University of the Western Territories in Warsaw. Her knowledge of Polish literature exceeded mine. And it all came so easily to her, even the task of reading heaps of Orzeszkowa's and Wyspiański's novels. Sometimes, I couldn't take it anymore, and she would summarize these novels' plots for me. Her grades were also much better than mine. She was a born valedictorian; I was a born eccentric. Effortlessly, modestly, with good-natured irony, she one-upped us all.

What was Maryna's background?

Her father was an officer, an army doctor. He had died young, but loomed large as a mythic presence. Before the war, she and her mother lived on Wilcza Street in Warsaw; she was an only child. Her red hair drew attention during the German occupation; some people tried to blackmail her mother, claiming that Maryna was Jewish. She wasn't. However, she did belong to the Home Army, so she had reason to fear denunciation. Still, she knew how to defend herself. She had poise; I don't know whether she had been born with it or she acquired it as a partisan soldier. She also spoke German beautifully, which helped. When we met, she still carried herself like an underground fighter, in the best possible sense. She told us stories about poems that she and her fellow partisans recited to each other on the eve of the 1944 Warsaw Uprising. It impressed me. In an interview she gave for Krzysztof Bukowski's documentary film about me, *Obłoki Marii Janion* [The clouds of Maria Janion, 1993], Maryna reminisced about these student days. She said that the historical context reminded her of the immediate post-Napoleonic era, when the teenage Adam Mickiewicz and the Napoleonic Wars veteran Onufry Pietraszkiewicz, both major

Romantic poets, met in the same classroom. Our friendship paralleled theirs in this regard: Maryna was four years older than me, and at that age, four years make a big difference.

You were the young Mickiewicz—down to the detail that, like him, you had been born on Christmas Eve in Vilnius. And she, a former partisan, was Pietraszkiewicz?

Yes, more or less; we didn't think too hard about the parallel. We formed a deep friendship, the single most important one in my life. It was also the first of my intimate friendships: I met my other dear friends, Alina Witkowska and Małgorzata Baranowska, somewhat later. All three women are dead now, so hopefully this ranking can't offend them. Maryna passed away in 2000, of lung cancer. She was a real addict, a chain smoker; it held her in thrall in a trancelike, self-destructive fashion. She did quit smoking eventually, but it was too late. Anyway, the four years' difference mattered a lot when we were young. She drew attention to it, calling me a child. She had a point: Unlike me, she had had an adult's experience of the war. Many of her friends and acquaintances were soldiers, veterans of the 1944 uprising. I moved in very different circles. She also had a side job as a typewriter at the National Repatriation Bureau. She typed fast and made good money there.

How did you make ends meet?

At first, I received some financial support from the university. Bratnia Pomoc also played a huge role in my life; I wouldn't have survived without them. And Ms. Kruszyńska let me stay in her apartment. Through these support structures, I was able to meet my basic needs. Ms. Kruszyńska's elderly servant gave me extra food; my mother helped me out as well. Whenever I could, I did freelance copyediting on the side.

What other peer relationships mattered most to you?

Tadeusz Drewnowski: he, Maryna, and I formed a friendly triad. Hania Kulągowska, who eventually became Piotr Słonimski's wife, was also an important person in my life. As was Alina Nofer, somewhat older than all of us, a very energetic person who studied Henryk Sienkiewicz and positivist literature. The poet Anna Pogonowska, who died recently.

Tadeusz Drewnowski writes about these student years in Łódź in his memoirs: about the coursework, the people he met, everyone's politics. "Like everyone in Łódź, we had come from every corner of Poland." He also writes that college-aged young people came to Łódź, "some by accident; some to study; and some, because they were homeless."

That's all true. Everyone yearned for closeness. Each of us had recently lived through a tragedy: the deaths of family members, the loss of friends. Most of my friends in Łódź were fellow students of Polish literature. Drewnowski, Żmigrodzka, and many others. Irena Draber and Helena Starzec were devout Catholics; we got along despite our huge ideological differences. They continually tried to convert us, and we continually tried to convert them. We all hung out at the café on Narutowicz Street, conveniently located on the way from the university to my apartment on Kilińska Street. They served us coffee and some dismal pastries . . . we had not yet taken up smoking and drinking. The Polish literature department was housed close by, right at the end of Narutowicz Street. I walked there from the apartment every day. Maryna and her mother also lived in the area, next to the train station. Drewnowski's flat was farther away, in the Julianów neighborhood. His father and brother had been killed in 1939, during the mass executions in Palmiry. His mother had been taken to the concentration camp in Ravensbrück. She had survived and come back home, but died soon after the war was over. Tadziupek—that's what Maryna and I called him—lived alone, if I recall, and I think some distant relatives sent him money. The three of us once hosted Stefania Skwarczyńska, the eminent prewar professor and one of our teachers, at Tadziupek's place in Julianów. Her visit meant a lot to us.

Drewnowski describes Skwarczyńska in his memoirs as a "young, beautiful" woman. But your social life remained chaste and well-mannered?

Private matters were not what brought us together. We met to discuss initiatives and put them into action. These practical planning meetings happened frequently; the students in our department saw a lot of each other. Ms. Kruszyńska left Łódź shortly after I moved there; once she had made it to London, the apartment became mine. My mother and Mirek moved in with me during my second year at the university. I hosted many meetings and get-togethers, as well as parties. I don't think there was anything special about the parties—but many people tended to show up, and my mother enjoyed having them there. They liked her, too. She found work at the musical theater Lutnia, which had moved to Łódź from Vilnius, the way we had. She did double duty there as an administrative assistant and as a prompter. Mirek became a student in the biology department. My mother worked hard to support her children; she wanted us to focus on our studies, to find good jobs, to escape the penury of our childhood. She took very good care of us. Before leaving for work in the morning, she would set out a breakfast plate: bread, hardboiled eggs, tomatoes, all ready for Mirek and me.

Did she find a boyfriend?

For a while, there was a man named Ryszard, whom she'd met back in Vilnius. He was a civil servant and an officer in the army; in 1939, he defended Warsaw. The Germans captured him, and he spent the rest of the war in a POW camp. He and my mother exchanged letters throughout the war; the Germans censored their correspondence, but they wrote to each other regularly all the same. Unfortunately, after the war ended, Ryszard never rejoined my mother. En route to her, he found someone else. A strange story. My mother never confided in me about her love life, but I think he hurt her deeply.

What about your love life? How did it evolve from your childhood attraction to King Kong?

I have always been attracted to girls. Early on, it was girls in general. During the war, while I was taking underground high school classes, I began to feel drawn to specific female friends.

Did you figure out how to seduce them?

Naturally. I did my best—and I was pretty good at it.

Were they freaked out by you?

No, not particularly.

Would you describe yourself as monogamous or polygamous?

I'm not sure how to answer that question. I am monogamous in some ways, polygamous in others.

I love that! Were you and Maria Żmigrodzka a couple?

No, not at all. She was attracted to men. Well, for the most part, she attracted the men around her, but the interest was mutual.

And yet, for as long as I can remember, I've heard the two of you described as romantic partners.

That's just not true. Maryna had her affairs, to be sure, but those involved men and not women. Sure, back in Łódź, we were inseparable. But I don't think anyone thought twice about it; young women often form close friendships at the university. And besides, with Drewnowski, we usually went around as a group of three. That triad didn't survive in the way Maryna's and my friendship did; but throughout many years, she and I never crossed lines with each other. We did scandalize people, but for a different reason: we were young women who freely spoke their minds in public. Once, we incited a much gossiped-about scandal at a Zjazd Kół Polonistów [Polish Literature Association Meeting] in Kraków.

What had you done?

Not much—basically nothing. "They just stood there and talked" is what my mother's friend related to her. The witness from whom she'd heard about it had been appalled to see young women behave that way. To get into polemics with everyone around you, that's just not proper female behavior. The story emphasized gender norms and rules of propriety, and how we'd contravened against them. There was also a different ideological and political matter at stake. The papers we gave were Marxist in their method; we talked about social class. At the time, most Polish literature scholars held a much more traditional outlook. Terrible clashes erupted repeatedly around this divergence.

Did the gossip upset you?

Hardly. My mother wasn't upset to hear it, either—maybe just in the general sense that hearing anyone criticize Mirek or me bothered her. Maryna and I also never cared to deny the rumors circulating about us; they felt irrelevant. Back in Łódź, we were a close-knit community. Our group had taken over the local branch of the Polish Literature Association. We constantly held executive committee meetings, open gatherings, discussions, panels. Once, we invited the poet Konstanty Ildefons Gałczyński to speak to us. He accepted, showed up, and recited poems; it was a great success. One of our events shocked the general public: an open discussion during which we criticized the actor Hanka Bielicka. Popular in Łódź, she frequently performed on local stages; we attacked her as a petite-bourgeoise starlet. At the time, all news spread through the city quickly—even minor news such as our negative opinion of her. My mother was furious with me when it reached her, and, for once, she did not take my side. Bielicka was a theatrical actor, so my mother, who worked at the theater, felt personally wounded by the criticism.

The Institute of Literary Research at the Polish Academy of Sciences

For how many years have you worked at the Institute of Literary Research? It seems like you've been there since its incipience.

Nearly sixty years—though in the last few, I have been a professor emerita. The Institute came into being soon after the war, in 1948. Initially, it was housed on Krakowskie Przedmieście, in a few rooms inside a building that had survived the war. Then, for some time, we moved to Śniadecki Street. Pałac Staszica [Staszic Palace], the institute's current home, was just a pile of rubble when we were starting out.

At first, the institute was not part of the Polish Academy of Sciences.

Well, the Polish Academy of Sciences hadn't been founded yet. So, yes, ours was a self-standing institute. Żółkiewski proposed it as a way of continuing the work of the prewar Polish Literature Association. Prewar scholars like him—Dawid Hopensztand, Żółkiewski, as well as Fryde and Kazimierz Budzyk—were close to Manfred Kridl and deeply influenced by Russian Formalism. They wanted to found an institute in which new ways of thinking could be pursued. Through the Institute of Literary Research, Żółkiewski brought this project to fruition. At first, our budget came from the Ministry of Culture.

Were any women scholars employed there?

Yes—Maria Renata Mayenowa, an eminent scholar of poetics and literary theory—though she did join us rather late. Early on, the institute employed few people. The women employees tended to be academics whom Żółkiewski had known before the war. Then there was Maryna and me. Maryna already had her master's degree; I didn't. Żółkiewski hurried me along, and I finished it quickly. I don't even remember the topic of my master's thesis; the institute absorbed me. I conversed with Żółkiewski; we made plans [. . .] His charisma is worth underlining. He knew how to organize a project, unite people around it, delegate roles. Above all, he wanted to renew our understanding of Polish literature, to help us read it with fresh eyes.

Was he the one who convinced you to specialize in Romanticism?

He was. Specifically, he wanted me to focus on Romantic poetry written within Polish territories between the uprisings of 1830–31 and 1863–64. Not émigré poetry from this period, which was glamorous and well-known; its humbler, poorly known domestic cousins. The poets I researched included Kornel Ujejski and Lucjan Siemieński. I devoted my first monograph to the latter. I also worked on Edmund Wasilewski, Ryszard Berwinski, and Wincenty Pol. Pol, like Siemieński, evolved from a progressive to a reactionary writer over the course of his life. Though minor, their poems were often surprisingly progressive, occasionally revolutionary. I like to stress that this poetry remains my main specialization. Maryna focused on novels from this period; I focused on the poems. We committed ourselves to this research. Domestic Polish Romanticism fascinated us in its difference from mystical, messianic émigré writing. Ideologically speaking, we sought in this domestic literature the roots of contemporary progressivism. Maryna eventually wrote a synthetic history of novels written in nineteenth-century Poland; I did the same for the period's poems. These histories became part of a multivolume, collaborative endeavor, *Obraz literatury polskiej XIX i XX wieku* [An account of Polish literature in the nineteenth and twentieth centuries]. This project did not see publication until some years later. By then, our contributions had lost their early, obsessive tic of labeling our sources' progressive and reactionary elements.

The literature you worked on was second-rate, especially compared to émigré Romanticism; did it repay your focus?

We wanted to undo the ways in which, and reasons why, scholars valued works of literature and literary periods. To that end, we had to examine these works from the ground up and articulate their contexts and concerns. The Enlightenment and late nineteenth-century positivism obviously resonated with Marxism as we understood it. Romanticism, by contrast, seemed alien to it. We strove to subvert this appearance of alienness. The task compelled me, especially since no one had worked on these minor Romantic writers before us. We discovered them.

What bonds tied you to Żółkiewski? Would you describe them as friendship? Or obedience?

Definitely friendship. We first became friends in Łódź; during the years we all lived in Warsaw, our bond continued to deepen. He often had us over for tea, as did his close friend, the former underground fighter and conspirator Wanda Leopold. Żółkiewski was a Viennese neopositivist. Before the war, he gave a talk about the Vienna Circle that eventually appeared in a Festschrift for Kazimierz Wóycicki. He expanded our methodological horizons. We nicknamed him Metodolo.

Sławek Sierakowski recently bought a copy of Żółkiewski's book Spór o Mickiewicza [The quarrel over Mickiewicz, 1952]; he tells me that it opens with a quotation from the first secretary of the People's Republic of Poland, Bolesław Bierut.

Żółkiewski wrote that book in 1952. It laid out his Marxist literary critical method, which hinged on the conflict between progressivism and reactionism that we've been talking about. I composed an essay about the positivist writer Piotr Chmielowski around the same time that includes a quotation from Lenin. As we saw it then, every scholarly stance was also an ideological stance—indeed, a party stance—caught within the antinomy between reactionaries and progressives.

I wouldn't worry about the Lenin quote—what you said in your book wasn't untrue, though you expressed it strongly. The conservative Polish President Lech Kaczyński also cited Lenin in his doctoral dissertation. He was maligned for it, especially by Janusz Palikot.

I remember the ruckus over Kaczyński's citations. All the same—I did write one sentence in this early book that now embarrasses me.

Maria Janion, Lucjan Siemieński: Poeta Romantyczny [Lucjan Siemieński: A Romantic poet, 1955]. I reread parts of it recently—though I confess I didn't get through the whole thing. It's such a painstaking, carefully footnoted, erudite piece of scholarship; it would have taken a scholar lesser than yourself half of their academic career to write it. I hereby recommend it to all my right-wing colleagues.

I don't know if I'd recommend it to anyone. I've come to find it boring.

Let readers struggle through it; they'll learn something.

The sentence in that book that I regret described the unification of Russia and Ukraine in the seventeenth century as a positive development. I count this sentence among my intellectual misdeeds. Ah, I remember one more misdeed: in *Humanistyka, poznanie i terapia* [The humanities, understanding, and therapy], I cited a poem by Brecht that praised the collective wisdom of the Communist Party.

Come now—you've expiated those sins manyfold. And, surely, it's still politically acceptable to cite Brecht?

Right. But the citation came out wrong in that passage. All our talk about progressiveness and backwardness conveyed our implied positive attitudes toward Russia. But the progressive literary scholarship from Russia carried a predatory, colonial undertone that became increasingly noticeable to us. Alongside so-called great books, we read many works by these Soviet literary scholars. I even wrote a detailed review of a monograph one of them wrote about Dostoevsky. The content of his book wasn't particularly predatory; it performed detailed sociological work on the relationship between Dostoevsky's writing and his life.

Were you fluent in Russian?

Before leaving Vilnius, I spent a year at a Soviet middle school. Its language of instruction was Polish, but we were taught Russian history and Russian as a foreign language. A chasm separated this new, Soviet curriculum from the prewar Polish one. Afterward, I learned more Russian on my own. I think I spoke it well. . . .

What projects did the Institute of Literary Research undertake?

At first, we imagined it as an institution that would hold big debates about major literary trends and movements. But then a serious conflict erupted among us; Maryna, Henryk Markiewicz, and I were on one side of this conflict, Żółkiewski on the other. We wanted to publish single-author monographs about individual authors' life and writing. Maryna planned to write about Orzeszkowa; Markiewicz, about Prus; and I, about Krasiński. Żółkiewski thought these kinds of books were useless and petit bourgeois to boot. The particulars of a person's biography don't reveal enough about the world, the times, the intellectual movements around her. It's not real research. That question mattered tremendously to all of us: what counted, and what did not count, as real research. For Żółkiewski, only grand methodological syntheses deserved that label; single-author monographs did not.

So, what kind of output would he have wanted you to produce?

Something neopositivist, Marxist, methodologically innovative. A description of the current order of things that prescribed how they ought to change in the future. Or a book about the development of literature across an entire literary era. A grand synthesis.

How were such syntheses politically useful?

They helped one understand how popular literary venues can be used to educate the general population. And they had a well-articulated, consistent cultural and scholarly politics. [. . .]

Were you and Żółkiewicz on first-name terms?

Yes! At some point, we all drank the *Brüderschaft* and switched to first-name terms.

What did he call you?

Misia.

Your friend Henryk Markiewicz wrote a limerick about you; it rhymed Misia Janion with wiedzy kanion [a canyon of knowledge].

Is that too much of an inside joke? Henio Markiewicz joined us early on, when Marxism interested him as well. He lived in Kraków, so we didn't see each other every day—but ours was an important, close friendship.

Marxism interested him, but he ended up writing a petit bourgeois biography of Bolesław Prus.

We did not resolve our quarrel over literary and scholarly genres—over what was worth writing about. As a result, since then, I've remained interested in the social contexts in which literature comes into being, in its location within social structures. And, of course, in questions of scholarly method. Those have always fascinated me. In 1958, at a Conference of Polish Literature Instructors, I gave a long talk with a boring title: "Tradycje i perspektywy metodologiczne badań genetycznych w historii literatury" [Traditions and methods of genetic literary history]. Clocking in at a hundred pages, an expanded version of this talk came out in the conference's proceedings in 1960. I described how Polish, German, and French scholarship approached genetic criticism, aiming to showcase the tension between a historicist and a structuralist understanding of Marxism.

It's an incredible essay: thicketed with footnotes, yet very clear—in your usual way—about the conceptual problem at stake. If Marxist literary scholarship is historicist at its core, then it's a form of genetic criticism. If it is structuralist, then its stakes are ultimately formal: They concern the internal patterns and dynamics of the text at hand. At the end of this essay, you reconcile these two alternatives. Do you ultimately advocate an eclectic approach?

Yes, you could say that. I meant to show that no ideologically driven methods were ever "pure." To assume that they could or ought to be pure goes against the necessary complexity of thought; it also goes against the broad-minded, erudite curiosity that I saw as the scholar's principal task. I believed—and I still believe—that literary theories should serve literary texts, not the other way around. Theoretical essays are themselves part of literary history and should be interpreted in its context. One should not treat them as mechanical, doctrinal tools of interpretation. My article mounted a critique of Marxism in this spirit—or rather, not of Marxism itself, but its frustratingly doctrinal uses. My colleague Głowiński claims that the group to which I belonged saw Marxism as the single most important, groundbreaking scholarly method—and structuralism, with which he sympathized, as Marxism's second-rate subordinate. But let me cite his own words, which capture the idealism of the times we were both living in. In *Kręgi Obcości* [Circles of otherness], Głowiński writes that "the Institute of Literary Research was an oasis of intellectual freedom. It did not subordinate research to any ideological dicta; and whenever some outside force tried to impose such dicta, we joined forces in pushing against them."

Revisionism

You've described the open-mindedness of mentors such as Kott and Ważyk as an early sign of the Thaw. When did you begin to suspect that the Thaw might be coming?

In Poland, Stalinism was short-lived. Stalin died in 1953, when I was already living in Warsaw. I should pause here to say a few words about revisionism. Leszek Kołakowski defines it as the belief that the Communist Party can sustain within itself a subgroup that is critical of it. That's how we defined revisionism as well, and it seemed crucial to appraise the party from the inside. To criticize it from the outside would have felt futile. Kołakowski rapidly lost hope that such internal critique can occur. After all, he argued, how could a platform that saw itself as uniquely attuned to reality accept negative feedback? Right before the Thaw, the members of the institute traveled to Czechoslovakia at the invitation of the Institute of Czechoslovak Philology. For the first time, philologists from the two countries encountered one another. For the Czechoslovaks, literary research was an inherently, necessarily Marxist pursuit. I gave a lecture that—my Czech colleagues later told me—nearly gave the head of their institute a stroke. I opened this lecture by stating that there are two versions of Marxism. That, in itself, constituted an incredibly revisionist statement.

What were these two Marxisms?

One of them was dogmatic; the other, revisionist. But the former position naturally presumed that there could only be one Marxism. No qualifiers could be appended to it.

In an interview you gave to Marta Zielińska and Anna Nasiłowska, you said that "the official version of Marxism stifled reflective thinking. This fact is so obvious that there's no point in debating it." Did you hold this view as early as the 1950s?

I did. In general, my community's discontent was palpable. We were all intellectuals and experts in our fields; we found it difficult to accept top-down party prescriptions about what we should or should not say.

How would you describe your revisionism?

It stemmed from the Enlightenment. Voltaire inspired me most of all; he inspired Maryna as well. Our anticlericalism borrowed from this eighteenth-century tradition.

Is it true that when Maryna was single and still living with her mother, she pretended to go to church every year the week before Easter? She'd take a walk around the block and return with a basket of food that had supposedly been blessed by the priest. Her mother expected her to perform this Catholic ritual, and Maryna could not bear to refuse her directly.

That's all true. Each year, Maryna feared that a bolt of lightning would strike the unblessed basket, along with the other food she prepared for Easter. But, as she put it, "year after year, nothing happened."

How did scholars of Polish literature respond to the political changes brought about by communism?

I thought a lot about this question as a student. But later, I became preoccupied with my own work. [. . .]

One could not draw a simple distinction between loyal and disloyal members of the Communist Party.

Certainly not. Between 1956 and 1968, many of us who were party members wondered if we should hand in our resignations. But we insisted that it should be possible to critique the party from the inside; that one shouldn't leave it unless one was officially expelled. I shared this attitude. Many of my friends handed in their member cards; I waited until the leadership threw me out. Which, eventually, it did.

When did that happen?

As late as 1978. [. . .] I was almost cast out in March 1968, but somehow it didn't happen. I hoped to provoke a dramatic expulsion that would reflect badly on those who expelled me. I was naive. But that's how we saw things at the time; we thought that expelling a series of serious, prominent intellectuals would cause the party embarrassment and censure. Like me, Maryna waited for the party to expel her; she finally left on her own in 1981, when Poland came under martial law. [. . .] For years, party meetings ignited futile political discussions that rapidly became personal. They irritated me. My friend Małgorzata Baranowska pointed out to me, in the early seventies, that I was obviously distraught by these meetings and ought to quit. But I clung on to my belief in internal critique, in the possibility of changing a system from the inside.

Occupy the University

You like to describe yourself simply as a teacher.

I always have. I've wanted to be a teacher since childhood, which tended to annoy those around me. I read an encyclopedia and tried to explain to my younger brother what I'd learned. I became a university teacher at an exceptionally young age. I didn't even have a master's degree when I led my first course at the University of Warsaw.

Your seminars in Gdańsk modeled how the university can be an engaged, participatory institution. Today, we often think of universities as politically neutral grounds where we learn to work within the capitalist market. But legends still circulate about your courses and your view of higher education; you treated it as a space where people could form and fashion themselves.

I believe in the inherent sensitivity and open-mindedness of every human being; this leftist as well as Romantic belief grounds my vision of education. I reflected on this conjunction of leftism and Romanticism in *Romantyzm, rewolucja, marksizm* [Romanticism, revolution, Marxism], a book I dedicate to "the University of Gdańsk as it celebrates the first anniversary of its foundation." This book came out in 1972. I began teaching my seminar on transgressions in the mid-seventies, as the political tides were starting to turn toward freedom. I framed it as a seminar, but too many people signed up, and we had to move to a lecture hall. The hall filled with the young, some of them students, some passersby from the streets of Gdańsk. Once, the mother of a high schooler filed a complaint with me: Her son had been attending my lectures instead of his classes. Many of my auditors had been driven to desperation by the emptiness and provinciality of life in communist Poland. That's how Ewa Graczyk retroactively described the ambiance of our seminar sessions. These young people's desperation seems to have drawn them to my approach toward literature as an existential endeavor, a space for thinking about the meaning of life.

Transgresje, your series of seminars on transgression, introduced these young people to new thinkers and movements; it sparked in them a thirst for intellectual freedom.

We were buoyed by the energy of May 1968. It took some time before we became able to reflect on that historical moment, but we all urgently desired to do so.

What about March 1968?

The events of March 1968 made it difficult to communicate across social boundaries; we worked hard to resolve these difficulties. March 1968 had divided society into the "people" and the "intelligentsia." The students belonged to the "people." The "intelligentsia," to which their teachers belonged, could offer them nothing beyond disillusionment.

You see students as part of the "people"? That's curious. You were teaching in Gdańsk in 1968, during the student strikes. There's a scene in Andrzej Wajda's Man of Iron *where the younger Birkut reminisces about his days as a student activist. He and his friend, played by Bogusław Linda, rush to the older Birkut, a construction worker, who forbids his son to go on strike. Linda bares his back, which the police have bruised black and blue with their batons. Still, the older Birkut is adamant. The son comments on this memory as follows: "We, the students, went on strike in 1968, and the workers didn't help us; so when the workers went on strike in 1970, we didn't help them either." That scene puts students on the side of the intelligentsia.*

It does. But in 1968, few students actually went on strike. At that point, their movement was indecisive and vague, nowhere close to the force it assumed in 1980 or 1981. Moreover, many of my students came from impoverished, long-suffering, working-class families. The people I taught were the children of what Ewa Graczyk called "Soviet rabble." They saw Transgresje as something *colorful*; the word recurs throughout their reminiscences about it.

What colors did you offer them? Were they political colors? Were these students aware that you were teaching them how to contest the norms around them?

We didn't talk about politics. But these seminars did inspire later, more politicized initiatives. Alongside the seminar, we set up a poetic circle called the New Privacy, whose members wrote intimate, personal poems. In Adam Mickiewicz's *Dziady* [Forefathers' eve, 1832], one of the great Romantic works I regularly teach, a young introspective poet named Gustaw metamorphoses into a politically engaged poet named Konrad. This history repeated itself in our poetic circles: Young poets of the private sphere went to the docks to join the dockworkers' strike. In that sense, Transgresje helped prepare the ground, at least here in Gdańsk, for the events of 1980 and 1981.

But you didn't discuss politics during the seminars themselves?

Not directly—though we did frequently discuss Poland. We talked about representations of it as a suffering, subjugated country, and about writers who rebelled against these patriotic mimetic conventions. Calling this seminar series Transgresje in itself constituted an act of rebellion, a repudiation of our patriotic duties. We also discussed transgressive forms of patriotism that lead to insanity. In Polish literature, they find their most famous incarnation in Rejtan, the patriot driven mad by his love of his country. We often returned to this figure.

Which of these two famous writers would you pick as the patron saint of Transgresje: Stanisław Brzozowski or Witold Gombrowicz?

I have to pick Brzozowski; he influenced my thinking deeply in that period. In his novel *Płomienie* [The flames], he starkly depicts the political impasses of precommunist Poland. Polish elites eat herring in cream sauce and play cards with Russian soldiers while bemoaning their occupied homeland's misfortunes. This combination of indifference and self-satisfaction, this game of appearances—I constantly pointed out and criticized instances of it to my students. "The white walls of the traditional Polish home," as his novel describes them, seemed to contain only dishonesty. Everyone talked about caring for Poland, but nobody did anything. I was commuting between Gdańsk and Warsaw in this period, constantly taking the train between these two cities. I talked to a lot of people on these commutes, and those conversations shaped my sense of contemporary Polish culture.

Transgresje emphasized individual freedom of expression and questioned preexisting cultural norms. Today, we might describe it as engaging in identity politics.

It's true. I would describe the status quo I fought against as universalism. Along with *objectivism* and *humanism, universalism* was the dominant academic catchphrase and ideology of the day. Studying literature was supposed to expose students to universal human values, to help them embrace our shared humanity without ever defining what "humanity" was, while vaguely encouraging them toward pursuing freedom. Everyone stressed the importance of "Christian values" or "human values." Academia was stuck in the kind of positivism once practiced by Piotr Chmielowski. Transgresje, by contrast, focused on otherness and difference, which comes through even in the first edited volume that emerged from these seminars, called *Galernicy Wrażliwości* [Under the yoke of sensitivity]. One of the French writers we read, Emma Santos, depicts herself as a mute madwoman who struggles against her voicelessness. Her memoirs, which some decry as hysterical, represent the perspective of an excluded being. Universalist truisms cannot explain this kind of writing. Transgresje was accused of eccentricity, worshiping pathologies, overfocusing on diseased minds. Of course, those were the themes that the students loved most.

How did your students connect these seminar discussions to the "here and now"?

You raise an important point. From the start, I insisted on making everyone aware of the specific subject position from which they speak. I drew attention to their individual sensitivities and consciousnesses, and the ways in which their qualities informed their acts of expression and interpretation. I described their subjectivity as an intellectual opportunity: Each of them can potentially contribute to our shared understanding in a unique way. Transgresje thus staged both a series of hermeneutic exercises and a process of subjective consciousness-building. Each student—or really anyone who spoke—stated, often quite bluntly, from what perspective they wanted to speak. Meanwhile, all other humanities seminars on offer encouraged students to strain toward universalisms and generalization, as if addressing some invisible, disembodied tribunal of academic wisdom.

Now your approach reminds me of Gombrowicz rather than Brzozowski; you were fighting communism by strengthening people's sense of themselves as individual, unique beings.

I agree. We also questioned conventional assumptions of what counts as research or scholarly intervention. Our universities taught students to memorize facts, titles, and dates; final exams reinforced that principle. Naturally, a humanist does need some factual knowledge; I often enjoined my students to aspire toward historical and literary erudition. But my seminar aimed to break down academic bureaucracies and hierarchies, within which students were "lower-ranked" academic staff members. Students did sometimes talk in other settings, but nobody cared what they said. Instead, knowledge was pounded into them. Transgresje fostered a diversity of voices; we heard from otherwise successful students as well as less successful ones. Many of the essays students wrote for me ended up being published. Now that was truly unheard of. How can one publish student essays, discussions, or comments? The very idea seemed offensive and scandalous to the academic establishment. They criticized me sharply for including "inappropriate" pieces of writing in the edited volumes that came out of the seminar: personal opinions and responses that literature incited in its members.

You were destroying the university and demoralizing the working classes.

Precisely. Many frowned on me. Local reviews of these edited volumes underlined that they threatened cultural hierarchies and canons.

What about your fellow faculty members? How did the university hierarchy respond to you?

Nobody spoke to me about the seminars directly. I generally enjoyed a good reputation, but people also saw me as an eccentric. A weird old lady pursuing a weird idea—this seems to have been everyone's perception. It astonished everyone when I secured a publisher for the book series: Edward Mazurkiewicz, the head of Wydawnictwo Morskie. The Central Committee of the Polish United Workers' Party even held a special meeting about me in Warsaw. I was accruing too much power, between editing the Library of Romanticism series in Kraków and the Transgresje series in Gdańsk. The matter was investigated by the academic branch of the Central Committee. People pointed out that my influence was becoming excessive . . .

You were invading Polish academia from all sides: from the north as well as from the south, from the sea and from the mountains?

[Laughs] Exactly. In 1968, I was fired from the College of Pedagogy in Gdańsk, which was supposed to cut me off from working with young people. But the young continued to reach out to me; they could not be driven away. Eventually, student petitions caused me to be restored to my faculty position. Transgresje, which I began to teach after returning to the College of Pedagogy, was shut down in similar fashion. I led it for six, maybe seven years, until I was fired once more when martial law came into force in 1981.

Would you describe Transgresje as an attempt to marry Polish Romanticism to avant-garde twentieth-century French thought?

I would. My first inspirations for the seminar came from so-called humanistic psychiatry, the work of Ronald Laing and Antoni Kępiński. Then there was Georges Bataille and Jean Genet—and Michel Foucault, of course. I introduced my students to their writings and published translations of them in the Transgresje book series. These were often the first translations of these authors' work into Polish; I know for sure that was the case for Foucault. We wanted humanists to think with social categories such as gender and class, with an emphasis on the former. To that end, we discussed forms of exclusion and otherness, of marginality to normative social structures and conventions.

You discussed people who were excluded because they were deemed insane, because they were women, because they were children. Did you see the mechanisms of socioeconomic and cultural exclusion as analogous to each other? Did becoming a madman and becoming a proletarian seem like versions of the same social process?

At the time, I thought they had a lot in common.

What did you want these comparisons and discussions to bring about?

The political emancipation of Poland.

Did you believe that could happen?

Certainly. I remember asking a graduate seminar if they knew Michał Sokolnicki's argument that Poland regained independence in 1918 through the initiative of only two hundred individuals. Two hundred! I felt a shiver go through the students. There were fifty people in the room. They only needed another hundred and fifty to liberate Poland once more. I imagined it that way myself: Two hundred people suffice to kindle a movement, to develop a new mode of thinking that will reshape reality.

But at the time, you were a member of the Polish United Worker's Party, which controlled Poland's communist regime. Didn't that commitment limit you?

It didn't. I suppose I was able to set my own, unusual terms within it.

Until you left the party after some years of teaching Transgresje.

Yes. I did give up on the party in 1978. Well, it gave up on me. Of course, when I joined the illegal, antigovernment Towarzystwo Kursów Naukowych [Society for Academic Courses], I knew what consequences I might face. I had always been among those who refused to leave the Worker's Party. Let it expel me if it needs to. And so it did. I continued to teach my seminar. Nobody criticized me to my face, but I heard back-channel reports of how my case had been discussed at party meetings. Something was found to be wrong with me. My position at the University of Gdańsk remained solid because other faculty saw me as a marginal figure. Meanwhile, I drew crowds to my courses. In some semesters, Transgresje had over two hundred participants.

You drew crowds; you invited students to contribute; the sessions ran over. What else was unusual about these seminars?

We only met once a month. I wanted to introduce my students to the French humanistic tradition, to diverse critical methods and perspectives. Regular master's seminars did not make room for such learning. But before my students could read French theory, we had to translate it—since none of them knew any foreign languages. Some of my fellow faculty used these sources' foreignness and difficulty as a pretext to draw students away from my seminars. They told students that my courses would be too hard for them. Fortunately, this rhetoric didn't work. I became very good at organizing book shipments from abroad by one trick or another. Then came the immense labor of translation. Maryna Ochab produced a masterful translation of Georges Bataille's writing; she took on this labor despite knowing that I wouldn't be able to pay her much, or promptly. My closest junior faculty collaborators, Zbigniew Majchrowski, Stanisław Rosiek, and Stefan Chwin, played a major role in initiating and carrying out these translations. Xerox machines didn't exist yet, so students shared typescripts with each other and copied them by hand. Transgresje was effectively a semilegal publishing house, a grassroots book factory. The effort this required electrified us all.

What kinds of students did you attract? Did they conform to a type, or did they come across your classes by serendipity? Were they unhinged? Brave? Politically aware?

Some were unhinged. Above all, I attracted brave ones. I had many outstanding students. When I described them as "outstanding," it took the other faculty aback. How can a student be "outstanding"? It didn't make sense. A student was just a student.

You taught French philosophy and Polish Romanticism. How would you describe your idea of the university as an institution? Was it Eastern European?

Yes, it stemmed from an Eastern and Central European tradition. I saw the university as a force of enlightenment, fueled by the imperative to educate the common people. Our contemporaries don't see it that way anymore. Nor do I know current university life; I take on doctoral students through the Polish Academy of Sciences, but master's students don't reach out to me anymore.

They have no time for that. The university has become pragmatic in its values.

How could it be anything other than pragmatic? What other special skills does it promote? The university no longer seems capable of fostering critical perspectives on the world. But perhaps it no longer needs to do so. Poland has now been liberated. We can read and buy books freely. The transgressive themes of my seminar don't seem outré anymore; popular culture has absorbed them. And aren't present-day students confident in their subjecthood?

You're kidding.

Maybe a little.

Maria Janion, the Non-Émigré Poet

Let's return to the distinction between émigré and non-émigré, "major" and "minor" Polish Romanticisms. Leszek Kołakowski left Poland after March 1968, as did many of your other friends. The reputation of the Workers' Party's had been seriously damaged after it persecuted and expelled its Jewish members. Members of the oppositional group Komandosi [Commandos] had been sent to jail. I've asked you this before, but I'll ask again. Weren't you tempted to get out of Poland at that point? You could have left it all behind, including your party card, and started a new career, say, in Paris. Instead, you chose the fate of the minor Romantics, the non-émigré poets.

After March 1968, I sensed a calamity looming over us. I wanted to prevent it by harnessing and mobilizing the energy of young people. To leave Poland at that moment would have been to abandon them. The catastrophe I saw on the horizon would have, I think, brought about the end of this country, its cultural annihilation. I had to save myself, but I also had to salvage what remained here. My employer in Gdańsk was a pedagogical college; my intra- and extramural courses educated future teachers. I wanted to have an impact within Poland; it mattered to me that the work I had already put into this teaching not go to waste. I quelled the fears that March 1968 raised in me through frantic, constant teaching. I recently looked back over *Romantyzm, rewolucja, marksizm,* which came out in 1972, and which I dedicated to "the University of Gdańsk as it celebrates the first year of its existence." In a subtitle, I called this book *Colloquia gdańskie* [the Gdańsk colloquia]. Małgorzata Czermińska, whose name features prominently in the introduction, played a great role in bringing this book into being. I owe a debt of gratitude to her for the extremely meticulous, accurate notes she took during my lectures, which proved invaluable as I turned them into a monograph. People no longer appreciate the old art of note-taking; it involves dipping into the stream of someone's speech to fish out key concepts and patterns. I recently read that the physical act of writing things longhand helps one focus. Or so it did in the old days. I wrote out my lectures before delivering them, but I didn't just read them. Instead, I spoke from memory, occasionally glancing down at my notes. Each chapter of *Romantyzm, rewolucja, marksizm* concludes with a long supplementary bibliography. These were my nontechnological means of ordering and preserving the knowledge I acquired during this period. Eventually, Transgresje began to be recorded on an old reel-to-reel audio system.

In 2008, you officially retired from teaching. Attending your last seminar session made for an intense experience. After Gazeta Wyborcza announced the seminar would come to a close, generations of your students showed up to it. Someone gave a presentation. You lectured. Discussion followed. Finally, everyone stood up and clapped. And that was that. Many of us had chills running down our backs. I had attended your seminars for over a dozen years, and you'd always led them the same way. First, you would ask students to propose paper topics and describe their academic interests; then you would prepare your lectures for the term in response to their needs. Your openness to your students' requests and suggestions helped you reinvent yourself year after year; that's how you always remained in the intellectual avant-garde. Some of us, me included, became graduate students late in life, but most of the people who joined your seminars, and to whose interests and concerns your teaching responded, were very young. I know I sound like the teacher's pet, saying all this to you—but it's true.

Well, it is nice to hear. Though I have to tell you that rereading *Romantyzm, rewolucja, marksizm* left me appalled. Horrified, even. The standard of erudition to which this book holds itself is overbearing and excessive, as if I were trying to say everything all at once. Why did I read and write so much, I wonder? Looking back at it, this older version of myself seems manic.

Weren't you doing it for the students?

Sure. But the process felt physical and alimentary: it's as if I was ramming books down my throat. However fast you gobble them up, you can't consume them all. But as the Russians say, *надо стараться:* You have to try. And so I did. In one of the documentaries made about me, Małgorzata Czermińska recalls how we would assemble at the College of Pedagogy, which was situated in Wrzeszcz on the outskirts of Gdańsk. The campus extended halfway into a forest, in the middle of nowhere; but even there, I repeated to students that we were part of Europe, and our intellectual standards could and should match those of the top European schools. I did everything I could to match these standards. After the events of March 1968, I threw myself into French and German books and journals with renewed force. My interest in Western Marxism had long preceded that political moment. But after

Polish Marxism had been discredited, this interest took on a different, revisionary meaning. I recommitted myself to it while knowing it to be a lost cause, just as I always used to defend Poland's least successful insurrection, the one that erupted in January 1861. It seems to be in my nature to defend lost causes.

In Main Currents of Marxism, Kołakowski writes that "the year 1968, which was also that of the Soviet invasion of Czechoslovakia, virtually marked the end of revisionism as a separate intellectual trend in Poland. At present, the opposition, which articulates itself in various forms, makes scarcely any use of Marxist or Communist phraseology, but finds fully adequate expression in terms of national conservatism, religion, and traditional democratic or social–democratic formulas. Communism has ceased in general to be an intellectual problem, remaining simply a matter of government power and repression."[1] Jacek Kuroń and Karol Modzelewski's Socialist Manifesto for Poland (1967) stated that Poland's communist party had become an exploitative social force; to break free from it, Poland needed a revolution of the proletariat. Your revisionism was apolitical by comparison. It aimed to highlight the cultural dimensions of leftist thinking. In this sense, it resonated with the student movements of March 1968, since, as Kołakowski also writes, communist ideology did not subtend them. . . .

I desired a less dogmatic Marxism, one that commented on specific cultural phenomena instead of offering rigid cultural norms. Many found this desire to be astonishing. Party members read my book to figure out its allegiances. That Marxism and revolution featured in the title seemed like a good sign. But when they read further, they discovered that the book disconcerted them and defied their expectations. "What does this have to do with Marxism?" people would ask. They found the views I expressed deeply odd. A man named Szlachcic, the minister of the interior, spoke about it at a high-up government meeting as the harbinger of a dangerous political movement. But again, amid all this talk, nothing happened to me or immediately around me. It would have been hard for dogmatic Marxists to write an ideological takedown of my book because its arguments were too complicated for them. So they decided to dismiss it as a "weird" book.

The book's intellectual heroes are Althusser, Lukacs, Marx in his struggle against Hegel, Freud, and Nietzsche. It also features Derrida, the Tel Quel group, Camus, Sartre, the surrealists, and the Marquis de Sade . . . too many figures for me to list here. You show how these philosophers illu-

minate some of the oldest myths of Western culture, such as the stories of Oedipus and Prometheus. You depict them as philosophers of literature following Marx's dictum that "philology must become philosophy." The revolution you call for is intellectual rather than proletarian; it involves a radical freedom of imagination and aesthetic expression.

I like this summary, even though the book overspills with details. But what else was I going to do? I had found out what Marx meant in France, and I wanted to relate this knowledge to my students. Kołakowski sees his French reception as insignificant and ludic; he dismisses it out of hand for its lack of seriousness because it doesn't reckon with the political realities of communist countries. Like most émigrés, Kołakowski became a conservative. I did not. I remained convinced that Poland needed an intellectual space in which art could be seen as autonomous from social structures and self-awareness could be recognized as a tragic condition. So-called vulgar Marxism did not allow for that; it did not accord art, literature, or culture any independent agency.

Did you wish to attain total knowledge? Did you believe that, eventually, you could come to know everything?

No. I always knew there were aspects of the world that I would never come to understand, things that would remain mysterious. I write a lot about dreams in this book, about what the Romantics and Freud thought about the unconscious, about how views on the imagination evolved between Romanticism and surrealism. The problem of evil remained my main preoccupation, as it had always been. Alongside the French Marxism I read for *Romantyzm, rewolucja, marksizm,* I went through many books about fascism, Hitler, and so forth, and wove these books into my writing. It offended my mother that a book I wrote had Hitler's picture in it.

Plyushkin, Harpagon, and Me

You allowed yourself to indulge in film and theater; didn't these entertainments compromise your work ethic?

I treated watching plays and films as part of my work. I used to say that I take on a research topic the way a hungry person gnaws on a bone. I needed to suck out every drop of marrow. Another metaphor pertains here as well: As a researcher, I'm greedy, like a miser or a hoarder. I don't just consume knowledge; I amass it, forage for it, collect it unrestrainedly. Each little bit seems worth keeping. As you know, I still haven't lost that habit.

I know that all too well. I've seen you balance plates and glasses of hot tea on stacks of newspapers. This isn't safe: You could burn yourself! But you insist that one mustn't throw out read newspapers because one might have overlooked something interesting in them. In 1997, Marta Zielińska and Anna Nasiłowska did a wonderful interview with you, which came out in Teksty Drugie. The interview is titled "Kuferek Harpagona" [Harpagon's money box]. In it, you describe yourself as follows: "As visual culture (the culture of the moving, blinking image!) triumphs over other cultural forms, I put ever more value in books as cultural capital. I am like the miser in Molière's play. Harpagon carries his wealth with him in a money box. He compulsively caresses his gold, listens to the noise it makes, enjoys its physical closeness. If he allowed this gold to circulate by investing it, what joy would it bring him? None. With a delight like Harpagon's, I like to dip my hand into my library stacks." So, you are a Harpagon . . . or a Plyushkin?

Plyushkin! Maryna used to call me that. He's one of the main characters in Gogol's *Dead Souls,* a skinflint and a hoarder. An awful miser, but above all, a collector of everything. Maryna compared me to him in amusing ways. The way Gogol describes him is incredible. Plyushkin displays the dregs of an old liqueur in a bottle filled with dead flies on his dining table. He looks like an elderly house steward, walking around in a greasy bathrobe that no longer resembles anything at all except a piece of yuft, the bark-tanned leather that Russian shoes are made of. The bathrobe splits into four pieces along his back, slowly shedding its cotton stuffing. "It was . . . impossible," as Gogol describes it, "to make out what he had tied round his neck: a stocking, a garter, or a stomach-belt, but it was certainly not a cravat." Plyushkin may be a landowner; but as he walks around the village he owns, he looks under every little bridge and plank and takes whatever he finds. "An old sole, a bit of a peasant woman's dress, an iron nail, a piece of broken earthenware, he carried them all off home and put them in the pile which Chichikov had noticed in the corner. The peasants feared him. 'He is out fishing again!' the peasants used to say when they saw him stalking his prey. . . . If a careless peasant woman happened to forget her bucket at the well, he would grab it too." Once an object entered his collection, "there was no redress."[2] I, of course, did not go so far as to pilfer.

Marek Bieńczyk recalls that back in the eighties, when he used to drive you to your seminar meetings, you would say to him, "Panie Mareczku, you're going to Paris. People discard amazing things there. You find books and newspapers by the roadside. Please investigate some trash bins, I'm sure you'll find something wonderful to bring back to us."

I daydreamed about the things Marek might find: pieces of writing penned by an unknown hand, books, newspapers. Keep in mind that French newspapers were a precious commodity in the People's Republic of Poland.

That's the literary historian in you speaking. Any sentence, any word you come across might turn out to be useful for as-yet-unforeseen reasons. You spoke about this possibility frequently—for example, in your conversation with Zbigniew Majchrowski, which appeared in a 1994 issue of Tytuł. *You make many important points in this interview, including the following declaration: "My interest in literary history relates to my more general proclivity toward collecting and poring over the remains of things." You describe your chosen profession as "a particular form of foraging." Sometimes the foraging yields trash, but sometimes it yields treasures. The forager cannot be certain of her outcome as she sifts through trash bins, dusty catalogs, forgotten pieces of text. Gradually, you put these fragments together into what you call "literary-historical wholes" [*całostki*]. This expression is so typical of you: You forage for fragments and fashion them into wholes. At other times, you've compared your work to that of an artisan, a cobbler who spends her entire day at the last and creates a complete shoe around it by the evening.*

I enjoy thinking of myself as an artisan. Yes, I could see myself wearing an apron to do my research. A cobbler's apron—or a carpenter's, since I also sometimes imagine myself sanding blocks of wood.

And a butcher's apron for when you write about freneticism, vampires, and revolutions?

Exactly. I like aprons in general, and the idea of putting one on for work. I never wore an actual apron to write, but I had what I called my rags—at-home clothes in which I did my academic work. Maryna and I often had the following phone exchange: "What are you up to?" "Not much, just working in my rags." An artisan's workshop is a calm, pleasant place, even if it's not a wizard's castle. The workshop creates order and facilitates production. It allows the artisan to do something real from morning until sundown—at which point, the cranky but spiritually fulfilled cobbler can leave his post and go to sleep. It's not always easy for me to get past the initial collecting stage; I get worked up over the smallest, irrelevant details.

That's also true in a literal sense. All kinds of things inhabit the recesses of your apartment, each of them precious: Here's a newspaper clipping, there's a postcard, a teddy bear gifted to you by grateful students, your famed collection of Napoleonic toy soldiers, a khanjali dagger, a cracked blown-glass Christmas ornament. Student gifts constitute a vast resource in themselves. Małgorzata Baranowska describes your apartment as follows: "Nobody dares to touch any of it, even the squeaky rubber owl with pom-poms on its gilded ears. Or the postcards sent by people who might now be too old to remember they had ever visited the places pictured in them. She received and kept all of them, as well as wind-up birds, a Play-Doh condor, a student-made Easter egg with a book etched into its shell."

They're souvenirs! One must keep them because . . . well, I'm not sure why. But I think one ought to. As far as master's theses go, I only kept those for a while after they'd been defended and then discarded them. I once watched a documentary about Jacques Derrida in which he describes a more extreme habit. He put all his students' essays in a garden shed. He couldn't bear to throw them out; his nineteenth-century academic sensibility prevented him. My own passion for hoarding comes from a childhood experience of poverty and wartime deprivation. I saw so much destruction! My father would come home in a drunken rage and break our plates. We were left with piles of useless shards nobody could repair. I was young when all this happened, but I still remember my fear, shock, and grief over the plates' instant, irreparable ruin. Then came the war and the Holocaust. Members of my generation gravitate toward the image of a person sitting on a rubbish heap. Beckett repeats it, as do the Polish writers Szajski, Kantor, and Różewicz. The heap is all that's left of the world; the fragments it contains must be cared for and protected. I also often describe existence as an archive that must be collected and preserved. This idea comes out of Borges, but it also echoes Plyushkin's ethos. Susan Sontag and Walter Benjamin would describe it as a form of melancholia. And Claude Lévi-Strauss would see in its obsession with parts and wholes a form of bricolage: The humanist as bricoleur.

What you're saying also reminds me of the shop windows in prewar Vilnius about which you reminisced earlier. When you were a child, each shop window seemed like a world unto itself; then the Russian army took over Vilnius, and all the displays were gone within twenty-four hours.

Yes. As a child, I also liked to dig in the sewer along with other ill-behaved neighborhood children. It made me feel like an old-fashioned highway robber. That childhood memory remains lodged within me. But one must keep one's hoarding tendencies in check. The horrors of the war were real and horrifying; still, one must strive to keep a tidy apartment. Can't let yourself go. When you're old, the temptation to do that intensifies. You abandon your rituals of cleanliness, of self-maintenance. One mustn't let this self-abandonment show in public. Though one of my old friends, Rysieńko Przybylski, has long adopted the inverse attitude: He makes himself out to be older and more decrepit than he is. As he tells me, if you limp around, easily lose your breath, and helplessly drop into a chair in company, people will readily let you reject their invitations. "Poor Przybylski," they will say, "he's aged." Meanwhile, Rysieńko can enjoy his peace and quiet at home, reading and writing what he calls his "little books." I do observe some tendencies toward letting myself go within me. I see a dirty glass, but I don't care to clean it. I put silverware on the table for breakfast, and it's still there; I don't have the energy to fight it.

Come on. Wisława Szymborska's silverware was never clean, even when she was younger. If that bothered her guest, they could step into the kitchen and wash it themselves. And someone comes to clean up your apartment these days.

One day, you'll come to understand me. I have great empathy for Plyushkin. Having amassed so many books and papers keeps me alive. It muddies the river of time—or maybe deepens it, or lets it meander. I'm not sure. Amid this paper and rubbish, I find it easier to go on.

"A passion for spiritual collecting—and constant mourning for spiritual deposits that have gone to waste." That's how you described it in conversation with Majchrowski. Tomek Kiliński describes your notion of the archive as follows: The archive is a "shifting place, a symbolic place, a trace, a space of hospitality, a lack." What animates it is "a will toward overcoming and commemorating an absence." "Polka. Medium. Cień. Wyobrażenie" *[The Polish woman: A medium, a daydream, a shade], an art exhibit curated by Agnieszka Zawadowska in 2005 under your patronage embodied this imaginative as well as physical labor of saving, collecting, and ordering traces of existence, with a focus on the traces of women who had not previously been accorded a place in Polish history. Kiliński deconstructs the Polish equivalent of Derrida's term "hospitality" as* gość-inność, *literally the hosting or welcoming of otherness. This is apt wordplay. An archive needs*

to offer a place of refuge into which various fragments and traces can be welcomed and within which they can be embraced. Plyushkin represents the opposite of hospitality and meaning-making. He receives no one; he does not dust; he does not air the room. He does not differentiate. The forces of desire and repression mingle within him.

Gogol's grotesque narratives are particularly good at representing this ambivalence: Plyushkin holds up a dark mirror to the passions of cognition, creation, and love. His desires could be seen as obscene and anal—but they are also recognizable as desires, with love at their point of origin. Gogol describes him in these terms, as an ordinary man who succumbed to avarice and of hoarding, filth and suspicion. These passions overcame him. As I've said before, one must tread carefully in these matters. Knowledge and writing are sublimated preoccupations. They bring gratification and occasionally intense pleasure because they are buoyed by a libidinal drive, a half-hidden rapaciousness. And envy, of course. The social respectability of a university professorship does not protect one from these dangers. For these reasons, I cannot imagine doing research without teaching; I need the higher-order, ritualized responsibility of sharing my work with students. That is the only thing that gives me a sense of safety amid the dangers of my profession. I repeat: Literary scholarship is dangerous work. Wilhelm Dilthey, another figure whose work is important for me, classifies literary and social history as studies of the spirit. The immediate objects of literary historical study are texts and ideas, but there is also a spiritual aspect to our endeavors. Olga Tokarczuk aptly describes writing as strenuous, physical labor. It makes one's joints stiffen and bows the body under the weight of hefty, dusty tomes. In a more profound sense, it's also an experience of the existential heaviness of literary archives and the painfully thin line that separates the collection from the heap, cosmos from chaos. As I've confessed to Barbara Łopieńska, I sometimes fear that the floor underneath me—which is also my neighbors' ceiling—might collapse under the weight of my personal library. My compulsion to hoard books and papers has nothing ordinary about it.

But at least you don't keep your shoes in the oven, or a shopping cart in a tree, or the cremated remains of your loved ones on the mantelpiece—all of which Kasia Bratkowska and I recently encountered in a friend's apartment in London. It's true that you don't let anything be thrown away. Still, your papers compose themselves into a personal library, a labyrinth of books across the rooms, kitchen, and bathroom of a tight, post-Soviet flat that stays in one piece and does not breed mice. Sure, sometimes a book falls here and there, but you always put it back in its place. You don't keep a fly-infested bottle of old liqueur; you don't hang a foot wrap around your neck or don a tallow-stained bathrobe. Your cardigan, which Agnieszka Zawadowska bought for you, is rather fashionable. You only imagine yourself as Plyushkin.

You reassure me. But I recall how Maryna and I once went to a conference in Budapest and shared a hotel room. We brought some books with us—at the time, one traveled with one's books—and upon arrival, I proceeded to lay mine out across the floor. "Look at you, piling up your heap," Maryna commented: Plyushkin had disembarked and was making himself comfortable. She had a point. Maryna's teasing was good-natured. My more bourgeois friend, Alina Witkowska, sometimes got furious with me. She rarely visited me toward the end of her life, but she saw *Bunt Janion* [Janion's rebellion], the documentary Agnieszka Arnold made about me, when it was broadcast on public television. Agnieszka shot much of the footage in my apartment. Alina called me the day after the film aired to say how much I'd disappointed her. "Look at the state of your home! How can you let people film it and display it in public? It looks like a dump, a ruin, a mad hermit's hollow." She hurt my feelings. What can I say? She lived in a post-Soviet flat like I did, but the way she set it up was palatial. I told myself it was a question of taste.

It is. Paulina Reiter, who writes for the women's section of Gazeta Wyborcza, describes your apartment as the most beautiful place she'd ever seen. Agnieszka Zawadowska, a set designer, calls it incredibly stylish.

Really? I find that hard to believe.

Notes

1. Leszek Kołakowski, *Main Currents of Marxism,* trans. P. S. Falla (New York: W. W. Norton, 2005), 1161.
2. Nikolai Gogol, *Dead Souls,* trans. George Reavey (New York: W. W. Norton, 1985), 121–22.

Translator's Acknowledgments

It is a privilege to bring Maria Janion's critical voice into English. I thank Kazimiera Szczuka, her literary executor, for trusting me with this task. Leah Pennywark at the University of Minnesota Press, as well as the editors of UMP's Cultural Critique book series, saw *The Bad Child: A Maria Janion Reader* to completion with good-humored professionalism. My research assistant Yasmine Chokrane, my copyeditor Nicholas Taylor, and my anonymous readers at *PMLA* and the University of Minnesota Press provided careful feedback on earlier drafts of this translation, saving me from many infelicities and errors. Ayesha Ramachandran tirelessly encouraged this project, making time and space for me to work on it since the summer of 2020 when news of Janion's passing moved me to begin translating her writing.

I would not have seen this *Reader* to completion without Ayesha's support. I dedicate this translation to my grandmother, Maria Figlerowicz (1934–2020), whose death coincided with Janion's and who first taught me how to be a humanist.

Publication History

Chapter 1 was originally published as "Sami sobie cudzy," in *Niesamowita słowiańszczyzna* (Kraków: Wydawnictwo Literackie, 2006), 7–46.
Chapter 2 was originally published as "Polska w Europie," in *Niesamowita słowiańszczyzna,* 165–210.
Chapter 3 was originally published as "Między śmiechem a śmiercią," in *Żyjąc tracimy życie* (Warsaw: W.A.B., 2001), 271–88.
Chapter 4 was originally published as "Patriota-wariat," in *Wobec zła* (Warsaw: Verba, 1989), 9–32.
Chapter 5 was originally published as "Powstrzymać Prometeusza," in *Wobec zła,* 147–57.
Chapter 6 was originally published as "Marzący: Jest tam, gdzie go nie ma, a nie ma go tu, gdzie jest . . . ," in *Projekt krytyki fantazmatycznej* (Warsaw: PEN, 1991), 30–59.
Chapter 7 was originally published as "Teoria literatury ze stanowiska teorii arcydzieł literackich," in *Odnawianie znaczeń* (Kraków: Wydawnictwo Literackie, 1980), 301–19.
Chapter 8 was originally published as "Próba teorii fascynacji filmem," in *Odnawianie znaczeń,* 320–56.
Chapter 9 was originally published as "Legion żydowski Mickiewicza," in *Bohater, spisek, śmierć* (Warsaw: W.A.B., 2009), 223–55.
Chapter 10 was originally published as "Fragmenty dyskursu miłosnego," in *Kobiety i duch inności* (Warsaw: Sic!, 1996), 136–51.
Chapter 11 was originally published as Maria Janion and Kazimiera Szczuka, *Transe, traumy, transgresje* (Warsaw: Wydawnictwo Krytyki Politycznej, 2012), vol. 1: 33–40, 56–62, 99–107, 117–19, 145–51; vol. 2: 31–35, 43–50.

Index

Aeschylus: *Prometheus Unbound,* 109, 111, 112

aesthetics: Borderlands, 33; cinematic, 161; Cossack, 32; of cultural history, 146–47; Freudian, 161; of horror and melodrama, 170–71, 172–73; idiolects of, 149; Janion's writings on, xx; literary, 145; Near Eastern, 39–40; of pleasure, 122, 160; Romantic, 78, 156–57

Anderson, Benedict: use of term "imagined communities," ix

Andrzejewski, Jerzy: *Hospital Notes (Notatki szpitalne),* 97–98

Angelus (literary award), 15, 16

Annales school, 141

Anonimus, Gallus: on Old Church Slavonic, 42

Antczak, Jerzy: film adaptation of *Nights and Days,* 167

anti-Semitism: in Western Europe, 196, 199. *See also* Poland: anti-Semitism in

Arnim, Bettina von: relationship with Goethe, 210–11

Arnold, Agnieszka: *Janion's Rebellion (Bunt Janion),* 253

Aron, Jean-Paul: *The Art of Eating in France (Le Mangeur du dix-neuvième siecle),* 141

art/artworks, 144, 148, 153; coherence in, 147, 150–51; idiolects of, 149–50; masterpieces, 146–47; Romantics' new kind of, 156–57. *See also* Malczewski, Jacek, art of

Ascherson, Neal: on Poland's Orientalism, 40–41

Auschwitz (concentration camp), 55–58

Austria, 8, 16, 45, 179; partitioning of Poland by, 8, 45

Bachelard, Gaston: phenomenology of poetry, 147

balkanization, 14–15

Balzac, Honoré de: novels of, 162

barbarians, 12, 38

Bar Confederation: instigation of 1830 insurrection, 89

Barthes, Roland: *A Lover's Discourse,* xxi, 206, 207–9

Bataille, Georges, 241, 243

Battle of Grunwald (1410), 44

Battle of Maciejowice (1794), 86–87

Baudelaire, Charles: on the imagination, 120; "Le Gouffre," 73

Beauvoir, Simone de: on women's roles throughout history, 46–47

Beauvois, Daniel: on Polish mythologies, 34; on the Ukrainian Triangle, 35–36

Beckett, Samuel: dislike for Bertolt Brecht, 143

Belarus: Poland's relationship with, xv

Belmont, Leo: *A Modern-Day Moses (Mojżesz współczesny),* 197, 198

Bem, Józef, 195; influence on Mickiewicz, 180–81

Bergeret, Jean: on Freud's theory of phantasms, 125

Berlant, Lauren: on melodrama, xiv

Berwiński, Ryszard Wincenty: *Bogunka on the Lake Gopło (Bogunka na Gople),* 22

Besançon, Alain: on psychoanalytic history, 150; on Russia, 52–53
Bessler, Gabriele: on Polish culture, 70
Bettelheim, Bruno: on concentration camps, 57
Białoszewski, Miron: play about Janion, ix–x
Birkenmajer, Józef: on Bogurodzica, 44
Blake, William: on the imagination, 155
Blüth, Rafał: on creation of a Jewish legion, 198
Bogurodzica (Mother of God), 44–45, 51
Borderlands *(Kresy),* 30–38; concentration camps in, 54–58; Eastern, xv, 30–33, 37, 39; Germans and Russians in, 45–54; mythologies of, 30, 34, 37; Polish, xv, 36; Romantics' views of, 32–33; Sarmatians in, 38–41; Ukranian, xviii
Borges, Jorge Luis, 174
Borowski, Tadeusz: short stories by, 54, 55–58
Bosnia: Serbian genocides in, 24–25
Brakoniecki, Kazimierz: on mythologized Slavdom, 16–17
Brandstaetter, Roman: on Armand Lévy, 195; on creation of a Jewish legion, 189–90, 191, 200; on Władysław Mickiewicz's biography of father, 196–97, 198
Braudel, Fernand: theory of history, 144
Brooks, Mel: *Young Frankenstein,* 175
Brzozowski, Stanisław: *The Flames (Płomienie),* 239
Buñuel, Luis: film adaptation of *The Monk,* 169; *The Phantom of Liberty,* 160
Byron, Lord, 121; on myth of Prometheus, 111

Caillois, Roger, 173–74, 209; description of the fantastic, 146–47
Camus, Albert, 55; on myth of Sisyphus, 114
Cape Arkona: fall of, 12
Catholic Church/Catholicism, 21, 114, 195; Orthodox churches' relationship with, 30, 37–38, 41, 43–44; Polish, xvi, 9, 17, 45, 50–51, 181. *See also* Christianity; George XVI, Pope; Jesus Christ; John Paul II, Pope; Virgin Mary
Cato, 93, 94, 95
Central Europe, xvii, 13, 15–16, 137, 243
Chaunu, Pierre: on lines between Eastern and Western Europe, 29–30
Chmielnicki, Bohdan: rebellion led by, 35, 36
Christianity, 10, 44, 110, 186–87; East–West divisions, 41, 42–43; eroticism condemned, 168–70; Polish, 9, 22–23, 35, 38, 41, 43; Slavic forced conversion to, xvi, xviii, 11–13, 18, 22, 42. *See also* Catholic Church/Catholicism; Orthodox churches
Ciccarini, Marina: on European attitudes toward otherness, 39–40
cinema: contemporary, 153; daydreams in, xx, 160–61, 162; dreams in, 155, 171; fantasies in, 155, 160, 162; Gothic, 173–74; hero types, 169; mainstream, 163–64; phantasms in, xx, 130, 155, 159–61, 171; Romanticism and, 156–58, 174. *See also* horror; melodrama
Cixous, Hélène: on Genet, 206; on Müller's novel, 215–16
communism/Communist Party, 16, 51, 232; Janion's membership in, xiv–xv, 240, 242; Polish, xxi, 6, 54, 97, 235–36, 246. *See also* Marx, Karl; Marxism; Stalinism
Conrad, Joseph: *Under Western Eyes,* 54
Cooper, James Fenimore: portrayals of Native Americans, 32–33

Corm, Georges: on the Balkans, 14–15
Cossacks, 31–32, 36, 181, 189–90; Jewish legion in, 191, 192–93
creativity, 108, 113, 124, 135; artistic, 76, 153; forgery and, 72–73; Freud's essay on, 153–61; literary, 128, 153–54; role within history, xi, xix. *See also* art/artworks; cinema; literature
Crimean War (1853–56), 179–83, 196
Croce, Benedetto: distinguishing between poetry and literature, 151
culture, 39, 160; history of, 146–47; mass, 155, 171; of Romanticism, 51–52; of the West, 29. *See also* folk culture; folklore/folktales; Poland: culture of
culture, popular, xiii, 5, 21, 29, 122, 157; incorporating Freudian theory into, 160, 162; Janion's description of, xiii–xiv; melodrama, 170–71; phantasms in, xvi, 155, 159, 161
Curtius, Ernst: account of topoi and myths, 144–45
Custine, Marquis de: *Russia in 1839,* 53
Cyril and Methodius: mission to Slavdom, 41–44
Czajkowski, Michal (Prince): *Adam Mickiewicz in the Cossack Encampment (Adam Mickiewicz w obozie kozackim),* 196–97; conflict with Zamoyski, 182; conversion to Islam, 191, 195; on creation of a Jewish legion, 191, 192–93, 196; jokes about the Israelites, 188–89; leader of Ottoman Cossack regiment, 181, 189, 192–93, 196
Czapliński, Przemysław: on mass communication, 6
Czapska, Maria: on Jewish–Polish entanglement, 25
Czermińska, Małgorzata, 245; contributions to *Gdansk Colloquia,* 244

Dąbrowska, Maria: book about, 101–2; *Nights and Days (Noce i dnie),* 102, 167
Dąbrowski, General: patriot-as-madman, 89; Polish legions led by, 183–84; and third partition of Poland, 201n14
Davis, Norman: on Western studies of Eastern Europe, 7
daydreams: cinematic, xx, 159, 160–61; distinction between phantasms, dreams, imagination, and, 132–33; Freud's theory of, xiii–xiv, 125, 128, 162–63; Gombrowicz's theory of, xiii–xiv; heroes of, 161, 162; phantasms as, 119, 121, 123. *See also* dreams; fantasies/phantasies; phantasms
Declaration of the Rights of Man and Citizen, 110–11
Defoe, Daniel: *A Journal of the Plague Year,* 54–55
democracy, vii–viii, 155; Polish, 5, 6, 40
Derrida, Jacques, 250; on hospitality, 251–52
Descartes, René: understanding of the human, 135
Dilthey, Wilhelm: on literary and social history, 252; use of term *Einfühlen,* 7–8
Dostoevsky, Fyodor: *Crime and Punishment,* 132; monographs on, 232
Doubrovsky, Serge: on subjective existence, 124
Dracula, 174–75
dreams, 71, 113–14, 128, 150, 153; cinematic, 155, 171; distinction between phantasms, daydreams, imagination, and, 132–33; Gombrowicz's attitude toward, xii, xiv; Gothic literature's connection with, 173–74; Romantics' treatment of, 155–56. *See also* daydreams; fantasies/phantasies; phantasms
Duker, Abraham G.: on Adam Mickiewicz, 185, 188; on Armand Lévy, 195–96; on Jewish emancipation, 192; on Polish–Israeli legion, 189

Dumas, Alexandre: *Count of Monte Cristo*, 158; *The Lady of the Camellias*, 158, 165, 166–67, 172; *Three Musketeers*, 158
Duras, Marguerite: on Barthes, 215–16
Dvořák, Antonin: *Rusałka* (opera), xviii. *See also rusałki*
dziady ritual, 25–26. *See also* Mickiewicz, Adam: *Forefathers' Eve (Dziady)*

East, the, 7, 156, 195; colonizers of, 13–14, 33; Mickiewicz's purpose in, 179–83, 196; Poland's relationship with, 34, 40; West's relationship with, 41, 42, 44. *See also* Borderlands *(Kresy)*: Eastern; Eastern Orthodoxy
Eastern Europe, xx, 17, 39, 243; Janion's writings on, ix, x, xvii–xviii, xix; Jews in, 187–88, 196, 198, 199; Old Church Slavonic in, 41–43, 45; opportunities within European Union, xiv–xv; pagan beliefs, xvi, xviii; Poland's relationship with, xv, 50–51; Western Europe's relationship with, 14–15, 29–30, 35. *See also* East, the; Slavdom/Slavs
Eastern Orthodoxy, 37–38. *See also* Greek Orthodoxy; Orthodox churches; Russian Orthodoxy
Eco, Umberto: on language of artwork, 149; on literary idiolects, 151
Enlightenment, the, 123, 187; Marxism and, 231–32; revisionism stemming from, 235–36; Romanticism and, 120, 155–57. *See also* Herder, Johann Gottfried
Erdman, Jan: *The Way to Ostra Brama (Droga do Ostrej Bramy)*, 103
Erhard, Jean: on history of ideas, 139–40
Erofeyev, Viktor: on Russia, 53–54
eroticism, 159, 163–64, 167, 168–70
Europe: emotional and erotic spheres, 171–72; myths of, 29; Poland's location in, 29–61; totalitarianism's rise in, 57–58. *See also* Borderlands *(Kresy)*; Central Europe; Eastern Europe; Germans/Germany; Poland; Russia/Russians; Ukraine; Western Europe

fantasies/phantasies, x, 17, 73, 119–20; cinematic, 155, 160, 162; of German Romanticism, 125; Gombrowicz's attitude toward, xii, xiv; Janion's writings on, viii, xix; of Poland as a chosen nation, 8, 15, 18; in popular culture, xiii–xiv, xvi, 67, 158, 159; reality and, 132; Romantics' treatment of, xi–xii, 120–23, 125. *See also* daydreams; dreams; eroticism; imagination; phantasms
fascism, viii, 17, 49, 175
Faust: Prometheism of, 112
Feuerbach, Ludwig: on myth of Prometheus, 111
Fielding, Henry: *Tom Jones*, 163
Fisz, Zenon: comparing Borderland and U.S. landscapes, 32–33; on mid-eighteenth-century Ukraine, 30–31
folk culture, 20–21, 120–22, 156, 157; in Malczewski's art, xviii, 71
folklore/folktales, 68, 122, 174; Polish, xviii, 71–75, 157; *rusałki*, 67–72, 74–75, 79; Slavic, 20, 67–68, 79, 157. *See also* mythologies/myths; storytelling
Fontane, Theodor: on phantasms, 127
Foucault, Michel, 241; concept of the archeology of knowledge, 140
Frankenstein, 174–75
Frankism (Jewish sect), 187, 188, 200
Freud, Sigmund: "Creative Writers and Day-Dreaming," 153–61; daydreams theory of, xiii–xiv, 125, 128, 153–61; *Familienroman*, 136, 162–63; inspirations for, 123,

142; literary method of, 136–37; *Moses and Monotheism,* 136; phantasm theory of, 123–29, 133–37, 155–56, 159, 163–64, 168; on pleasure, 160–61, 173; on popular novels, 161–62, 162–63; prephantasm theory of, 125–29; on Romantics' view of the unconscious, 121, 247. *See also* psychoanalysis
Friday, Nancy: erotic phantasies in books of, 130; *My Secret Garden,* 158–59
Furet, François: on the French Revolution, 110–11

Gadamer, Hans-Georg: on Herder's philosophy of history, 24
gender, xiii, 205–6, 229, 241
Genet, Jean, 241; *Balcony,* 132; vision of homosexuality, 206
genres, 144–45, 149; cinematic, xx; fantasy, 174; foundling narrative, 162–63; Gothic, 45, 157, 161, 163–64, 168–76; musical-mythical, 7. *See also* horror; melodrama
George XVI, Pope: condemnation of Poland's 1830 insurrection, 47. *See also* Catholic Church/Catholicism
Germans/Germany, xxi, 68, 171; in the Borderlands, 45–54; Lithuanian occupation by, 219, 222; nationalism in, xiii, 13–14; Nazi, x, 16, 52, 222; Poland occupied by, vii, viii, 8, 46, 52, 58; Romano-Germanic Empire, 42–43; Slavs oppressed by, 18, 42. *See also* Holocaust, the
Gieysztor, Aleksander: on Slavic folklore, 20
Ginzburg, Carlo: on popular culture, 21
globalization, viii–xvi, 6, 9, 19
Głowacki, Aleksander. *See* Prus, Bolesław
Głowacki, Leon: in 1863 insurrection, 100–101
Gnosticism: myth of Prometheus compared to, 112
Goethe, Wolfgang von Johann: accusation of espousing Pelagianism, 110; Bettina von Arnim's relationship with, 210–11; *Elective Affinities,* 212; *Faust,* 48; "The Fisherman," 69; on myth of Prometheus, 111; "On the Divine," 115; poems of, xix; "Prometheus," 109–10; *The Sorrows of Young Werther,* 211, 212
Goffman, Erving: on theater of everyday life, 127
Gogol, Nikolai: *Dead Souls,* 248, 252; *Taras Bulba,* 32
Golden Book (Złota Hramota) decree, 36
Gombrowicz, Witold: daydreams theory of, xiii–xiv; fighting communism, 240; notion of art, 142, 150–51; thesis on secret dreams and fantasies, 159–60
Goszczyński, Seweryn, 85; *The Castle of Kaniów (Zamek kaniowski),* 32; grim images of the "motherland," 92; *The King of the Castle (Król zamczyska),* 99–100; on patriot-as-madman, 92
Gothic: genre of, 45, 157, 161, 163–64, 168–76; horror, xiii, xx. *See also* horror: Gothic
Great Moravia (medieval state), 43
Greek Orthodoxy, 41, 43–44. *See also* Eastern Orthodoxy; Orthodox churches; Russian Orthodoxy
Greer, Germaine: on mythology of romantic love, 167
Grzybkowska, Teresa: on Malczewski's art, 63, 65, 75
gulags. *See* Soviets: gulags run by

hallucinations, 119, 129–30
Hawthorne, Nathaniel: "The Minister's Black Veil," 133–34
Hegel, Georg Wilhelm Friedrich: as Gnosticism, 112; on history, 145–46, 147; on Slavdom, 19

Heine, Heinrich: "The Lorelei," 69–70
Herder, Johann Gottfried: on ancient Slavs, 18–19, 20, 22; philosophy of history, 19, 24. *See also* Enlightenment, the
Herling-Grudziński, Gustaw: on myth of Sisyphus, 114; *A World Apart,* 54–55
Herodotus: discourse of alterity, 38
Herschel, Abraham Joshua: on Jews in Eastern Europe, 188
Herzl, Jacob, 197, 198
Herzl, Theodor: Belmont on, 197; creator of Zionism, 198, 200
Hesiod: on Greek Promethean myth, 108–9
Hess, Moses: calls for Jewish national Renaissance, 200; *Rome and Jerusalem (Rom und Jerusalem),* 194–95
history, 148, 156, 252; Hegelian notion of, 145–46, 147; Herder's philosophy of, 19, 24. *See also* culture: history of; ideas, history of; literature, history of; politics: history of
Hoffman, E. T. A.: on subconscious, 121, 125
Holocaust, the, 25–26, 54–58
homophobia: Polish, viii, xii
homosexuality, xxi, 130, 186; in Müller's novel, 206–7; romantic love and, 209–14; writing's connection to, 214–16. *See also* sexuality
homosociality, 182
horror, 72, 122; demons, vampires, monsters, 168–71; Freud's theory of phantasm and, 153–61; Gothic, xiii, xx; melodrama's differences from, 171–73; myths of, 174–76; Romantic writers' treatment of, 153–61
Hugo, Victor, 165; *Les Misérables,* 111; *Toilers of the Sea,* 111
humanism/humanists, xiii, 7, 113, 126, 129, 239; psychiatry based on, 131, 241
humanities: imagination and, 15, 135–36; phantasms' importance to, 129–37; Polish, 5–8. *See also* art/artworks; literature
Hungarian Uprising of 1848–49, 179, 180

ideas, history of, 139–52; antagonism between history of literature and, 140–43; contained in history of literature, 144–45; methods of, 148; politics of, 239; temporalities of, 142, 144, 150–51
identity, 10, 123, 146, 222; national and ethnic, 17–18, 40; politics of, 239; Slavic, 22, 24, 43. *See also* Poland: identity in
ideology, 103, 195, 239; communist, 231–32, 246; differences in, 225, 227, 229; literature and, 139, 142–44; nationalist, xxii, 37. *See also* ideas, history of
imagination, ix, 127; contemporary cultural, 162–63; distinction between phantasms, daydreams, dreams, and, 132–33; First Enfranchisement of the Imagination, 120–23; humanities and, 135–36; liberating, 155–56; phantasms and, 119–23; Romantics' treatment of, 156–57, 158–59
immortality, 46, 90, 173; in Freud's phantasm of, 162, 168. *See also* Kundera, Milan: *Immortality*
Institute of Czechoslovak Philology, 235
Institute of Literary Research (Polish Academy of Sciences), 229–34
Ionesco, Eugène: notion of art, 142–43
Israel: Poland's destiny intertwined with, 25–26, 187–91; spiritual superiority of, 183–87. *See also* Jews/Judaism; Mickiewicz, Adam, Jewish legion created by; Zionism/Zionists
Iwaszkiewicz, Jarosław: "Zarudzie," 36

Jakobson, Roman: on Old Church Slavonic, 41–42
Janion, Maria: Arnold's documentary about, 253; as artisan, 249–50; Białoszewski's play about, ix–x; childhood, vii–viii, x–xi, 250–51; Communism Party membership, xiv–xv, 236, 240, 242; conversation with Zbigniew Majchrowski, 249, 251; on Eastern Europe, ix, x, xvii–xviii, xix; as forager/hoarder, 247–49, 252–53; friendship with Maryna Żmigrodzka, 221, 225–26, 227, 228–29, 248, 253; at Institute of Literary Research, 229–34; life in Vilnius, x, xxi, 219, 226, 228, 232; on Marxism, viii, xvii, xix, 237, 244–45, 247; membership in Polish United Workers Party, 242; on nationalism, viii, xiv, xvii, xix; as *non-émigré* poet, 244–47; on popular culture, xiii–xiv; professorship at University of Gdansk, 237–43; revisionism concept of, 235–36, 246; Transeje concept of, xii–xiii, xvii–xviii, 238–43, 245; on Ukraine, xv, xviii; at university in Łódź, 224–29; World War II experiences, 219–24
Janion, Maria, works by: *The Gdańsk Colloquia (Colloquia gdańskie)*, 244; *Hero, Conspiracy, Death (Bohater, spisek, śmierć)*, 221; *The Humanities, Understanding, and Therapy (Humanistyka, poznanie i terapia)*, 232; *Let Us Join Europe, but Bring Our Dead along with Us (Do Europy tak, ale razem z naszymi umarłymi)*, 221; *Lucjan Siemieński*, 232; "The Project of Phantasmatic Critique," xix–xx; *Romanticism, Revolution, Marxism (Romantyzm, rewolucja, marksizm)*, 237, 244–45, 247; "Traditions and Methods of Genetic Literary History" ("Tradycje i perspektywy metodologiczne badań genetycznych w historii literatury"), 234; Transgressions (Transgresje, book series), xii–xiii; *Uncanny Slavdom (Niesamowita słowiańszczyzna)*, xv–xvi, xvii–xviii
Jasinowski, Bogumił: on southeastern Borderlands, 33
Jauss, Hans Robert: on history of literature *vs.* history of ideas, 141; on Kracauer's critique of historiography, 145–46
Jensen, Wilhelm: *Gradiva*, 125, 136, 155
Jesus Christ, 45, 147, 186
Jews/Judaism: Eastern European, 187–88, 196, 198, 199; emancipation of, 192, 194; jokes about, 188–89; mysticism of, xxi, 198; in Poland, xx, 22–23, 194; stereotypes of, 186; during World War II, 219–24. *See also* anti-Semitism; Holocaust, the; Mickiewicz, Adam, Jewish legion created by; Zionism/Zionists
John Paul II, Pope, x, 51, 114–15; encyclical on Cyril and Methodius' mission, 42–43. *See also* Catholic Church/Catholicism; Christianity
John III Sobieski, King, 32, 40
Jung, Carl: on imagination, 121; on phantasms, 126, 134

Kafka, Franz: *Metamorphosis*, 113
Kajsiewicz, Hieronim: sonnets on 1830 insurrection against Russia, 92–93
Karadžić, Radovan, 24
Karamzin, Nikolai: *History of Russia*, 22
kitsch, 135, 146–47
Kittler, Friedrich: writings on cinema, xx
Klein, Melanie: on phantasm as a concept, 129
Klinger, Witold: on *rusałki*, 79

Klotz, Claude: *A Vampire in Paris,* 175
Kniaźnin, Franciszek: on Lithuanian patriotism, 90; Mickiewicz on, 87; patriot-as-madman, 89
Koestler, Arthur: on Promethianism, 107
Kołakowski, Leszek: leaves Poland, viii, 244; on Marxism, 107, 112, 113, 246, 247; on revisionism, 235; on Sisyphus, 114
Kościuszko, Tadeusz, 86; insurrection leader, 36, 191; patriot-as-madman, 89
Kossak-Szczucka, Zofia: *The Raging Fire (Pożoga),* 36
Kracauer, Siegfried: on historiography, 145–46
Krasiński, Zygmunt, 22, 49, 50, 194; *Adam the Madman (Adam Szaleniec),* 98–99; *Irydion,* 99; letters to European religious leaders, 46, 47
Kraszewski, Józef Ignacy: on insurrectionists, 100; on Polish oppression in Borderlands, 35; on the Slavic uncanny, 22
Krzysztoń, Jerzy: *Madness (Obłęd),* 97, 98
Kundera, Milan: on Freud's novel writing, 137; *Immortality,* 210–11; protesting Russian despotism, 16
Kuroń, Jacek: *Socialist Manifesto for Poland,* 246
Kusturica, Emir: *Underground,* 24

Lacan, Jacques: on the symbolic order, 124
Laing, Ronald David: *Bird of Paradise,* 133; *The Divided Self,* 133; on humanistic psychiatry, 131, 241; on psychoanalysis, 130–33; *Self and Others,* 131–33; understanding of the human, 135
Lanson, Gustave: on history of ideas, 139–40; on representative literary works, 145
Laplanche, Jean: study of Freud's theory of phantasm, 124
leftism/leftists: Janion's writings on, xix–xx
Le Goff, Jacques: *Making History (Faire de l'histoire),* 141–42
Leiris, Michel: *Manhood,* 130
Lem, Stanisław: on contemporary Polish culture, 5; separating art from kitsch, 146–47
Leśmian, Bolesław: "The Barn" ("Stodoła"), 73; folktales, 71–75; *Klechdy polskie,* 73; on *rusałki,* 79
Levi, Primo: *Survival in Auschwitz,* 57
Lévi-Strauss, Claude: on Freud's writing, 137; on the symbolic order, 124
Lévy, Armand: accompanying Adam Mickiewicz on his travels, 179, 183; on creation of Jewish legion, 189–90, 191, 198; on death of Adam Mickiewicz, 188, 197–98; as early Zionist, 195–98; negotiations with the Rothschilds, 196, 197; patriotism of, 181, 193; travels around duchies of the Danube, 194–95. *See also* Mickiewicz, Adam; Mickiewicz, Adam, Jewish legion created by
Lewis, Matthew Gregory: *The Monk,* 168, 169, 172
literature, 150, 151, 205; dreams in, 154–56; Gothic, 172, 173–74; phantasms in, 103, 129, 154–56, 160; popular novels, 157–58, 161–62, 163–64; renewal of, 6–7. *See also* humanities; poetry
literature, history of, 139–52; antagonism between history of ideas and, 140–43; Janion on, 252; masterpieces of, 146–48, 151; temporalities of, 142, 144, 145–46, 149, 150–51
Lithuania: occupations of, 219, 222–23. *See also* Vilnius, Lithuania
Logos (Word): myths of, 206, 216
love, romantic, 166–68; homosexual, 209–14. *See also* Romanticism/Romantics

Lovejoy, A. O.: on history of ideas, 139–40; on representative literary works, 145
Luther, Martin, 49. *See also* Catholic Church/Catholicism; Christianity
Luzitsi tribes (Łużyczanie), 12

Machnicki, Jan: insanity of, 99–100
Maciej of Miechów: descriptions of European and Asian Samartia, 38
Majchrowski, Zbigniew: conversation with Janion, 249, 251
Malczewski, Jacek: on Polish nationhood, xx–xxi; rusałka narratives, 65–71, 72, 74–75, 79
Malczewski, Jacek, art of, xviii, 63–81; *Childhood (Dzieciństwo)*, 63; *The Drowned Man Embraced by a Swamp Demon (Topielec w uściskach dziwożony)*, 65, 67 (*fig.*); *He and She (On i ona)*, 65, 66 (*fig.*); *Melancholia*, 64, 104, *104* (*fig.*); *My Funeral (Mój pogrzeb)*, *78–79* (*fig.*); *The Nix and the Mermaid (Wodnik i syrena)*, 65; *The Painter's Dream (Sen malarza)*, 64; *Possessed (Opętany)*, 65, *65* (*fig.*); *Rusałki*, 66; self-portraits, 77–78; *Self-portrait with Fauns (Autoportret z faunami)*, *76–77* (*fig.*), 78; *A Strange Catch (Osobliwy połów)*, 65; surrealism in, 75–77; *Swamp Demon amid the Mullein (Rusałki: Boginka w dziewannach)*, 65; *Tickled to Death (Załaskotany)*, 65, *67* (*fig.*); *Vicious Circle (Błędne koło)*, 64; *Water Demon amid the Mullein (Boginka w dziewannach)*, *66* (*fig.*)
Malczewski, Rafał (son of Jacek Malczewski): on Jacek Malczewski's art, 75, 76
Mann, Thomas: on German problem, 49; on myth and fascism, 17; novels by, 176
Marcuse, Herbert: on myth of Prometheus, 113–14
marginalized people/marginalization, x, xiii, xix, xxi, 15, 34, 45, 115. *See also* homophobia; Other/otherness; racism; xenophobia
Marody, Mirosław: on intertwining of Catholicism and nationalism, 51
Marx, Karl: ideas of, 147; on myth of Prometheus, 111–13; view of human nature, xix
Marxism, 235; Enlightenment resonating with, 231–32; Janion's writings on, viii, xvii, xix, 237, 244–45, 247; Polish, 246; Soviet, viii, ix, xix; Western, xii–xiii
Maurer, Jadwiga: on creation of Jewish legion, 181, 196, 198–99; on Władysław Mickiewicz's biography of father, 197
Mauron, Charles: on Freud's theory of phantasms, 134
Mazurkiewicz, Roman: on Bogurodzica, 45
melodrama, xiv, 122, 166; features of, 166, 170–71; Freud's theory of phantasm and, 153–61; history of, 164–66; horror's differences from, 171–73; Psyche and Eros in, 161–68; romantic love in, 166–68, 170, 172–73; Romantic writers' treatment of, xx, 153–61
messianism, Polish, 8, 46–47, 51–52, 107–8, 114, 231
Methodius. *See* Cyril and Methodius
Michelet, Jules: on history methods, 141, 150; on myth of Prometheus, 111
Mickiewicz, Adam, 19, 52, 87, 200; attempt to create a Polish legion, 179–84, 186–87; *Ballads and Romances*, 68, 69; "Concerning Madmen and Reasonable People" ("O ludziach rozsądnych i ludziach szalonych"), 88–89; *Crimean Sonnets (Sonety krymskie)*, 211–12; death of, 188, 196; *Forefathers' Eve (Dziady)*, 22, 25–26, 47, 48–49, 92, 108, 122, 213, 238; friendship with Onufry Pietraszkiewicz,

225–26; messianism of, 20, 46–47, 183, 185, 186, 188; *Pan Tadeusz*, 89–90, 94; *Statement of Principles (Skład zasad)*, 184–85, 194, 198; travels to Turkey, 182, 184, 188; Zionism of, 199–200
Mickiewicz, Adam, Jewish legion created by, xx–xxi, 179–204; Crimean War's relationship to, 179–83; Israel's spiritual primogeniture, 183–87; Poland–Israel mystical union, 187–91, 193–95; precursors and successors to, 198–200; preserving Jewish observances within, 190–93, 198, 221; visit to Burgas military encampment, 182–83, 189–90, 196–97. *See also* Lévy, Armand
Mickiewicz, Władysław (son of Adam): biography of father, 182, 185, 189, 192, 195, 196, 197, 198–99
Mieszko I, King: Polish state created by, 12–13
Miłosz, Czesław, viii; condemnation of religious patriotism, 47; translation of Simone Weil's works, 51; *Unattainable Earth (Nieobjęta ziemia)*, 115; on *A World Apart*, 55
Mirabeau, Octave: *The Torture Garden*, 69
Mniszek, Helena: *The Leper (Trędowata)*, 170
Modzelewski, Karol: on Christian missionaries, 12–13; *Socialist Manifesto for Poland*, 246
Morin, Edgar: differences between melodrama and horror, 171–72; melodramatic femininity, 167
Mrożek, Sławomir: on East–West division, 8
Müller, Nicole: *Because That's the Most Terrible Thing about Love (Denn das ist das Schreckliche an der Liebe)*, 205–17
Munich Agreement (1938), 14
Musil, Robert, 176
mysticism, xxi, 120–21, 184, 198
mythologies/myths: of American Wild West, 32, 33; of the Borderlands, 30, 34, 37; Celtic, 9; cultural, 161–62; Ernst Curtius's account of, 144–45; European, 16, 29; Greek, 108–13; of horror, 174–76; of *Logos* (Word), 206, 216; phantasms compared to, 120, 135; Polish, 23, 37–39, 71–75; of Romanticism, 68; of romantic love, 167; Slavic, 9–17, 20, 68, 79; of the Ukranian steppe, 31; Western, 247; in works of art, 143. *See also* folklore/folktales; storytelling

Naruszewicz, Adam, 87; on Slavic mythology, 10
nationalism, x, xxii, 17, 51; in Eastern Europe, xviii; German, xiii, 13–14; Janion's writings on, viii, xiv, xvii, xix; Jewish legion in terms of, 191–92; Polish, vii, 37, 186; Slavic, 18–19
Nebuchadnezzar: biblical legend of, 114
New Privacy, 238
Niekricz, Aleksander: *Utopia in Power (Utopia u władzy)*, 107
Niemcewicz, Julian Ursyn: description of Retjan's suicide, 93–94; on Michał Walewski, 87
Nietzsche, Friedrich: conception of humanity, 110; on romantic love, 212
Nora, Pierre: *Making History (Faire de l'histoire)*, 141–42
Norwid, Cyprian Kamil: criticism of Statement of Principles *(Skład zasad)*, 185

Ogiński, Michał Kleofas: on the Battle of Maciejowice, 86–87
Old Church Slavonic, 41–43, 45
Orientalism, Polish, xvii, 7, 29, 39–41
Orthodox churches: Catholicism's relationship with, 30, 37–38, 41,

43–44. *See also* Eastern Orthodoxy; Greek Orthodoxy; Russian Orthodoxy
Orzeszkowa, Eliza: *The Pompaliński Family (Pompalińscy),* 101; religion of, 49
Other/otherness, 7, 29, 39–40. *See also* homophobia; marginalized people/marginalization; racism; xenophobia
Otto, Rudolf: concept of the holy, 85–86
Ottoman Empire, 40. *See also* Eastern Europe

paganism: Eastern European, 37–38; Slavic, 9–15, 17, 43
Paracelsus: imagination theories of, 119, 121
Pasha, Sadyk. *See* Czajkowski, Michal (Prince)
patriotism, 57, 89, 90, 102
patriotism, Polish: dark side of, xviii–xix; Lévy's, 192, 197; Mickiewicz's, 183, 197; patriot-as-madman image, 85–105, 238–39; religious, 47
Pawlikowski, Paweł: *Serbian Epics,* 24
Pelagianism, 110
phantasies. *See* fantasies/phantasies
phantasmagoria, 122, 163, 167
phantasmatic critique, 119–38; First Enfranchisement of the Imagination, 119–23; Freud's phantasm theory, 133–37; humanities importance to, 130–37; imaginings, delusions, hallucinations, 129–30; Janion's writings on, xiii, xvi, xix–xx; Prometheism and, xi–xiv; romantic love as, 167
phantasms, 122, 153; cinematic, xx, 130, 155, 159–61, 171; daydreams as, 119, 121, 123; distinction between daydreams, dreams, imagination and, 132–33; in folk culture, 122–23; Freud's theory of, 123–29, 133–37, 154–61, 163–64, 168; haunting Polish literature, xix–xx, 103; imagination and, 119–23; importance to the humanities, 129–37; Janion's writings on, xix–xx; in literature, 129, 154–56, 160; notion of love, 166–68; in popular culture, xiv, 155, 157, 159; prephantasms, 125–29; Romantics' treatment of, 120–23, 155–58. *See also* daydreams; dreams; fantasies/phantasies; imagination
phantoms, 121, 122, 171, 173; Freud's theory of, 153–61
philology, 7–8
philosophy, 103, 112, 139, 142. *See also* humanism/humanists; Marxism
Pigoń, Stanisław: on Adam Mickiewicz's plans for a Jewish legion, 189, 191, 195; anti-Semitic perspectives of, 202n36
Piłsudski, Józef, General: on politics, 49; "We, the First Brigade" ("My pierwsza brygada"), 103
Piotrowski, Rufin: Polish–Russian identity struggle, 93–94
Pixérécourt, Gilbert de: plays by, 164
Plato, 57, 90, 200, 209
pleasure, 48, 128–29; aesthetic, 122, 160; principle of, 161, 173, 176
poetry, 10, 25, 73, 147, 151, 158, 179; Romantic, xi–xii, 103, 213, 230
Pol, Wincenty: *Mohort,* 33
Poland: anti-Semitism in, viii, xxi, 23, 24, 119, 194, 197, 199, 221, 244; Borderlands, xv, 36; Catholicism in, xvi, 9, 17, 45, 50–51, 181; as a chosen nation, 15, 18; Christianity in, 9, 22–23, 35, 38, 41, 43; as colonizer, 33; communism in, xiv, xxi, 6, 54, 97, 232, 235–36, 242; culture of, viii, x, xi–xii, xvi, 34, 39–40, 48–49, 70, 98, 184, 191; democracy in, 5, 6, 40; Eastern Europe's relationship with, xv, 50–51; Eastern–Western national consciousness, 29–30, 39–40, 41, 44, 45; forced conversion to

Christianity, 22–23; homophobia in, viii, xii; humanities in, 5–8; identity in, xv–xvii, 6, 21, 24, 37, 47, 51, 53, 186; inclusion in the Soviet Bloc, vii; independence of, xix, 13, 24, 25, 95–96, 242–43; Israel's destiny intertwined with, 25–26, 187–91; Jews living in, xx, 22–23, 194; under martial law, 236, 241; Marxism in, 246; messianism in, 8, 46–47, 51–52, 107–8, 114; military conflicts with Tatars, 40–41; modernization/ transformation of, 5–6, 35; mythologies of, 23, 37–39, 71–75; nationalism of, vii, 37, 186; nationhood of, xxi, 12–13; neofascism in, 17; 1968 student strike, 237–38, 244, 245, 246; occupations of, vii, viii, x, xiii, 8, 45–54, 239; Orientalism of, xvii, 7, 29, 39–41; partitions of, 8, 45–46, 86–91, 93, 94–95, 96–97, 105, 201n14; politics in, xi–xii, 5; religion in, 49, 194; Russians living in, 8, 30, 46–58; Stalinism in, 235; stereotypes of, x, xv–xvi, 38, 54; struggles for independence, xxi, 34, 46–47, 50, 51, 88–89, 93, 103, 105, 179; Ukraine's relationship with, xv, 30–38; Western Europe's relationship with, vii; West's relationship with, xiv–xvi, 11, 40. *See also* Romanticism/Romantics, Polish

Poland, insurrections by: of 1830, 47, 89, 92–93, 98–99; of 1861, 246; of 1863, 36, 100–102, 103, 108

Polanski, Roman: *Fearless Vampire Killers,* 175

Polish Academy of Sciences, 230

Polish–Soviet War of 1919–21, 50

Polish United Workers Party, 242, 244. *See also* communism/ Communist Party; Marxism

politics, 238–39; cultural, 164–65; history of, 144–45; identity, 239; morality and, 49–50; Polish, xi–xii, 5; violent, 13

Porębski, Edward: *Celtic, German, and Romance Folk Songs (Pieśni udowe celtyckie, germańskie, romańskie),* 72–73

positivism, 123, 231, 239

postcolonialism, 7, 8

Prometheism: of French Revolution, 110–11; in Greek myth, 108–13; metaphor of, xix; phantasmatic critique and, xi–xiv; Romantic, 108, 111, 112, 122–23, 157–58; socialism as, xii, xix, 107–16; Stalinism's relationship with, 107, 113

Prus, Bolesław: religion of, 49; view of Polish patriotism, 100–101

Przesmycki, Zenon: on Jacek Malczewski's art, 75–76

psychiatry, 131, 241

psychoanalysis, 37, 136, 150; Freuds' development of, 125–29; Lacan's views on, 124; Laing on, 130–33

Puig, Manuel: *Kiss of the Spider Woman,* 130

racism: anti-Ukrainian, viii, 35. *See also* anti-Semitism; homophobia; marginalized people/marginalization; Other/otherness; xenophobia

Rank, Otto: *Myth of the Birth of the Hero,* 136

Ranke, Leopold von: on European history, 29

Ratzinger, Joseph Cardinal: on Catholic Church as one, true church, 44

reality, 125, 126; alien, 173, 174; alternative, 153–54; distortions of, 143; everyday, 128, 154, 165, 170; Freud's investigation of, 123–24; monstrous, 171; mythologizing, 163; public, 131–32; Romantics' treatment of, 121, 156–57; twentieth-century urban, 160

Rejtan, Tadeusz: patriot-as-madman, 89–103

religion, 103, 246; indigenous, 9; of

love, 167, 170; mysticism and, 120–21; of patriotism, 47, 57; Polish, 49, 194; pre-Christian, 10–11; unity of, 186. *See also* Catholic Church/Catholicism; Christianity; Eastern Orthodoxy; Greek Orthodoxy; Jews/Judaism; Orthodox churches; paganism; Russian Orthodoxy
revisionism, 235–36, 246
right, the, xvi–xvii, xxi, 37
Rikhlin, Mikhail: on Russia, 53
Robert, Marthe: on Freud's literature, 136; *From Oedipus to Moses,* 137
Roeg, Nicolas: *Don't Look Now,* 174
Romanticism/Romantics, 31, 78; cinema and, 156–58, 174; culture of, 51–52; dream theory of, 155–56; Enlightenment and, 120, 155–57; on fantasies/phantasies, xi–xii, 120–23, 125; French tragedy, 165; German, 68, 125, 153; hero image of, 122–23, 157–58; history of, 146–47; ideas about oppressed nations' struggles of freedom, 193–94; imagination theories of, 119–23; Janion's writings on, 237, 244–45, 247; mythologies/myths of, 68; phantasm theory of, 120–23, 155–58; poetry of, xi–xii, 103, 213, 230; popular novels of, 157–58, 163, 166; of Slavdom, 20, 21–22, 24; on the subconscious/unconscious, 120–21, 247; view of the Borderlands, 32–33. *See also* love, romantic
Romanticism/Romantics, Polish, 19, 32, 33, 49, 50, 51, 188, 230–31, 247; aesthetics of, 78, 156–57; art of, 68–69; cross-fertilization with Zionism, xx–xxi; culture of, 51–52, 107; *émigré* status of poets, 233, 244; on patriot-as-madman concept, 85–86, 91–92, 93, 95, 98, 102–3; Poland depicted as Polonia, 46–47; on pre-Christian religions, 10–11; Prometheism and, 108, 111, 112; of Slavdom, 20–22, 25. *See also* Malczewski, Jacek, art of; messianism, Polish; *rusałki*
Rousseau, Jean-Jacques, 110, 115; *Nouvelle Héloïse,* 213; understanding of the human, 135
Rudaś-Grodzka, Monika: on Kraszewski, 22; on Polish Romantics, 21
rusałki, xviii, 67–72, 74–75
Russia/Russians, 17, 32; in the Borderlands, 45–54; despotism of, 16, 52–53; Karamzin's *History of Russia,* 22; in Poland, 8, 30, 46–58; Polish insurrections against, 36, 47, 89, 92–93; stereotypes of, 52–53; Ukraine's relationship with, xviii, 34, 232; Vilnius occupation, 250–51; war with Turkey, 179, 180–81; Western Europe's relationship with, viii, 15–16, 52–54; during World War II, 219–24. *See also* Cossacks; Soviets; USSR
Russian Orthodoxy, 30, 41. *See also* Eastern Orthodoxy; Greek Orthodoxy; Orthodox churches
Russian Revolution, 107
Ruszkowski, Janusz: on Mickiewicz, 180, 184
Rzewuski, Henryk: on Retjan's suicide, 94; *Soplica's Tales (Pamiątki Soplicy),* 90

Sabbateanism (Jewish sect), 187, 200
Said, Edward W.: on Western conceptions of the East, 7, 29
Sarmatians, 38–41
Sartre, Jean-Paul: *No Exit,* 132
Schiller, Friedrich von: division between real and ideal, 49–50
Schlegel, Friedrich: on artistic irony, 78
Schoedsack, Ernest: *The Most Dangerous Game,* 168
Scholem, Gershom, 187; on Mickiewicz as a Frankist, 200
Schulz, Bruno, 159–60, 174; *Familienromane,* 163; *Sanatorium under the*

Sign of the Hourglass, 163; *Street of Crocodiles,* 163
Serbia/Serbians: genocide of, 24–25
Ševčenko, Ihor: on Polish cultural influence in Ukraine, 34
sexuality, 168, 206. *See also* homosexuality
Shakespeare, William: *Hamlet,* 136
Shelley, Percy Bysshe: on *Prometheus Unbound,* 111
Siege of Vienna (1683), 40
Sienkiewicz, Henryk, 32–33, 35
Singer, Isaac Bashevis, xviii; *King of the Fields,* 22–23
Sisyphus, myth of, 114
Slavdom/Slavs, 5–28; attempts to self-Westernize, 30; conflict with Germany, 18, 42; deities of, 79; *dziady* ritual, 25–26; fears regarding, 15–18; folklore/folktales of, 20, 67–68, 79, 157; forced conversion to Christianity, xvi, xviii, 11–13, 18, 22, 42; idylls of, 18–19, 20, 22; in Ireland, 10; Janion's writings on xv–xvi, xvii–xviii; Latinization of, 42; mark of Iranian culture on, 39; mythologies of, 9–17, 20, 68, 79; nationalism, 18–19; Old Church Slavonic, 41–43, 45; old tribal name, 19; origins of, xviii, 20; paganism of, 9–15, 17, 43; Polabi, 11–13, 46; in Poland, 22, 41–42, 46; on Polish–Russian hostility, 50–51; Romanticism of, 20, 21–22, 24; slave image of, 13–14, 18, 19–22
Słowacki, Juliusz, 107; *Father Marek (Ksiądz Marek),* 188; *Kordian,* 47; religion of, 49; *The Spirit-King (Król-Duch),* 22
Śniadecka, Ludwika: on Adam Mickiewicz's plans for a Jewish legion, 190, 192
socialism: as a Prometheism, xii, xix, 111–16
Sofsky, Wolfgang, 17–18; on violence, 56–57
Solon: beliefs regarding life in captivity, 95
Sophocles: Freud's inspiration from, 142; *Oedipus Rex,* 136
Soviets: Bloc formed by, vii, 15, 16; gulags run by, 54–55; influence of, xiv; Lithuanian occupation by, 219, 222–23; Marxism of, viii, ix, xix; Poland occupation by, vii, x, xiii, 239. *See also* Russia/Russians; USSR
Spitteler, Carl: *Imago,* 125
Springtime of Nations, 179, 193, 195
Stachniuk, Jan, 15; on Slavic nationhood, 17
Stalinism, xii, 107, 113, 235. *See also* communism/Communist Party
Stanisław August, King, 91, 96
Stender-Petersen, Adolf: on Bogurodzica, 44–45; on Old Church Slavonic, 41–42
Stendhal, 55
stereotypes, 52–53, 111, 155; collective, xix; Jewish, 186; of male homosociality, 182; nationalist, xiii, 13, 161; phantasms compared to, 135; Polish, x, xv–xvi, 38, 54
Stoker, Bram: *Dracula,* 174–75
storytelling, 7, 24, 73. *See also* folklore/folktales; mythologies/myths
Sue, Eugène: *Mysteries of Paris,* 158, 162
Sulimirski, Tadeusz: on Polish nobility's "Sarmatian" roots, 38–39
surrealism/surrealists, 160, 169, 247; Malczewski's, 75–77; psychoanalysis' relationship with, 129–30
Szczepanowski, Stanisław: comparison of *Faust* and *Dziady,* 48; on Schiller's division between real and ideal, 49–50
Szczuka, Kazimiera: Janion's interview with, xxi, 219–53
Szyc, Joachim A.: *Slavic Gods (Słowiańscy bogowie),* 10

Tatars: Poland's military conflicts with, 40–41
Tazbir, Janusz: on Polish presence in the Borderlands, 38
Thomas Aquinas: ideas of, 147
Tokarczuk, Olga: description of writing, 252
Tokarzówna, Krystyna: on Aleksander Głowacki, 100
Tolkien, J. R. R.: retelling of Celtic mythology, 9
Tomashevsky, Boris: comparing melodramatic novels with the cinema, 164, 165
Towiański, Andrzej: goals of, 186, 188; as Mickiewicz's mentor, 180, 185; mysticism of, 184
Transgresje, Janion's concept of, xii–xiii, 238–43, 245
Trentowski, Bronisław: on Slavic beliefs, 10–11
Turkey: Mickiewicz's travels to, 182, 184, 188; organizing Jewish legion in, 96, 179, 191, 196, 198; war with Russia, 179, 180–81

Ugrešić, Dubravka: on Radovan Karadžić, 24
Ukraine: Janion's analyses of, xv, xviii; literary works from, 232; Polish relationship with, xv, 30–38; racism against, viii, 35; Russia's relationship with, xviii, 34, 232; steppe, 30–31, 33
Uman, massacre of, 36
Union of Brest (1595–96), 37
universalism, 42, 239
University of Gdansk: Janion's professorship at, 237–44; student strike of 1968, 237–38, 244, 245, 246
USSR, 16, 52, 54, 107. *See also* Russia/Russians; Soviets

Valabrega, Jean-Paul: on phantasms, 124, 134
Valery, Paul, 209
Vico, Giambattista, 7; on Western culture, 29
Vilnius, Lithuania: Janion living in, x, xxi, 219, 226, 228, 232; Jews of, 219–24; Soviet occupation of, 250–51
violence, 13, 22, 35, 50, 56–57. *See also* Holocaust, the
Virgin Mary, 44–45, 51
Visconti, Luchino: *Death in Venice,* 174
visions: cinematic, 173; Mickiewicz's, 193; Retjan's, 97–98; Romantics' treatment of, 121; of Slavdom, 19, 22
Voegelin, Eric: on Marx's understanding of Prometheus, 111–12

Wajda, Andrzej: *Man of Iron,* 238
Walicki, Andrzej, 52; on Catholic–Orthodox Christian dialogue, 43–44
Wallenrod, Konrad: as traitor, 103
Weil, Simone: on Promethean myth, 109; on religion, 51
Weintraub, Wiktor: on formation of Jewish legion, 198–99
West, the, 29, 247; missionaries from, 11–12; Poland's relationship with, xiv–xvi, 11, 40
Western Europe, xix, 14; anti-Semitism in, 196, 199; Eastern Europe's relationship with, 14–15, 29–30, 35; Jews in, 187–88; Poland's relationship with, vii; Russia/Soviet Union's relationship with, viii, 15–16, 52–54
White, Hayden: list of narrative genres, 7
Wilson, Andrew: on the Cossacks, 31–32
Witkiewicz, Stanisław Ignacy (aka Witkacy): on Borderland mythologies, 37
Wójcicki, Kazimierz Władysław: *Legends, Ancient Tales, and Stories of the Polish and Russian Peoples (Klechdy, starożytne podania i*

powieściludu polskiego i Rusi), 68–69
Woronicz, Jan Paweł: on old Slavic tribal name, 19; poem after partitioning, 96
Wyka, Kazimierz: on Jacek Malczewski's art, 63, 75
Wyspiański, Stanisław: on the Slavic uncanny, 22; *The Wedding,* 64

xenophobia: Polish, viii, xii

Yugoslavia, former: war in, 24–25

Zaleski, Józef Bohdan: on Adam Mickiewicz, 180, 185–86
Zamoyski, Władysław, General: conflict with Czajkowski, 182; military action, 181
Zawieyski, Jerzy: play about Retjan, 95, 96–97; on Rejtan, 92, 95–96
Żbikowski, Andrzej: on Borderland people, xv, 37
Żeromski, Stefan, 107
Zionism/Zionists: Christian, 198, 199; cross-fertilization with Polish Romanticism, xx–xxi; Theodor Herzl as creator of, 198, 200. *See also* Jews/Judaism
Žižek, Slavoj: on national and ethnic identity, 17–18; on Serbian genocides, 24–25
Żmigrodzka, Maryna: Janion's friendship with, 221, 225–26, 227, 228–29, 248, 253; Marxism of, 235–36; on Romantic irony, 78; work at Institute for Literary Research, 31, 230, 231

Maria Janion (1926–2020) was the greatest Polish leftist intellectual of the past century. The author of twenty-three books and hundreds of articles and essays, she mentored and inspired several generations of Eastern European scholars and political activists. Originally trained as a scholar of Romanticism, Janion ranged widely in her writings; she is best known as a theorist of nationalism, fascism, and collective cultural consciousness. She held appointments at several Polish academic institutions, including the University of Gdańsk and the Institute of Literary Studies in Warsaw. For her Eastern European students and readers, her death in 2020 marked the end of an era.

Marta Figlerowicz is professor of comparative literature at Yale University. She is a Guggenheim Fellow and author of *Flat Protagonists: A Theory of Novel Character* and *Spaces of Feeling: Affect and Awareness in Modernist Literature* as well as over a hundred articles, reviews, and essays. Her translations from Polish have appeared in *PMLA* and *The Paris Review.*